life
colors

Also by Pamala Oslie

Make Your Dreams Come True

REVISED EDITION

life
colors

What the Colors in
Your Aura Reveal

PAMALA OSLIE

NEW WORLD LIBRARY
NOVATO, CALIFORNIA

New World Library
14 Pamaron Way
Novato, CA 94949

Revised edition copyright © 2000 by Pamala Oslie
Cover design: Kathy Warinner
Author photo: Connie Adams
Text design and typography: Tona Pearce Myers

Originally published by New World Library in 1991.
Library of Congress Cataloging-in-Publication Data
Oslie, Pamala.
Life colors : what the colors in your aura reveal / Pamala Oslie. — Rev. ed.
p. cm.
ISBN 1-57731-169-8 (alk. paper)
1. Aura. 2. Typology (Psychology) — Miscellanea. I. Title.
BF1389.A 085 2000
133.8'92—dc21   00-056871

First printing of the revised edition, September 2000
Printed in Canada on acid-free paper
Distributed to the trade by Publishers Group West
ISBN 1-57731-169-8

10   9   8

This book is dedicated to All.
May we remember that we are One
And that we are playful, unlimited Creators.
May we all live together in love,
joy, light, and harmony.

contents

acknowledgments

I wish to express my love and gratitude to the following friends who have all been inspirational teachers to me.

My appreciation to the three people who helped me the most with this book:

To Bo Fox whom I love and cherish beyond words and who has been a wonderful, joyful light in my life.

To Janet Mills whom I love and appreciate for her friendship, love, inspiration, and wisdom.

To Becky Benenate for all her support and devoted time and energy in putting this book together.

My deepest love and appreciation to my mother, Beverly, for her encouragement, love, and support; and to my father, Palmer, for his inspiration and dedicated love.

To my sister, Paula, and my brothers, Larry and Scott, who have been incredibly loving, patient, and supportive toward me. And to their lights: Michael, Christine, Kari, Keith, Kory, Kyle, Kalen, Kip, Walter, and Diane.

Thank you to all my wonderful friends who have brought so much love and joy to my experience in this lifetime — Connie

Adams; Chandler and Sandy Armstrong; Lynne and Frank Babb; Ray and Sylvia Benenate; Joyce Bleiman and family; Diana and Dan Brown; Lee Bryant; Joan Bueling; Tom Callahan; Joan, Linda, and Mike Clifford; Lenie Colacino; Noel and Betty Cooke; Caitlin Crest; Bonita, Bret, Bryan, and Mike Dehn; Lori and Kevin Dunne; Alexis Ells; Kathryn Grove Garcia; Michelle Gysan; Dinny Harter; Pat Harwell; Ann and Bruce Stephen Holms, Joyce Johnson and Gary Jurich; Linda Jones and family; Mary Judge; Darcia Kleinsmid; Helen Kramer; Peggy and Richard Lamb; Rod Lathim; John Leonard; Kenny Loggins and family; Diane Matsinger; Lori Mazzuca; Amy and Michael McDonald; Hank McMonigle; Leslie Moed; Sandy Park; Glen and Patricia Posner; Jane Asher Reaney; Carolyn Ringo and Geoff Levens; Star Riparetti; Rob Robb; Barbara Rollinson; Darai and Jeff Roundy; Monica Ryker; David Schenkel; Susan and Ted Shaffer; Kim Fox Shockley; Bruce and Kim Stanwood Terranova; Kelly and Mike Stark; Anne Stewart; Alli Stillman; Marilyn Tam; David Tate; Linda Thornton and family; Duncan Westley; Kati Zimmermann; Arthur and all my other friends who hopefully know who they are and that I love them.

To all my clients who have become such special friends, thank you for your trust and support.

Thank you Michael Bromley and Barbara Bowers for helping me awaken my abilities.

Thank you Kathy Warinner for the cover design and Connie Adams for the author photograph and Georgia Hughes for editing.

Thank you Marc Allen, my publisher, for believing in this book.

Thanks to all those who have inspired my awakening, especially Seth, Jane Roberts, Richard Bach, Deepak Chopra, and Terry Cole-Whittaker.

foreword
Joyce Bleiman, Ph.D.

The technological advances of the past century have taught us to believe in and rely on only what we can see, hear, touch, taste, smell, and measure with instruments. A consequence of our growing reliance on technology is that we lose touch with our innate humanness, our intuition, unlimited potential, and connection to the process of life

For much of the western world, this is an age of material wealth and abundance, expanding longevity and prosperity. And yet, despite unprecedented wealth, many people experience a deepening sense of disillusionment, isolation, and loss. There's a void that cannot be filled with relationships, food, drugs, alcohol, or shopping. Something's missing.

We have adopted endless ways to distract our attention from our inner voices, and from the messages our innate intelligence is trying to get across to us — vital messages about who we are and what our purpose is.

The information in *Life Colors* gives us a fuller understanding of the unique design of the human personality, and from this understanding a road map to inner peace and wholeness. Over the course of my career as a professor of human and organizational systems, I have avidly sought out ideas and theories that might help people break free from cultural shackles and perceptual boundaries. *Life Colors,* both in the classroom and in my work as a consultant, has been an effective tool for helping people better understand themselves and others in new ways, free from judgment.

Pamala Oslie has a rare gift: she can see and interpret the human aura. This gift is remarkable in and of itself and makes Pamala an extraordinary person. But she is also blessed with integrity, compassion, and a wonderful ability to communicate what she knows for the benefit of people from all walks of life.

Reading *Life Colors* leads to a change in our perception of reality and our understanding of what true human potential really is. What Pamala Oslie, using her intuitive gift, teaches about the human aura is corroborated by discoveries in the field of neuropsychology.

Nuclear spect scans provide graphic images of the human brain and give researchers insight into behavioral and psychological characteristics. An in-depth understanding of the human aura provides similar insights. In fact, I asked an experienced neuropsychiatrist to compare common categories found on spect scans with those defined in *Life Colors,* and not only was he fascinated by the similarities, he was astounded.

In the same way that the personal computer and the technologies it has spawned give us greater freedom to expand our horizons, *Life Colors* helps us restore and reclaim our ability to trust in things we cannot see, things we knew when we showed up in this life, whole, complete, and possessing unique gifts of our very own.

Joyce Bleiman, Ph.D.
co-author of *Love Among the Wild Gods:*
Reclaiming True Power and Peace

introduction

What kind of personality are you? What are your goals and purposes for being here? How do you process life — physically, mentally, or emotionally? What kind of marriage partner is best suited for you? What are your attitudes about career, money, family, sex? What kinds of occupations are best for you? What is your definition of success? What are your positive qualities and negative tendencies? How do you maintain and enhance your positive characteristics? Where are your weak spots concerning health? These are questions that interest most people. Over the years I have discovered that valuable clues and answers to these questions lie hidden in our auras.

The aura is the electromagnetic or energy field that radiates from all matter, although some matter is so dense and vibrates so slowly that it is often difficult to detect its aura. Throughout the ages artists have depicted the aura as a halo or glowing light that appears around the heads or bodies of highly evolved, enlightened spiritual masters and saints. Apparently, the auras around these beings were so clear and powerful that others could easily see, feel, or sense them. Recently, the aura has been scientifically detected through Kirilian photography.

I became interested in the aura in 1983 after attending a psychic development class taught by Michael Bromley and discovering that I was able to receive information about people clairvoyantly. Then, after attending numerous aura workshops led by Dr. Barbara Bowers, who was able to see the aura physically, I noticed that I was receiving psychic information about people that corresponded with her descriptions and data on the various aura colors. Eventually, through my psychic work I also developed the ability to see these colors. I discovered there are basic and consistent personality traits that coincide with each color.

I see the aura as glowing bands of different luminescent colored lights that completely surround the body. Everyone has an aura that comprises many different-colored bands of light that radiate approximately six feet out in all directions from the body. I can tell if a person is healthy or ill, happy or frustrated by the intensity and vibrancy of the color as well as by the expansiveness and size of the aura. One person's aura may be bright, vibrant, and expanded, showing a sense of openness, well-being, positive self-esteem, and health; another's may be faded and tightly drawn to the body, showing fear, illness, lack of self-esteem, hopelessness, or a perceived need for protection. A dark, densely colored aura usually reveals depression, anger, or self-pity. Each colored band tells a story. Each color contains information about the person.

Being able to "read" the aura and understand the meaning behind each color has helped me understand the way I process information, my interactions with people, how I handle love relationships, and my purpose in life. My purpose in writing about the aura is to bring this knowledge to others, to enable them to understand how and why they process life in a particular way. This knowledge gives them permission to be themselves, to become more accepting of themselves and others while learning effective ways of changing their unwanted behaviors and attitudes.

The different colors of an aura are created in much the same manner as sounds are created. With sounds, the faster the vibration the higher the frequency of sound. The vibration of a bass note on a piano resonates at a slower rate than the high C note. Similarly, as the waves of energy that make up the aura change their speed of vibration, the colors change. In the aura, a slower vibration creates red and orange. Faster vibrations create blue, violet, and indigo. A bass note is not better than or worse than a high note. It is just a different sound. Likewise, orange in the aura is not better than or worse than blue. Different colors signify our different desires for a variety of experiences on the planet. Life would be mundane and uninspiring if we all had the same aura colors, just as a song would be quite monotonous if it were composed of only one note.

In writing about aura colors, it is not my intention to establish any kind of limitation, separation, or "superior" attitudes among readers. There are no good or bad colors. The colors in the aura reflect people's choices in this lifetime, but this does not mean they are limited to a particular goal or way of processing. We are all free to expand, grow, and change in any way we choose. By understanding the attributes of each color, people can even consciously draw in a color for a specific purpose, such as healing, prosperity, or compassion. My goal is to show that although we may all have different methods, goals, and purposes, we are all part of the whole. We are each a part of a colorful rainbow.

AURA LIFE COLORS

Your aura contains many different-colored bands. The one or two bands closest to your body reveal your priorities, methods of processing life, and primary purpose for being on the planet. These are your Life Colors, the aura colors described in this book. These bands do not usually change. The outer bands of the aura, however, frequently change colors and positions, reflecting what is happening with you at a given time.

For simplification, I have categorized the Life Colors into three families: the physical colors, the mental colors, and the emotional colors.

Those with physical colors process information predominantly through their physical bodies, through touch. These colors include Red, Orange, Magenta, and Yellow.

Those with mental colors process life intellectually, by first gathering information, then analyzing it. These colors include Logical Tan, Abstract Tan, Sensitive Tan, Environmental Tan, and Green.

Those with emotional colors — Blue, Violet, Indigo, Lavender, and Crystal — process life primarily through their feelings, emotions, and intuition.

Some Life Colors are predominantly in males; others are predominantly in females. The use of "he" or "she" throughout the book, however, is usually arbitrary.

I believe that, on a deep level, we have all chosen our Life Colors. However, we are not restricted to living only within our colors. Choosing to come into this life with particular Life Colors does not mean we cannot experience the qualities, purposes, priorities, and methods of other Life Colors. Although we have our original Life Colors, we also continuously add other colors into the outer bands of our auras. Through years of working with people, however, I have discovered that people cannot usually ignore or discard the attributes of their original Life Colors without experiencing a sense of disconnection, confusion, and disharmony within themselves. Most people need to fulfill their original Life Colors before they can expand to the other colors. They must first love and accept who they are before they can satisfactorily experience the qualities of the other colors.

Some people are born with one Life Color; others are born with two Life Colors, which I call Combination Colors. Combination Colors show up as the two bands of color that are consistently the closest colors around the body. Having two Life

Colors can be a powerful combination, giving an additional dimension to one's abilities, or it can create a great deal of inner conflict.

The reasons for choosing two Life Colors vary with each individual. Some people choose two Life Colors because the qualities of the second color add more power, energy, fun, or creativity to their main goals in life. Another reason is to ensure balance, practicality, responsibility, or self-reliance.

When people have two Life Colors in the same aura family — for example, a Blue/Violet combination, which has two Life Colors in the emotional family — they may be living the equivalent of two lifetimes at once. Perhaps they are in a hurry to experience their life lessons so they will not have to physically incarnate on this planet again. Or perhaps they did not learn all the lessons (or receive all the benefits) from their last life, and so have carried them over into this lifetime.

People with this Combination Color often sense they are living two lifetimes at once. As they switch from one life experience to another (without needing to die or change bodies), they usually feel a dramatic shift in their lives. Their personalities may change drastically. The loving Blue who has held marriage and relationships as main priorities throughout this life suddenly discovers a burning desire to go into the world and make an impact on the planet. She can no longer stay at home and be a homemaker. Her familiar relationships, career, priorities, and emotions begin to feel alien to her. She feels like an entirely different being.

To discover if you are living two lives in one, first ask yourself if you believe, or if you feel that you are. (Always trust yourself and your feelings.) After answering the questions in the Life Color Questionnaire, notice if your two highest scores both appear in the same aura family. If they do, and you feel you are in the process of shifting — or have already shifted — into being an entirely different person, chances are you fall into this category.

Living two lifetimes at once applies only to those who have

two Life Colors in the same aura family. Many Combination Colors may experience a similar shift in their lives as they move their focus from one Life Color to the other. For example, as a Yellow/Violet (physical and emotional families) Combination Color moves his focus from his Yellow characteristics to his Violet, he may also experience a shift in his career or marital status. However, this person does not feel he is living two lifetimes at once the way a Blue/Violet Combination does.

Frequently, people add another color to their auras sometime during their lifetime, and that color becomes a part of their personality. You do not need to know whether you were born with certain Life Colors or added them later in life as long as you are happy and those colors benefit you. For example, if you came here as a Blue and have added Yellow to your aura, and the addition is having a positive influence on your life, then enjoy it. You have become a Blue/Yellow personality. If you feel, however, that you were born a Yellow/Violet, but added Logical Tan to please your parents or to be accepted by society, that extra color may be causing you to suppress who you really are. In this case, you may want to consider letting go of the characteristics of that color and allow yourself to explore the qualities of your true Life Colors.

IN THIS BOOK

The following chapters describe the general attributes, life purposes, goals, and qualities that each Life Color displays when we are "in power" (centered) and "out of power" (off balance). When we are in power, we are living our positive personalities and our true potential. When we are out of power, we are living in fear, self-doubt, and hesitancy. We are not living our full potential.

I provide methods that show how to regain balance and stay in power when we find ourselves out of power. I also describe the colors' characteristics regarding relationships, sex, children, problem-solving skills, definitions of success, and occupational interests as well as physical problems or weak health areas.

With the descriptions in this book, you can identify your Life Colors and use the information to enhance your life. After reading the descriptions, you may begin to recognize the personalities of your friends and family members. You can refer to the chapters on relationships to learn about your methods of relating to one another.

CHAPTER ONE

identifying your life colors

There are two methods to determine your Life Colors. The first is to read through the description of each color and see which most accurately describes your personality. Most people find it easy to discover their Life Colors or Combination Colors — as well as those of their friends and families — in this way. The second is to answer the questions that follow.

Keep in mind that frequently there are only subtle differences between some of the Life Colors. For example, Blues, Yellows, and Violets can all exhibit the same emotional qualities, the same desire for relationships (although for different reasons), and similar desires to help people, although in different ways. A Yellow, for example, usually helps people by fixing things for them — their cars, their kitchen sinks, or their physical bodies. A Yellow prefers not to get too heavily involved with people's emotional problems while helping them. A Blue usually helps people on a one-on-one, emotional level — counseling, teaching, or nursing. (A Blue nurse often cares about her patient's emotional well-being even more than his physical ailments.) A Violet usually wants to help many people at one time by inspiring and

1

empowering them. Rarely does a Violet have the desire or the patience to help one person at a time.

If you pay close attention to all the descriptions, you will intuitively feel which one or two colors are most closely aligned with who you really are. It is more common for us to have two Life Colors than it is to have one. It is also common for us to function primarily from one of our Life Colors more than the other.

Occasionally, we suppress our natural Life Colors because of family pressures or expectations. For example, someone with a carefree and energetic Yellow Life Color may have been forced by domineering, controlling, or "respectable" parents to behave in a more disciplined fashion. He may have been told that it was not appropriate to be silly, playful, or irresponsible. Consequently, the sensitive Yellow loses his natural enthusiasm, his creativity, and his desire to make people laugh. Parents frequently raise their children based on their own beliefs and their own Life Colors. They do the best they can given that they are not always aware of the differences in their children's Life Colors or even of their own purposes and challenges in this lifetime.

To discover your Life Colors, first answer the questions in the questionnaire. Be sure to give your true answers, not the responses you think you should give. After answering the questions, note the category in which you had the highest number of yes responses. This is your Life Color. Then note which category had the second highest number of yes responses. If that number is close to that of the first category, you probably have a Combination Color; both colors are your Life Colors. If, however, your second category has far fewer yes responses than your first, you probably have only one Life Color. If three or four colors rate high numbers, you probably have added one or two colors that have become part of your personality. (For example, adding Violet to a Yellow/Green combination is very common. Violet seems to be a color that can calm and balance the conflict that frequently occurs in a Yellow/Green combination.)

Next, read the list of occupations to see which category appeals to you the most. Your chosen category can further reveal your Life Colors. When you feel you have discovered your Life Colors, read the section on those colors for in-depth information. Then, if you have two colors, read the section on your Combination Color. If you relate to the descriptions in those sections, you have discovered your Life Colors. Ultimately, you are your own best judge.

The chapters on relationships may help you understand how you relate to people with other Life Colors. These chapters are meant to serve only as a guide. There are no limits or absolutes. It is possible for any relationship to succeed with enough desire, love, and commitment. The information can help you discover ways to enhance your relationships and give you insight into areas in which you may experience difficulties.

The last chapter gives information that may assist you in learning how to see the human aura and how to add colors to the outer bands of your aura.

DIRECTIONS TO IDENTIFY YOUR LIFE COLORS

1. Answer the questions in the questionnaire. Choose the one or two categories with the highest number of yes responses.
2. Read the career choices. Choose the list of occupations to which you are most drawn (or have been drawn).
3. Read the chapters on the Life Colors that correspond to your answers.
4. Read the section in chapter 5 on the Combination Color that corresponds to your answers.
5. To see which Life Colors are most compatible with yours, read the sections in the relationship chapter that involve your Life Colors.

LIFE COLORS QUESTIONNAIRE

Before taking this test, read *all* the questions in each category. This will give you a general feeling of the personality type of each aura color. Then, after taking the test, total the number of times that you answered yes in each category.

Be sure to respond with the answers you feel are truly you, not with what you feel is expected of you or what you think you should be. Taking the test during an emotionally distraught or traumatic time for you may skew or alter your true answers. Therefore, I recommend you don't take the test during emotionally stressful times.

Yes Sometimes No   Life Color #1

Yes	Sometimes	No	
☐	☐	☐ (circled)	I believe that life is physical and biological, not spiritual.
☐	☐	☐ (circled)	I tend to believe only in the existence of those things that I can physically touch.
☒	☐	☐ (circled)	I tend to be strong, honest, and blunt.
☐ (circled)	☒	☐	I often have a quick temper, but get over it quickly and do not hold grudges.
☐	☐ (circled)	☒	I prefer work that is physical and has immediate, tangible results.
☐ (circled)	☐	☒	I enjoy taking physical action on projects rather than discussing ideas and plans.
☐	☐	☒ (circled)	I believe the primary focus and purpose of my life is to work hard, but to experience all of life's physical and animalistic pleasures.
☒	☐	☐ (circled)	I tend to be a loner.
☐	☒	☐ (circled)	I tend to express myself through my sexuality and my physical body more than through my intellect or my emotions.
☐ (circled)	☐	☒	I have a hard time expressing my feelings to others.
☐	☒	☐ (circled)	I am usually powerful, independent, self-confident, and practical.
☐ (circled)	☒	☐	I am persistent and hardworking and usually keep the rest of the team going.
2/4	4/1	6/7	(Total each column here.)

5

Yes	Sometimes	No	Life Color #2
☐	☐	☒	I tend to be a physical daredevil and risk-taker.
☐	☐	☒	I relish dangerous, thrilling, physical challenges — the more dangerous, the better.
☒	☐	☐	Having a regular job and a family feels boring to me.
☐	☐	☒	I prefer occupations that allow me to experience raw, physical courage. Stunt double would be a perfect career.
☐	☐	☒	I tend to use money for daring adventures such as mountain climbing or car racing, rather than for investment.
☐	☐	☒	I prefer to spend time alone or in the company of other daredevils.
☐	☐	☒	Experiencing physical pain does not frighten or deter me.
☐	☐	☒	I prefer doing high-risk, individual sports rather than team sports.
☐	☐	☒	I enjoy the challenge of going beyond physical limitations.
☒	☐	☒	I do not need to share my emotional feelings with anyone.
☒	☐	☐	People often see me as self-absorbed and aloof.
☐	☐	☒	Spiritual beliefs and concepts do not interest me.

| 1 | 0 | 11 | (Total each column here.) |

6

Yes	Sometimes	No	Life Color #3
❏	❏	☒	My lifestyle tends to be flamboyant and eccentric.
❏	❏	☒	My clothes, home, actions, and thoughts tend to be bizarre (not advanced or visionary, just bizarre).
❏	❏	☒	Acting foolish and outrageous is fun and does not embarrass me.
❏	❏	☒	I see life as an Alice in Wonderland–type adventure.
❏	❏	☒	I am not interested in spiritual concepts or helping the planet, only in experiencing the strangeness of the physical world.
❏	☒	❏	I do not usually conform to society's rules or laws.
❏	❏	☒	Although I love parties and social events, I have trouble keeping friends because my behavior sometimes shocks people.
☒	❏	❏	I am a loner.
☒	❏	❏	I am a quick thinker, but people rarely understand my ideas.
☒	❏	❏	I enjoy outrageous artistic expression.
❏	❏	☒	I do not usually take responsibility for friends or family.
❏	☒	☒	I feel more comfortable living in a big city where I can hide out in the crowds.
$\frac{3}{0}$	$\frac{1}{1}$	$\frac{8}{11}$	(Total each column here.)

Yes Sometimes No Life Color #4

Yes	Sometimes	No	
☐	☐	☒	Having fun is a strong priority for me.
☒	☐	☒	I have a great sense of humor and love to laugh.
☒	☐	☒	I am very optimistic and upbeat, always wearing a smile.
☒	☐	☒	I tend to look younger than my age.
☒	☐	☒	I tend to be rebellious. I hate being told what to do.
☐	☐	☒	I need physical exercise or dance regularly.
☒	☐	☒	I tend to fidget or have high energy.
☒	☐	☐	I like to be creative or artistic or work with my hands.
☒	☐	☐	When there is conflict, my first impulse is to avoid the situation, retreat, or run away.
☒	☐	☐	I am sensitive. My feelings can be hurt very easily.
☒	☐	☒	I have or have had a tendency to regularly overdo at least one of the following: drugs, alcohol, cigarettes, caffeine, sex, exercise, chocolates or other sweets, or overeating.
☒	☒	☐	I believe that sex should be fun.

| 8 / 5 | 0 / 1 | 4 / 6 | (Total each column here.) |

Yes *Sometimes* *No* *Life Color #5*

Yes	Sometimes	No	
❏	❏	❏	I enjoy working with mechanical or electronic gadgets and machines — computers, calculators, appliances, and electronic games.
❏	❏	❏	I prefer secure, stable jobs that provide regular paychecks.
❏	❏	❏	I am not an emotional person.
❏	❏	❏	I prefer to see the proof, logic, and data behind ideas.
❏	❏	❏	I prefer to work on the details of a project or assignment.
❏	❏	❏	I am a very analytical, logical, and sequential thinker.
❏	❏	❏	My attitude is "seeing is believing."
❏	❏	❏	I am practical with money and prefer secure investments.
❏	❏	❏	I usually follow the rules and abide by the laws. I prefer structure.
❏	❏	❏	I tend to take a long time to make a decision. (Take as long as you want to answer this question.)
❏	❏	❏	I typically follow a regular routine.
❏	❏	❏	I tend to be a pack rat, hanging on to things just in case I need them.

4   2   6   (Total each column here.)

4   8

Yes	Sometimes	No	Life Color #6

☐ ☐ **☑** I enjoy analyzing and measuring the environment.

☐ ☐ **☑** I am able to judge weight, distance, and volume through inner physical senses. (I can tell how much something weighs by holding it in my hand.)

☑ ☐ **☑** I am a logical and practical thinker.

☑ ☐ ☐ I am slow to develop friends and usually spend my time alone.

☐ ☐ **☑** I am fascinated by such things as the control panels in airplanes or submarines.

☑ ☐ **☑** I am a responsible, dedicated employee who follows directions well.

☐ ☐ **☑** I perceive reality as logical and three dimensional.

☑ ☐ **☑** I am a very private person and keep my feelings to myself.

☑ ☐ **☑** I am quiet and reserved but independent and strong.

☑ ☐ **☑** I prefer stable jobs and reliable paychecks.

☑ ☐ ☐ I tend to be serious and self-controlled.

☑ **☑** ☐ When raising children, I would be a rational disciplinarian.

3   1   8   (Total each column here.)

7   5

10

Yes Sometimes No   Life Color #7

Yes	Sometimes	No	
☑	☐	☐	Home and family are two of my most important priorities.
☑	☐	☑	I feel that supporting community activities and attending functions such as PTA meetings are important.
☑	☐	☑	I prefer to work in a support role in which I take care of the details, for example, secretary, bookkeeper, homemaker, medical assistant.
☑	☐	☑	I am a sensitive, calm, patient, and rational thinker.
☑	☐	☐	Having a sense of security and stability in my home is important to me.
☑	☑	☐	I tend to be a patient listener.
☑	☐	☑	I tend to be quiet, reserved, and often shy.
☑	☑	☐	I prefer to understand the logic in a situation; however, I am also emotionally supportive of people's needs.
☑	☐	☐	I believe that service to humanity is true spirituality.
☑	☑	☐	I usually put my family's needs before my own.
☑	☐	☑	I prefer to work in a structured environment.
☑	☐	☑	I usually work out my emotional upsets in a calm, logical, and quiet manner.

4   3   5   (Total each column here.)

11   1

11

Yes	Sometimes	No	Life Color #8
☑	☐	☒	I prefer jobs that allow me to work randomly with all the *details* of a project.
☑	☐	☒	I can see all the details that need to be taken care of, but I have difficulty deciding which ones need to be done first.
☒	☐	☐	I usually see numerous solutions to a problem.
☒	☐	☒	I frequently feel scattered, often forget appointments, or overbook my schedule with conflicting appointments.
☒	☐	☒	I prefer the security of a paycheck.
☒	☐	☐	I tend to theorize about emotions rather than actually experience them.
☒	☐	☐	I know many acquaintances, but have very few close friends.
☐	☒	☒	I enjoy attending social functions where I can talk with a lot of people.
☒	☐	☐	I love humanity, but I am often uncomfortable maintaining an intimate relationship.
☐	☒	☒	I get so busy and things get so hectic that I often forget to pay my bills.
☒	☐	☒	My possessions are not very important to me so I have trouble taking care of them.
☒	☒	☐	I am constantly misplacing things.
7	1	4	(Total each column here.)

12

Yes	Sometimes	No	Life Color #9
☑	☐	☐	I can be a workaholic, have a hard time relaxing.
☑	☐	☐	I am often in a hurry.
☑	☐	☐	I tend to be a perfectionist and am usually demanding on myself and others. I can be blunt and critical.
☑	☐	☐	I like things to be organized, efficient, and well planned. I frequently write lists.
☑	☐	☐	My three strongest priorities are making a lot of money, accomplishing my financial and business goals, and being respected by other powerful and intelligent people. (These are more important to me than helping others or improving the planet. See Life Color #11.)
☑	☐	☐	I enjoy being in charge and delegating responsibilities.
☑	☐	☐	I can be strong willed and tenacious.
☑	☐	☐	I need to learn and to be intellectually stimulated.
☑	☐	☐	I enjoy the challenge of developing plans and ideas rather than doing detailed work.
☑	☐	☐	I have high standards in relationships and tend to be easily bored by others.
☑	☐	☐	I can become impatient and frustrated with people if they are not motivated and ambitious.
☑	☐	☐	I can intimidate people.
12	—	—	(Total each column here.)
3	1	8	

13

Yes	Sometimes	No	*Life Color #10*
☑	☐	☐	People frequently turn to me with their emotional problems and I usually lovingly listen and counsel them.
☐	☐	☑	I am emotional and can easily be moved to tears.
☑	☐	☐	One of my strongest priorities is to be in a loving, monogamous relationship.
☐	☐	☑	I have difficulty letting go of relationships.
☐	☑	☐	Spirituality, love, and people are the most important elements in my life.
☐	☐	☑	Money is not my first priority.
☑	☐	☐	I tend to help and take care of everyone.
☑	☐	☐	I feel guilty if I say no to someone.
☐	☑	☒	I frequently have cold hands and feet.
☑	☐	☐	When there is conflict, I want everyone to love one another.
☐	☑	☐	I tend to feel very empathetic toward other people.
☐	☑	☐	I tend to be intuitive.
5	4	3	(Total each column here.)

10   7

Yes	Sometimes	No	Life Color #11
☑	☐	☐	I feel that I have a message to get across to people.
☑	☐	☐	I have a strong desire to help improve the planet.
☑	☐	☐	I have always felt that I was going to be famous or do something important.
☐	☑	☑	I have had a desire to perform for audiences.
☑	☐	☐	If I had a lot of money, I would travel or become involved in humanitarian causes.
☑	☐	☐	Freedom and independence are major priorities for me.
☑	☐	☐	I would much rather be self-employed.
☑	☐	☐	I am very interested in cosmic and universal concepts.
☐	☑	☐	I frequently end up in leadership positions or at least at the center of attention.
☑	☐	☐	I have often felt different from others.
☑	☑	☐	I am passionate about sex.
☑	☐	☐	I can become involved in too many projects at the same time.
10	2	0	(Total each column here.)
3	2	7	

Yes Sometimes No Life Color #12

Yes	Sometimes	No	
☐	(☐)	☒	I enjoy fantasy and make-believe more than the real world.
(☐)	☐	☒	I am quiet, sensitive, and spiritual.
(☐)	☐	☒	I am often forgetful and frequently spacey.
☐	☐	(☒)	I seem to be out of my body more than I am in it.
☐	☒	(☐)	People accuse me of being irresponsible and unrealistic.
☐	☐	(☒)	I have difficulty dealing with everyday responsibilities.
☐	☐	(☒)	I have a difficult time managing money.
(☐)	☐	☒	I tend to spend a lot of time alone, daydreaming.
(☒)	☐	☐	I prefer pretty, gentle, and fine artistic things, and I am uncomfortable with dirt, bugs, or harsh environments.
(☒)	☐	☐	I am an imaginative and creative thinker; however, I usually have trouble following through with my ideas.
(☐)	☐	☒	I tend to want others to solve my problems for me.
(☒)	☐	☐	I prefer to work in relaxed, low-stress environments.

Yes	Sometimes	No	
$\frac{3}{7}$	$\frac{1}{1}$	$\frac{4}{4}$	(Total each column here.)

Yes Sometimes No   *Life Color #13*

Yes	Sometimes	No	
☑	☐	☐	I am extremely sensitive and can be overwhelmed by being around too many people.
☐	☑	☐	I often feel I have quiet, inner healing powers.
☑	☐	☐	Frequently, I am frightened and unsure of what I am supposed to do on the planet.
☐	☑	☑	I usually feel uncomfortable in social situations.
☑	☑	☐	My personality changes to match others around me.
☑	☐	☑	I tend to be withdrawn, quiet, and insecure.
☑	☐	☑	I feel safer and more secure with others taking responsibility and making decisions for me.
☐	☐	☑	I need to spend a lot of time alone in quiet meditation to replenish myself.
☑	☐	☑	I often choose to work in quiet, calm, and peaceful environments.
☐	☑	☑	Physical reality often feels cold, harsh, and threatening to me.
☐	☑	☐	My spirituality and my serene inner connection with God are the most important aspects of my life.
☑	☐	☑	I frequently spend quiet time reading or being in my garden.

$\frac{3}{6}$ $\frac{4}{3}$ $\frac{5}{3}$ (Total each column here.)

Yes	Sometimes	No	Life Color #14
❏	❏	❏	My appearance can seem androgynous or asexual.
❏	❏	❏	I have difficulty relating to my physical body.
❏	❏	❏	I have a highly sensitive physical, emotional, and psychological system.
❏	❏	❏	I am highly intuitive or psychic.
❏	❏	❏	I have clear memories of past lives or can see spiritual beings in other dimensions.
❏	❏	❏	Computers and other technologies are second nature to me.
❏	❏	❏	I have difficulty relating to the world in its current condition and often don't feel that I belong here.
❏	❏	❏	I "know" there is spiritual energy in all things.
❏	❏	❏	I am extremely sensitive and compassionate, yet strong and independent.
❏	❏	❏	I constantly question and challenge old, dogmatic beliefs and methods.
❏	❏	❏	I cannot be forced to operate against my beliefs even if it would make others happy. Guilt and punishment do not work on me.
❏	❏	❏	I feel more creative and spiritually "advanced" than others.

4   2   4   (Total each column here.)

4   6

Red Overlay

Finally, the following is a test to see if you have a Red Overlay. The Red Overlay is not a Life Color. If you answer yes to three or more questions, chances are you have one. Please read "The Red Overlay" in chapter 5 for more information.

Yes   Sometimes   No   Red Overlay

Yes	Sometimes	No	Red Overlay
❑	❑	❑	I frequently experience intense, often uncontrollable anger or rage.
❑	❑	❑	My life seems to be a constant struggle.
❑	❑	❑	I consistently experience conflict and frustration regarding relationships, health, money, career.
❑	❑	❑	I experienced at least one of the following as a child:

a) emotional, physical, or mental abandonment or rejection (i.e., unwanted child, adopted, alcoholic parent)

b) emotional, physical, or mental abuse

c) life-threatening situation before birth, at birth, or at a young age

0   1   3   (Total each column here.)

1   3

Identifying Your Aura Life Colors

List which Life Colors categories you answered with the most yes responses to discover your Life Colors.

Aura category with highest number of yes answers: #___9___

Aura category with second highest number of yes answers: #___11___

Red Overlay   yes _____   no ___✓___

Life Colors Key
#1 = Red
#2 = Orange
#3 = Magenta
#4 = Yellow
#5 = Logical Tan
#6 = Environmental Tan
#7 = Sensitive Tan
#8 = Abstract Tan
#9 = Green
#10 = Blue
#11 = Violet
#12 = Lavender
#13 = Crystal
#14 = Indigo

Sensitive Tan / Blue

Occupations

To further help you discover your Life Colors, choose which list of occupations appeals to you the most. Please note that just because you currently have one occupation, it does not necessarily mean that is the best or most fulfilling one for you. If you are not happy in your line of work, you are probably not in alignment with your Life Colors.

Check the occupation categories to which you are most drawn or would be if money and family approval were not considerations. Also check the occupations in which you have worked in the past.

Certain occupations may appear on more than one list. For example, "writer" appears on many lists. Notice which other occupations in those lists you are most attracted to, and you will probably discover your real Life Colors.

#1

Firefighter
Rescue worker
Police work
Military personnel
Football player
Boxer
Bodyguard
Truck driver
Heavy equipment
    operator
Construction worker
Repairperson
Mechanic
Furniture mover
Shop foreman
Tractor driver
Farmer
Surgeon
Bartender
Waiter/waitress
Butcher
Dancer

#2

Race car driver
Skydiver
Hang glider
Wilderness guide
River rafter
Wild safari hunter
Stunt double
Mountain climber
Explorer
Rescue worker
Firefighter
Police worker
Detective
Deep-sea diver
Bounty hunter
Trapeze artist
Private investigator
Guard
Lion tamer
Paramedic

#3

Clown
Artist
Comedian
Actor
Art dealer or
    collector
Inventor
Set designer
Costume designer
Photographer
Publisher (especially
    avant-garde
    publications)
Entrepreneur
Salesperson
    (especially for
    unusual items)

#4

Musician
Artist
Comedian
Writer
Laborer
Gardener
Bodybuilder
Lifeguard
Firefighter
Auto mechanic
Athlete
Surfer
House painter
Construction worker
Bartender
Chef
Waiter/waitress
Massage therapist
Healer
Doctor, paramedic, nurse
Nutritionist
Veterinarian
Court jester for the world

#5

Engineer
Architect
Bookkeeper
Accountant
Computer analyst
Researcher
Scientist
Office clerk
Data processor
Factory assembly worker
Librarian
Court reporter
Appliance or electrical
   repairperson
Technician
Computer operator

#6

Archaeologist
Geologist
Environmental researcher
Scientist
Explorer
Map maker
Forest ranger
Military personnel
Pilot
Shipping and receiving
   clerk
Purchase order clerk
City planner
Developer
Architect
Computer operator
Lab technician
Telephone repairperson
Aerospace engineer
Electrical repairperson
Farmer

#7

Bookkeeper
Receptionist
Secretary
Office personnel
Accountant
Arbitrator
Counselor
Therapist
Judge
Dentist
Hygienist
Welfare, social worker
Teacher
Child care worker

#8

Teacher
Consultant
City developer
Landscaper
Gardener
Salesperson
Computer programmer
Designer

#9

Corporate executive
Business entrepreneur
Banker
Producer
Fundraiser
Organizer
Office manager
Marketing and advertising
   coordinator
Planning and investment
   advisor
Real estate agent
Salesperson (especially
   involving expensive
   items such as cars,
   insurance, and homes)
Stockbroker
Business manager or agent
Politician
King (or at least owner of
   the world)

#10

Teacher, educator
Counselor
Nurse
Childcare worker
Assistant or director of
    nonprofit organizations
Secretary
Volunteer
Nun, priest
Homemaker
Parent
Housekeeper
Waitress/Waiter
Social worker
Psychic
Clergy
Astrologer
Psychologist
Spiritual advisor

#11

Performer
Actor
Singer
Musician
Artist
Writer
Designer
Producer
Director
Cameraperson
Teacher
Minister
Psychologist
Consultant
Lecturer
Politician
Lawyer
Corporate officer
Business owner
Developer
Investment broker
Leader
Astronaut
Activist

#12

Storyteller
Mime
Artist (especially fantasy)
Writer (especially
    children's books)
Dancer
Actor
Costume designer
Interior decorator
Teacher
Singer
Musician

#13

Librarian
Secretary
Receptionist
Massage therapist
Healer, medicine
Dental assistant
Artist
Interior decorator
Florist
Herb grower
Physical therapist

#14

Artist
Writer
Musician
Designer
Day care worker
Animal caretaker
Social worker
Teacher, educator
Counselor
Computer programmer
Computer operator

#15

Actor
Musician
Singer
Artist
Comedian
Performer
Dancer
Doctor
Acupuncturist
Psychotherapist
Physical therapist
Massage therapist
Dentist
Chiropractor
Beautician
Environmentalist
Politician

#16

Lawyer
Computer operator
Politician
Physicist
Mediator
Scientist
Government personnel
Space research and
  development personnel
Public speaker
News broadcaster
Journalist
Station manager
Psychologist
Editor
Writer
Land developer
Investment broker
Businessperson
Social agency worker
Minister

#17

Writer
Producer
Director
Manager
Station owner
Performer
Business owner
Seminar and workshop
  leader
Speaker
Coordinator
Publisher
Bank owner or manager
Financial broker
Stock marker investor or
  advisor
Corporate president or
  owner
Entrepreneur
Politician
Business consultant
Real estate agent
Advertising and marketing
  person

#18

Teacher
Psychologist
Minister
Missionary
Musician
Actress
Photographer
Writer
Artist
Travel agent
Tour guide
Director
Foreign language
  interpreter
Speech therapist
Social agency director
Volunteer for political or
  environmental causes

#19

Writer
Producer
Inventor
Doctor
Pilot
Chiropractor
Entrepreneur
Musician, composer
Jeweler
Car salesperson
Professional athlete
Owner, manager of
  restaurant
  sports team
  health club
  auto repair garage
  construction company
Attorney
Teacher
Judge

#20

Accountant
Insurance broker
Banker
Investment consultant
Employee in large
  business firm
Executive
Tax analyst
Civil servant
Government office jobs
Researcher

#21

Architect
Engineer
Draftsperson
Designer
Doctor
Dentist
Chef
Medical technician
Pilot
Postal worker
Graphic artist
Mechanic
Technician
Electrician
Musician
Writer

#22

Artist
Dancer
Actor
Aerobics instructor
Hairdresser
Manicurist
Musician
Florist
Waitress
Ski instructor
Elementary or preschool
   teacher
Physical therapist
Massage therapist
Art teacher
Writer
Flight attendant
Paramedic, nurse, doctor

#23

Director for nonprofit or
   service organization
Fundraiser
Personnel director
Career counselor
Hospital administrator
Real estate agent
Office manager
Loan officer
Events coordinator
Store owner
Public relations director
Business consultant

Which category had the kinds of occupations to which you are the most drawn? _____

Refer to your answers in the first questionnaire to see if your Life Color responses coincide with your occupation preferences. Whichever descriptions you feel most aligned with are probably your aura Life Colors. (Did you notice any occupation from your past or present that caused you to feel unhappy or unfulfilled? Were you going against your real Life Colors?)

Occupations Key

#1 = Red
#2 = Orange
#3 = Magenta
#4 = Yellow
#5 = Logical Tan
#6 = Environmental Tan
#7 = Sensitive Tan
#8 = Abstract Tan

#9 = Green
#10= Blue
#11= Violet
#12= Lavender
#13= Crystal
#14= Indigo
#15= Violet/Yellow
#16= Violet/Tan
#17= Violet/Green
#18= Blue/Violet
#19= Yellow/Green
#20= Tan/Green
#21= Tan/Yellow
#22= Blue/Yellow
#23= Blue/Green

introduction to life colors

The following are descriptions of all fourteen aura Life Colors and the most common Combination Colors. I hope that reading these descriptions will help you understand and accept yourself as you are and also help you learn how you can stay in power and balance. Many people have covered up one or both of their original Life Colors at a young age because they felt that their true identities were wrong, inadequate, or inappropriate. For example, because Yellows are such an energetic handful for their parents, they may learn to subdue their energies and become responsible Tan personalities instead. Violet children often learn to hold back on their incredible power and vision in order not to overwhelm or displease their more conventional parents. Many children are raised to be Tan or Blue personalities because that is traditionally what has been expected by society. Consequently, most children with other Life Colors grow up feeling confused or disconnected from who they really are.

CHAPTER TWO

physical life colors

RED

Reds are physical and sexual. They love expressing themselves through their sensuality and their physical bodies. They live their lives in the here-and-now with zest, strength, courage, and self-confidence. Reds love to live in physical reality, to manipulate their environments. Reality must be tangible to them. They must be able to see, touch, hear, taste, and smell it.

Reds are not abstract thinkers. A wall is a wall and there is no need for further discussion or speculation. Reality is literal, not ethereal or complicated. Reds require proof that something exists. It must have a concrete and tangible substance. Reds remind us that we have bodies, that we are matter — flesh and blood. These robust personalities enjoy the physical aspects of life. They don't try to see life as an illusion or try to escape from it into a fantasy world.

Reds do not focus on spirituality. If they have been raised to believe in God, they see God as a physical Being who is just and righteous, not as an esoteric idea, a consciousness, a life energy. They will go to churches or join other religious organizations because they enjoy the singing, dancing, and other physical expressions involved in the rituals of worship. Reds are the workers with their religion — moving pews, building churches, singing in the choir, or setting up booths for the bazaar. They will help take care of the practical needs of the organization.

Reds are most comfortable and alive when strength and stamina are required. They enjoy the challenges of moving physical objects rather than dealing with mental or emotional problems. They are the workers, able to bring the ideas of others into tangible substance by loading and unloading boxes, moving furniture or building houses. They are not afraid of physical labor or hard work. These personalities are practical, realistic, hard working, and action oriented. They love seeing the immediate results of their work.

Reds can be refreshingly honest or brutally abrupt in their interactions. They can be very blunt and outspoken. They are energetic, courageous, full of stamina and endurance, optimistic, loyal, honest, and trustworthy. In power they are slow to anger. When they do get angry, they get over it quickly and do not hold grudges. Reds who are out of power, however, become angry, easily frustrated, physically explosive, and potentially dangerous. Their rage is often released by punching holes in walls, starting fights, or having intense sexual encounters.

When Reds are in power, they find more appropriate outlets for their energy and anger, such as exercise or sports. When hurt, Reds respond to pain in much the same way that animals do, by withdrawing emotionally and lashing out physically.

Reds have an almost animalistic instinct for survival. They can sense the physical risk factors and potential dangers involved in a situation. They instinctively know what skills and resources are needed to overcome the challenges. They are adept at helping people survive such environmental crises as floods, fires, and earthquakes. They exhibit raw courage in the face of danger.

Reds can become very closed-minded, believing that the only reality is physical and that their way is the best way. They tend to defend their feelings and thoughts. It is a challenge for Reds to create sensitive, long-lasting relationships. They are hard to get to know. They are usually wary of opening up or trusting others and can often be hurtful with their hard, protective shells.

To stay in power, Reds must find acceptable outlets for their energy and their frustrations. They need to learn when to quit and when to be persistent with their efforts. When no amount of physical strength or endurance will keep the raging waters from flooding a town, for example, Reds continue to fight. They hate giving up. They can be so stubborn about staying on a course that they are not always able to see other options. If the town is flooding, a better attitude may be, "Save what you can, then come back and rebuild." Their never-ending energy and stamina can often wear out others who were enlisted to help. Reds need to learn the difference between being persistent and being stubborn. They would also do well to temper their frankness and allow others to express their beliefs and points of view.

Reds' life purpose is to live in the physical world with gusto, courage, and energy. They choose to experience life, with all it has to offer, through the five bodily sensations of touch, taste, smell, sight, and sound. They also love to give substance and tangible reality to ideas and plans. Reds understand action. They want to enjoy life as physical beings.

Relationships

Although Reds enjoy the companionship of mates, it is challenging for them to relate to and communicate with their mates on an emotional, intimate level. This can become frustrating to a mate who wants to bond emotionally with a Red. Although Reds will be very loyal and hard-working providers, they do not always know how to be available on other levels. Reds are very private individuals. They do not share their feelings easily. They are not known to be deeply introspective. Although Reds enjoy being around people at times, they are very guarded and cautious about getting into relationships. They enjoy being rowdy with their drinking buddies, but then they want their solitude. They tend to go back and forth between being loners and needing others.

It takes a very strong, independent, self-realized person to handle the fiery personality of a Red. This person must be able to withstand the Red's emotional walls as well as his violent and sometimes dangerous temper. Even though a Red will calm down as quickly as he flared up, a mate can soon become wary of his unpredictable outbursts. The Red's personality tends to be very compelling, forceful, and potent. Some people enjoy Reds' invincible power and dynamic energy. They also love the challenge and the excitement that the unpredictable Reds add to their lives. Most Reds are hardworking, down-to-earth realists who offer an honest, practical lifestyle to their mates. Sometimes, however, living with Reds can be compared to running with the bulls.

Sex

Sex for Reds is a lusty, sensual experience. Sexuality is an indispensable part of life for these robust personalities. They consider sex to be one of the animalistic pleasures of life, one of the joys of being in a physical body. Life is to be fully enjoyed with passion, zest, and a full appreciation of the physical sensations it has to offer. Sex is one of life's greatest pleasures for Reds. They relish the sensual experiences of taste, smell, and touch.

Sex does not, however, always involve love and compassion for Reds. It is usually about lust, passion, and the physicality of being "animal." To Reds, sex is not something that should be taboo. It is a natural, enjoyable bodily experience that should be savored. Reds have a difficult time being members of any society that restricts or denounces sexual activity. Complying would eventually cause Reds anxiety and frustration and would make them feel there was something intrinsically wrong with them. Reds need to feel free to completely experience their sexuality.

Red Parents

Although they are honest hard workers who will provide for their children, Red parents are not usually emotionally available to them. Reds are not comfortable with their own emotions or with discussing their feelings with their children. It is difficult for them to outwardly share intimate, tender moments. Tossing around the football or doing yard work together is their idea of bonding with their children.

Children can be intimidated by the physical power and explosive temper of their Red parents. Their children respond with either respect or fear or they feel rejected and unloved, depending on their own aura colors. Reds are not unloving parents, however. They can be very protective and concerned about their children. They just have a hard time communicating or expressing their emotions. What Red parents do teach their children is an understanding of honesty, the American work ethic, and the belief that life is what you make it.

Red Children

Red children are often a handful. Although they can be hard workers and are willing to complete their jobs, they can also be incredibly stubborn and have violent tempers, which can frustrate and upset parents. Red children are most likely the ones who will start fights at school. They understand physical force and brute strength. Although they don't want to be leaders, they also don't want to be pushed around. Reds have very independent and strong personalities.

At school, Red children prefer learning about subjects they can apply to their lives here and now. Auto mechanics, woodshop, sports, music, and cooking and sewing classes are much more interesting to them than a philosophy class. If the class has no practical application to their lives, they find no meaning in it. They are hard and honest workers as long as they see the practicality in what they are doing.

Even though every child needs and appreciates love, affection, and praise, Red children are embarrassed by open displays of affection. They prefer receiving tangible rewards such as toys or candy. They love to see the immediate results of their hard-earned efforts. Delayed gratification is frustrating and soon intolerable for them. If their reward is to go to Disneyland, they must go now, not a month from now. Otherwise, they do not understand the connection between the action and the reward.

The challenge for parents of Red children is to help them find healthy outlets for their frustration, anger, and inexhaustible energy. Being active in sports and doing physical chores are healthy outlets for Red children. Parents must also help them understand and learn to express their inner feelings in a sensitive and constructive manner. Teaching Red children to communicate by having frequent and nonthreatening discussions about their feelings will help them learn other methods of communicating.

Problem Solving

The Reds' method of problem solving is action oriented — action with power and positive expectations. Reds do not like to theorize. Although they can be very intelligent, they would rather just put the plan into action to see if it works. Reds prefer to work with physical problems, not mental ones. For instance, if the piano doesn't fit through the door, Reds move it through an open window, widen the door, or disassemble the piano. They don't sit around for hours discussing the options. They often arrive at solutions by instinct, persistence, or pure brute strength.

When in power, Reds have the optimistic outlook that every problem has a solution, although they may focus on fixing the symptom rather than the cause. They will stick with the problem, trying every possible method to move the piano out of the room. Reds usually find an option that works. They persist even after everyone else has concluded that the situation is hopeless. They also have the physical strength and stamina to push the rock up the mountain, enduring beyond everyone else's point of exhaustion. They do not like to let their physical environment get the best of them. They can inspire others through their sheer optimism and willingness to continue.

Out of power, Reds can become angry and frustrated. Others may find their never-ending need to persist and conquer intolerable. They can wear out their teammates and in the process accuse them of being weak and useless. Their need for conquering the opponent, overcoming the problem, and winning at any cost can soon alienate them from those who are there to aid and support.

When solving problems, Reds need to maintain a realistic perspective of the actual importance of the project. Although they can usually come up with practical solutions for physical problems, they also need to see that not every problem is best solved on a physical level. Using force is not always the answer, not even temporarily. (Because of their great courage and dedication, however, Reds can be dauntless heroes during wars.)

Money

Reds are usually very sharp in business and handle their money proficiently. Although there are always exceptions, most Reds do not strive to be rich. Money is not that important to them. As long as their basic needs are met and they have some creature comforts, they are content. Reds do like to have nice things — nice clothes, comfortable furniture, quality tools, and quality appliances. Their lives, however, are not ruled by material possessions. They don't usually worry about money because they know they are self-sufficient. They can always find jobs that can make them enough money to survive. They see money as a real and tangible necessity, but not as something that rules their lives.

Success

Success for Reds is measured tangibly. They look for immediate and concrete results from their labor. They love to take action and to bring a plan or idea into physical manifestation. Success is having the courage, energy, and stamina to overcome or manipulate their environment.

Occupations

Reds prefer jobs that require physical work, allow them manual dexterity, and have immediate, tangible results. They do not want to wait for something to happen. They want to feel they have control over the outcome. Reds prefer to be self-employed, which allows them control over their time and energy. They want jobs in which they can see they have accomplished something real and tangible.

Because they are so powerful and rugged, Reds have great respect for the power and magnificence of nature, and they often appreciate being able to work outdoors. They also enjoy the challenge of being courageous in dangerous situations.

Reds are frequently drawn to occupations such as the following:

Firefighter	Repairperson
Rescue worker	Mechanic
Police	Furniture mover
Military personnel	Butcher
Football player	Tractor driver and farmer
Boxer	Surgeon
Bodyguard	Bartender
Truck driver	Waitress, waiter
Heavy equipment operator	Singer
Construction worker	Dancer
Shop foreman	Model

Occasionally, Reds like Marilyn Monroe (Red/Yellow), Mae West, Dolly Parton (Red/Yellow), Sean Penn (Red/Yellow), or Madonna (Red with added Violet) show up in the entertainment field.

Health

Health problems for Reds are often work related. They may suffer from hernias or backaches from lifting too much, cut fingers from a butcher's knife, burns from a fire, or bullet wounds from an escaping suspect's gun.

To stay physically healthy, Reds need to learn when enough is enough, when not to push things too far. They need to gauge their exuberance when accomplishing a task. They also need to moderate their physical appetites. Because Reds love sensual, animal pleasures, they can tend to love food or alcohol too much.

ORANGE

Oranges are the thrill-seekers and daredevils of the aura spectrum. They love the challenge and excitement of physical danger. They love to challenge their environment and go beyond accepted physical limits. Oranges put their lives on the line just to feel alive; the stakes must actually be life and death for Oranges to feel a sense of accomplishment and satisfaction. They love the adrenaline rush of excitement in the face of danger. For Oranges, thrills, cunning skill, and excitement are the essentials in life. Everything else is just passive existence. Evel Knievel and actor-stuntman Jackie Chan are well-known Orange examples.

Oranges are realists, preferring to challenge and conquer physical reality rather than to discuss abstract philosophies. To these adventurers, life is real and tangible. Spirituality has no meaning to them. They don't want to be bothered by such concepts.

Oranges love to imagine and plan the strategy for the next adventure and then put it into action. They don't like safety devices, however. For Oranges, the greater the risk, the better.

They love to "boldly go where no man has gone before." They will plan and review all aspects of the feat until they feel comfortable with it and then take it to the next dangerous level.

Oranges are very good at seeing things through the eyes of their opponents. They strategize what the other driver will do or how the wild prey will react. They plan their actions accordingly. Oranges mentally, physically, and emotionally process what it will take to overcome all the elements involved. Their comprehensive mental preparation and planning stages are responsible for their survival.

In power, Oranges are incredibly resourceful, with amazing abilities to mentally become their opponents, to calculate every possible maneuver, and to boldly take action. They live life at its rawest level with energy and self-confidence. They awe others with their courage and daring. They are bold enough to go after challenges and live their dreams — even in the face of potential death. They can be found fearlessly risking their lives to save others. They have performed acts of great heroism — firefighters saving people from burning buildings, rescue workers scaling treacherous mountains, police risking their lives to free hostages. Most Oranges do not consider these to be heroic acts, but just part of their jobs.

Out of power, Oranges can become egotistical and self-centered, caring only to live in their own world regardless of how it affects their families. They do not show affection or compassion easily. Emotional, gentle characteristics do not make much sense to them. Consequently, they can tend to be cold and aloof. Oranges have problems facing the challenge of knowing themselves, of going inside and learning who they are emotionally, mentally, and spiritually. The only risks they appear to be willing to face are those that require physical courage and cunning.

For Oranges to stay in power, they need to realize that life involves balance — a balance of the body, mind, and spirit. By staying balanced, risking the challenge of exploring the inner world as well as the outer, Oranges can develop the ability to experience life on all levels. In this way they may live long enough to attain the wisdom that comes with age.

Oranges' life purpose is to experience physical existence to its fullest extent, to reach the apparent limitations of reality and dare to push past them. What is important to Oranges is the freedom to explore new territories, to face all the elements, and to emerge victorious. Oranges do not want to be limited. They want to challenge life face-to-face, with daring and courage. They desire to develop physical and mental cunning and the ability to challenge and overcome physical risks.

Relationships

Oranges are not usually interested in marriage or family. It is challenging for mates to accept the exploits of the daring Oranges. Most mates would watch helplessly as the Oranges prepared and packed their gear. The uncertainty of the outcome — never knowing if they would see them again — usually creates more tension than most mates can handle. The stress factor would be enough to cause most relationships to fail.

Oranges, therefore, tend to be loners. They are too interested in their own adventures to commit to the stability of long-term relationships. They tend to be self-centered in relationships. Facing life-threatening risks is for their own satisfaction, not others'. Nor are they willing to put aside their desire for adventure merely to calm the fears of loved ones. Living in suburbia with a spouse, children, and a nine-to-five job is a slow, torturous death for an Orange.

Being loners, Oranges do not usually need or want emotional bonding. Life to them has an almost raw, animalistic quality. They do not relate to sensitivity or compassion. Courage, boldness, and daring are the aspects that arouse them. Surviving their adventures creates more passion and excitement for them than do relationships. Accomplishing and surviving physical reality is what life is all about.

Because of their physical prowess and skills, Oranges are usually physically fit and trim — features that are attractive to the opposite sex. Oranges do not have problems attracting partners, just in maintaining lasting relationships. To maintain relationships, Oranges need to find mates who are independent, resourceful, and emotionally strong enough to handle Oranges' behavior. Perhaps Oranges can find people who are courageous and daring enough to share in their adventures. However, they must respect the Oranges' fierce independence and tolerate the lack of emotional sensitivity.

Sex

Sex is usually not a priority for Oranges, their primary goal being the thrill and excitement of their next exploit. In power, their attitude is typically that sex is fun, a nice release, a natural body function, but that real life is out there waiting to be experienced and conquered. Out of power, Oranges can see sexual conquests as their challenge. They use others sexually, then cast them aside or forget about them when it's time to start planning the next adventure.

Orange Parents

Oranges are not usually parents. Children are too cumbersome and restrictive for them. If they end up with children, however, they usually leave the responsibility of raising the children to their mates, causing their mates to become quite resentful of the Oranges' attitude. Being the risk-takers that they are, Oranges often do not set very good examples for their children. They also tend not to bond affectionately, communicate well, or relate emotionally with their children. Oranges are not usually concerned with providing a good standard of living or education for them.

Orange Children

Even as children, Oranges are adventurers. They will dive from the high diving board, climb to the tops of trees, or jump from roofs. Cuts and bruises do not bother these kids. They enjoy exploring and challenging their environment. Oranges are a handful for their parents, who are concerned for their physical safety. These children are constantly looking for the thrill of the next adventure.

Orange children become quite bored with school, not relating to its passive, intellectual, nonphysical attributes. They are daredevils and can create discipline problems. They are usually alienated from their peers. Most students will not take the dangerous risks that Oranges will take. Oranges would rather be racing motorcycles down steep mountains or rafting through treacherous rapids.

The challenge for parents of Orange children is to give them the freedom to explore their world without parents getting ulcers in the process. Because Oranges are determined to live life on the edge, parents can help them learn how to calculate the risks and successfully plan strategies. This is Oranges' best tool for surviving their exploits. If they can learn to think clearly under the pressure of life-threatening situations, they have a chance of living longer, fuller lives. (Many Yellows have similar interests and can act like Oranges. However, Yellows fear pain. As Yellows age, they become less adventurous and more cautious. Typically, as they mature Yellows will not take the same extreme risks Oranges will. Yellows need friends, whereas Oranges tend to be loners.)

Problem Solving

Oranges examine all the factors, calculate the risks, go over in their heads all the possible scenarios, make sure they have all the necessary equipment, remove all safety devices to make the challenge as physically exciting and life threatening as possible, and then take action. They prefer to work on physical challenges. They see life as a contest. They leave the more mundane challenges and questions of day-to-day living to others. Although Oranges are meticulous in their planning and their problem solving when it comes to potential life and death situations, other kinds of problem solving do not interest them.

Money

Because Oranges are such daredevils, they seem to sense that they will probably have a short life span and, therefore, tend to be irresponsible with money. They look upon money as the tool that allows them to obtain all the necessary equipment for their journeys. Quality is very important to Oranges, so when they go mountain climbing they take the best equipment money can buy. Money facilitates their adventures. Oranges are not interested in financial security or long-range planning. Most of them do not live long enough to enjoy retirement benefits. They tend to live more for short-term thrills. Working just for the sake of financial security is far too passive for them.

Success

Oranges succeed every time they overcome the challenge they set for themselves and survive to tell about it. Success is clearly and simply defined: reaching the top of the mountain, carrying off the stunt as planned, winning the race, getting through the fire unscathed and still alive.

Occupations

Oranges prefer to freelance, getting paid for what they enjoy doing and then having the freedom to move on to the next adventure. They typically do not choose the burdensome responsibility of having employees or being in charge. They also have no desire for administrative duties. Office jobs are too slow and tedious for them. These adventurers like to be as autonomous as possible. Being sponsored by a company to race cars, dive for hidden treasure, or do promotional stunts out of an airplane are the kinds of jobs Oranges love. They prefer to compete individually rather than with a team. This is the only way their skills can truly be tested. Consequently, they do not make great employees or team members.

Occupations to which Oranges are drawn include the following:

Race car driver	Rescue worker
Skydiver	Firefighter
Hang glider	Police or detective work
Wilderness guide	Deep-sea diver
River rafter	Bounty hunter
Wild safari hunter	Private investigator
Stunt double	Guard
Mountaineer	Lion tamer
Explorer	Trapeze artist

Health

Oranges seem to suffer more from cuts, bruises, scrapes, and broken bones than from mental or stress-oriented problems such as ulcers. Oranges' biggest health challenge is staying alive long enough to eventually have the physical problems related to old age. To stay healthy, Oranges need to consider carefully all aspects of their exploits and plan their feats very thoroughly.

In times past, when raw physical courage and strength were more required, more physical colors — specifically more Reds and Oranges — were on the planet. Now, however, because humanity seems to have mastered the more basic levels of physical survival, mental and emotional colors seem to be more prevalent.

MAGENTA

Magentas are the nonconformists in the aura spectrum and are not commonly found on the planet these days. They are usually seen as bizarre loners. They see life from a different and unusual perspective. They don't choose to abide by society's mores. These individualistic thinkers consider following the crowd to be boring and restrictive. They prefer to live beyond restrictions and limitations. Peer pressure has no effect on them. They follow the beat of their own drummers.

Magentas are very intelligent. They are also innovative and creative, fascinated by the latest gadgets and inventions. Often inventors themselves, Magentas love to figure out new ways of doing things. They enjoy creating bizarre, controversial objects that are arty, trendy — or even beyond trendy. Their imagination knows no limits. They do, however, deal with the tangibles on the planet. They like taking physical substance and stretching it into new forms that go beyond what people consider normal. Their art is unique and outlandish — Andy Warhol is a good example of a creative Magenta.

In power, Magentas have the willingness and courage to set their own styles. They love change, to go beyond the traditional and the familiar. They love to shock people, to shake them from their ordinary, humdrum existence. For example, Magentas will walk down the street wearing wild clothes and purple Mohawk haircuts. Other people don't usually have the nerve or the desire to live the lifestyle of the Magenta. Magentas act on unusual ideas, trying new things just for the experience. In power, Magentas accept and appreciate themselves and allow others to be themselves. They are generally happy and optimistic, and they prefer to look at life with a sense of humor. These unique personalities tend to be strong willed and determined to live life exactly the way they want to.

Out of power, Magentas can feel despondent, isolated, and lonely. Conforming to the crowd is unbearable for them and can cause severe depression. Yet, having friends is usually dependent upon their conforming to a certain degree. When they are out of power, Magentas don't live true to their own curious, innovative style. This creates low self-esteem, boredom, and despair. They lose their desire to experience life, which then seems like a burden or a punishment instead of the joyful experience they know it can be. To stay in power, Magentas have to love and accept themselves, give themselves permission to be different, see life from their own unusual perspective, and allow themselves to act on their creative impulses.

Because of their outrageous behavior, Magentas prefer to live in large, crowded cities where they don't stand out as much and aren't pressured to conform. These free spirits aren't usually concerned about what others think, but in large cities they are more apt to have the freedom to express themselves.

These liberal personalities do not usually join organizations. They do not want to be limited by rules or expectations. They are not ones for structure. They are not followers, nor do they want the responsibility of being leaders. They set their own pace, create fun for themselves and others, and then go their own way. They lead the way only by creating a hole in the wall of accepted limitations and boundaries. By stepping beyond these boundaries, they encourage others to go beyond their self-imposed restrictions as well.

Laughter and the absurd appeal to Magentas. Their strange sense of humor is often twisted and eccentric. They are also very outspoken. Magentas love being the center of attention. (The character of Auntie Mame is a perfect example of the outrageous Magenta.) They love entertaining people — acting, performing, and creating outrageous trends. In power, they like all kinds of people and can be comfortable with anyone they meet. Their assortment of friends can be as wild and eclectic as their taste in clothes or home decorating — and the more outrageous, the better. They can have trouble, however, keeping intimate friends.

They don't like being responsible for or tied down by friends. They prefer their relationships to be free and easy. Being emotionally responsible for anyone is too confining.

Although they like people, they are usually loners because most people cannot relate to their outrageous and bizarre way of thinking. Although people can be amused and entertained for awhile by Magentas, most people eventually become embarrassed by their bizarre behavior. Magentas' biggest challenge is dealing with the loneliness of being misunderstood and socially unaccepted.

Magentas are free spirits. They love to travel, talk with people, explore different cultures, and experience life to its fullest. They are always thinking of something new and different to do. However, they will invest their time only in those things they find interesting.

Because Magentas are not interested in discipline and order, their lives can become very confused. They can have trouble remembering to pay the bills — even when they have enough money to do so.

Magentas' life purpose is to explore the new and to experiment outside normal, everyday boundaries. They strive to keep life from becoming complacent. They love to keep us questioning and pushing beyond our accepted limits, to keep us from being satisfied with the status quo.

(Many Yellow/Violet aura combinations think they are Magentas because they have so many similar qualities and experiences. Magentas tend to focus on and enjoy the strangeness of the physical world. They are not concerned about spirituality or about humanitarian or environmental causes the way Yellow/Violets are. Magentas prefer to live in busy cities. Yellows prefer to live in more natural environments. Read also about the life purposes of Yellows and Violets to discover which are your real Life Colors.)

Relationships

Magentas like to be around people who have fun and are interested in life. They don't want to be serious or intense for long periods. They will eagerly learn about people, laugh, shock them, have fun with them, and move on. Frequent and short marriages are common. They believe in commitment because it is the best way to really become intimate with someone, to really learn all about a person. Long-term, intense relationships, however, are too much. When the relationship turns into a responsibility, they will move on. They stay married long enough to get to know their mates intimately, to share worlds for awhile. Even before the wedding, the Magenta's partner should be well aware that the marriage will probably be temporary.

Magentas also prefer an open marriage. They want the freedom to explore and experiment. They don't want to live with rules or expectations. After awhile, this experience wears on their partners. Magentas are unpredictable, surprising, quick, and energetic, but their different way of living eventually becomes tiring for their mates.

Magentas are kind enough not to hurt their mates when they leave. They usually remain very good friends with their mates. Their exits are made with tact and grace.

Sex

For Magentas, sex is a different adventure with each person. It can be an experiment with styles or an experience in getting to know the other person. As long as it doesn't lead to an intense or serious involvement that requires rules or limitations, sex is enjoyable for them. As long as sex is always different, exciting, and unpredictable, Magentas will stay sexually involved with their partners. Magentas, however, are not usually sexually monogamous. Monogamy takes the variety out of life.

Magenta Parents

Magenta parents enjoy the refreshing and unlimited perspectives of children. It is fascinating for Magentas to be around children to see how they participate in life. But Magentas do not usually cope well with the responsibility of raising children. They are not usually able to provide a stable or secure environment for them. Having no rules or boundaries can be wonderfully freeing and fun for children, but it can also create confusion for them, especially when they enter a more controlled environment such as school. As caring as they are, Magenta parents are more like creative but rebellious children themselves who would suffocate under the weight of parental responsibilities. Magenta parents can, however, encourage children to explore their imaginative and creative talents.

Magenta Children

There is not much difference between the child and the adult Magenta, only that the adults often have more freedom to express their creative, adventurous side. Magenta children usually have to abide by school rules or parental expectations. This can frustrate and even inhibit them. Although Magenta children are bright and curious, they stay interested and involved only in the classes they like. When a subject doesn't interest Magentas, they will look for diversions. School officials consider Magentas behavior problems because they don't want to live within rules. Magenta children — like the adults — are bright, innovative, and often social outcasts.

For parents of Magenta children, the challenge is to find acceptable outlets for them to express their unique creative talents. Classes such as art, drama, speech, or woodshop often provide a more flexible vehicle for Magentas to explore their remarkable styles. Although Magenta children can be very independent, they also have short attention spans so they often need extraordinary amounts of supervision to help them complete projects. Often, they need to be placed in special classes where they can receive more individual attention. A more unusual or avant-garde approach to education, as opposed to the traditional classroom setting and style, will keep Magentas more interested.

Magentas learn best when they are allowed to be creative with their assignments. They are very bright — bright enough to conceive innovative ideas and approaches to assignments. Their unusual way of thinking originates from a sense of the absurd, not from anger or rebellion. They are not malicious. Perhaps, the educational system will eventually discover that all children do not learn through the same processes and the system will be re-adjusted to include meeting the needs of Magenta children. (Again, Magentas and Yellow/Violet combinations are easily mistaken for each other. Violet children seem to have grand visions for their lives and wisdom beyond their years; Magentas are basically unusual nonconformists who love to see the world from bizarre perspectives.)

Problem Solving

Problem solving for Magentas is often innovative and outrageous. In power they can tackle situations from a unique perspective, one that can also seem unrealistic or impractical to others. Typically, Magentas surprise people by actualizing their zany ideas into physical reality. Out of power, Magentas can be so depressed, confused, and lost that they have no interest or energy to deal with problems. When humorously reminded of the absurdity of life, Magentas usually come back to life.

Money

Magentas can be practical about earning money. They know they need it to pay the bills, though they don't want to be run by it or work just because society says they must. They prefer to live life in the here-and-now, not put off living until after they retire. Consequently, they like to work at jobs that pay large sums of money. Then they will quit, take the money they have earned, and go on extended vacations. They will take other jobs only after they run out of money.

Magentas always seem able to make the money they need. They buy the necessities and play with the rest. They love to buy the unusual. Money allows them to try new things, but it is not essential because they will always find ways to do what they want.

Success

Magentas judge their success by how much freedom of expression they have and how far they can go beyond society's standards.

Occupations

Magentas are drawn to occupations to that give them freedom to express themselves and develop new ideas or products. They don't like traditional nine-to-five schedules. Instead, they prefer jobs that make them a lot of money quickly so they can travel or just enjoy life. Magentas love to live on the creative edge. They prefer to work on projects that allow them to explore, to be innovative and creative. They are good at imagining something, then producing the physical form. They like to take physical substances and twist them into bizarre works of art.

Magentas have short attention spans, however, so they don't always complete projects. They become bored and lose interest quickly. They are not always dependable employees. They enjoy jobs that are flexible, inventive, or creative. They are good writers and persuasive salespeople. Writing a script for a Monty Python movie would appeal to Magentas.

Other jobs include the following:

Artist	Costume designer
Clown	Photographer
Comedian	Publisher of avant-garde
Actor	publications

Writer	Entrepreneur
Inventor	Salesperson (especially
Set designer	for unusual items)
Art dealer or collector	Sculptor

Health

Magentas do not have specific areas that commonly cause them problems, although unusual, erratic lifestyles and bizarre eating habits can eventually affect their physical bodies. Lack of sleep from attending all-night social events or digesting a full dinner at 3:00 A.M. can stress their bodies, causing them to eventually burn out. Because modifying their activities or eating on a regular schedule does not appeal to Magentas, their bodies often wear out from abuse.

YELLOW

Yellows are the most fun-loving, free-spirited, energetic, and childlike personalities in the aura spectrum. Yellows are wonderful, sensitive, optimistic beings, whose life purpose is to bring joy to people, to have fun, and to help heal the planet. Yellows can be either very shy and sensitive or the life of the party. These playful characters have a great sense of humor. They love to laugh and to make others laugh. They believe life is to be enjoyed. They like to live life freely and spontaneously. With perpetual smiles on their faces, they remind people not to take themselves or their problems too seriously.

Yellows would prefer not to work at all, unless their work was fun, playful, or creative. They love nature and often have concerns for the survival of wildlife and the environment. Dogs are drawn to Yellows and often become their best friends. These Yellows are the perfect, fun-loving playmates.

On the one hand, these sensitive, childlike personalities like to please and want to be liked by everyone. They are some of the most optimistic and considerate people on the planet. Because

51

they want everyone to be happy, they can be generous to a fault. People find themselves drawn to Yellows because they feel lighter and happier around them. Yellows like being around people, but they also need their space and time to be alone.

On the other hand, Yellows can be extremely stubborn and rebellious. They hate being told what to do and often will do the opposite, just to prove they can't be controlled.

Yellows are some of the most suppressed beings from their childhoods because they were so energetic and curious as children. Many parents had a difficult time dealing with these active little hummingbirds. Yellows in power have abundant energy flowing through their bodies as if from an unlimited source. They can have a hard time sitting still. While they are listening to someone they will often tap their feet, fidget, or squirm. This is one of Yellows' most recognizable traits. Exercise moves this energy through their bodies and helps them stay happy, healthy, and centered. Long-muscle exercises such as bicycling, swimming, snowboarding, yoga, dancing, volleyball, tennis, and surfing are great releases for Yellows. Otherwise, their intense, bottled-up energy will create an inner battle, causing them to become frustrated, exhausted, depressed, and, eventually, ill. It is especially important for Yellows to release energy through their physical bodies when they are upset or angry. When Yellows stay active and fit, they are filled with joy, happiness, and a zest for life, and they are better able to deal with life's challenges. (See in chapter 5 the Blue/Yellow section to see the conflict that arises around exercise.)

Yellows also have addictive personalities. Positive addictions include exercise, sports, and creativity. When in power, Yellows like to keep their bodies fit. They love playing outdoors, exercising, and eating healthy foods. They are drawn to nature, sunshine, and warm weather. If they focus on positive addictions, they remain full of life, joy, and creative energy.

Negative addictions for Yellows include drugs, alcohol, cigarettes, caffeine, sweets (especially chocolate), and overeating. They can even become addicted to watching television or playing computer games. If they indulge in negative addictions, first they become high and full of energy, but then can hit bottom, becoming depressed, lethargic, and confused or angry and rebellious. Their bodies are so sensitive that they can experience the effects of negative substances for a long time. It is difficult to convince Yellows to stay away from negative addictions because they enjoy the substances and do not like being told what to do. They are natural rebels. It must be their choice. Yellows are also not very self-disciplined, so it can be difficult for them to refrain from negative addictions after they become involved with them.

Yellows usually become involved in negative addictions when there is conflict, unhappiness, or a lack of fulfillment in their lives, but they don't know how to solve their problems. Often their inner conflicts began in childhood. Feeling as if they are unable to please parents is a common problem for Yellows. (Yellows especially need to bond with their fathers. They can feel quite hurt if they feel emotionally disconnected or are physically abandoned by their fathers.)

Because Yellows are so sensitive, their feelings can be hurt quite easily. They can sense when someone is troubled or unhappy with them, but they usually do not want to face them. Not answering the phone is often their solution. When they know people are upset, Yellows will first attempt to cheer them up. Their next impulse is to run away. If this is not an option, they may then turn to drugs or alcohol to numb the pain, suppress their feelings, or hide from the confusing situation. They do not enjoy becoming involved with intense emotional problems. To make the situation better, they would instead prefer to help people by physically fixing something for them — their cars, their health, or their kitchen sinks.

Usually, if Yellows recognize that the consequences of negative addictions are a loss of energy, joy, creativity, and youthful appearance, they will choose positive actions instead, such as staying physically active. Facing their conflicts and maintaining a sense of humor can help Yellows veer away from negative addictions. Yellows need to learn to face their challenges rather than run away.

Not knowing which career to choose is another dilemma for Yellows. Often, they do not know what they want to be. In addition to not wanting to work at all, Yellows are afraid they may choose the wrong careers and then end up stuck and unfulfilled. Their work must be fun for them. Because they need variety in their lives, they need to give themselves permission to choose many careers. Yellows can also be afraid of choosing careers because they don't believe in themselves. They are often insecure about their creative abilities, their ability to make money, or their ability to please others.

Yellows are very creative. They especially love to work with their hands — painting, sculpting, planting gardens, building homes, fixing appliances, working on cars. They are also procrastinators, however, so the cars they took apart may take months to be put back together. Yellows can also be creative writers. Both physical and creative projects are therapeutic for Yellows.

Yellows are also very intuitive through touch. This quality makes them great with massage and healing. When Yellows give massages, they instinctively find the areas that need healing. They have the ability to move energy through their bodies, making them natural healers. When you receive a hug from a Yellow, you can feel energy coming from the Yellow's body and instantly feel better. Yellows are also very kinesthetic. They can sense energy from people and their environment. It is physically uncomfortable for Yellows to be near someone who is angry or to be in a room where there has been tension or unhappiness. Yellows' bodies are their barometers.

Yellows often have a fear of commitment. In their eyes commitment may take away options; it means they will have to grow up and accept responsibilities. They have a hard time committing to one person or to one career. Yellows prefer choices and freedom rather than restrictive responsibilities. Although Yellows appreciate being loved, love can also frighten them. Love often involves responsibility. Yellows prefer to be liked. They are the ultimate Peter Pans, actually having a fear of growing up and growing old. Usually, Yellows look younger than their age. Unless they become involved in negative addictions or there are people making stressful or unreasonable demands on them, they will look and feel young throughout their lives.

The tendency to avoid commitment and hard work, as well as consistently being late for appointments, often earns Yellows the reputation of being lazy and irresponsible. (Yellows live so much in the moment that they lose track of time.) People with other Life Colors, although enjoying Yellows' generosity and playfulness, can become quite frustrated and judgmental of their easygoing attitude. (See in chapter 6 the relationships with Yellows.)

Yellows need to understand that commitment can help them reach deeper levels of intimacy and self-awareness and therefore add more fun, excitement, and freedom to their lives. Otherwise, they can drift aimlessly, confused and penniless, forever searching for something to bring them joy and fulfillment.

Relationships

In relationships, Yellows can be very sensitive and caring with their mates. Because they are considerate and want to please, it is painful for them to feel they have caused anyone unhappiness, especially those they love. Yellows can have an idealistic picture of what relationships can be. They want playmates who can laugh and play with them, take care of them (without over-mothering them), and not take away their freedom. Yellows still need their time alone.

Yellows like to flirt, but become nervous if the other person wants to explore more than flirtation. Because they like the excitement of catching someone's attention but don't like to be trapped, Yellows have a tendency to play games. If you chase after a Yellow and come on too strong, the Yellow will run away. If, however, you then back away or seem disinterested, the Yellow will come back to see if you still like him. He will be cute and entertaining and will bring gifts to assure your affection. When he has accomplished that, he is out the door again. To prevent Yellows from playing games, their partners must learn to stand firmly committed to the relationship and not react to the Yellows' habitual tendencies to run away. Yellows usually will return. When Yellows feel safe, they typically calm down and form committed relationships.

Even though Yellows often truly believe they want committed relationships, their history of relationship choices can reveal a different story. Fear of commitment can take the form of being attracted to people who are unavailable, unattainable, or have a similar fear of commitment. This kind of person is safe for Yellows. When Yellows truly allow themselves to fall in love, they are loving, faithful, and committed. They will do everything in their power to assure that their mates are happy.

If Yellows are in restrictive or domineering relationships and feel they are trapped — because of children, financial insecurities, or other commitments — they can become unhappy and depressed. At this point, they will close down, lose their energy, and give up on their lives, or they will develop subversive and rebellious behavior toward their mates. (See chapter 5 regarding relationship conflicts with the Blue/Yellow, Yellow/Violet, Yellow/Green, and Yellow/Tan Life Colors.)

Sex

Yellows are very sexual. Their lovemaking can be very playful. They like to laugh, have fun, and make jokes. At the same time they can also be very sensitive and considerate of their mates. Sex is both a pleasure and a physical release for Yellows. Sex can help them feel connected to the other person. It is challenging for Yellows to commit to one sexual partner. Monogamy takes away their choices and options. However, when Yellows really fall in love, they are as faithful as puppies. (They also have a fear of being caught or of hurting someone's feelings if they stray.)

Yellow Parents

Yellows love to play with children, but they do not necessarily want the responsibilities of raising them. Getting up at 2:00 A.M. to change a diaper or feed a baby is not their idea of a good time. Yellows are such children themselves that a woman married to a Yellow man will often complain of having three children rather than two children and a husband. Children love to be around Yellows because they can be great playmates. Because Yellow parents are more like children themselves, they do not usually want to be disciplinarians with their children, but want to be liked as friends.

If Yellows are in power, they are great with their children and can become very attached to them. They find creative ways to teach their children about life.

Out of power, Yellows tend not to be good examples to their children. They tend to be lazy and often abandon their responsibilities. Sometimes, Yellows out of power can become physically abusive or develop drug and alcohol problems. When Yellows are upset or frustrated, they tend to react physically. Alcohol and drugs can intensify that reactive behavior.

Yellow Children

Yellow children can either be painfully shy and insecure or exactly the opposite. When shy Yellows are around people they do not know, they run away or withdraw. They seem to be intimidated by people or are afraid of not being liked. When Yellows feel comfortable and familiar with those around them, they become charming little entertainers. Some Yellow children often cause trouble at school by being the class clowns. They love to make their friends laugh.

Yellow children are very active and curious. Physically, they are constantly on the move, getting up and down and into everything. Because of their physical energy and short attention spans, they have a difficult time focusing or sitting still for long periods of time. They fidget, squirm, and entertain their classmates. Yellow children are frequently diagnosed with ADD (Attention Deficit Disorder) or ADHD (Attention Deficit Hyperactive Disorder). During the long hours of school, it is beneficial to have these high-energy Yellow children draw or otherwise work creatively with their hands while the teacher is talking. Otherwise, it is difficult for Yellows to sit still and pay attention; their minds wander. Taking time out to run around the track at school is also a good release. As long as there is some form of movement for the children, they can concentrate. (This also applies to Yellow adults.) The physical disciplines of Tai Chi or yoga are excellent forms of meditation for Yellows because they involve slow movement.

Because movement is so meditative for Yellows, they also tend to calm down and develop creative ideas when they are riding in cars. If the ride is too long or restrictive, however, they become restless. Any type of movement relaxes Yellows and allows them to concentrate. Parents can often lull their Yellow babies to sleep by driving them in the car. Yellows are happier when there is movement of some sort.

Parents will want to encourage Yellow children's creativity by supplying them with crayons, paper, building blocks, or musical instruments. Directing their physical energy into sports, dance, or other positive outlets is also important for their children's well-being. In addition, parents can enjoy, rather than discourage, Yellows' ability to make others laugh. Yellow children need to know they are bringing joy to other people.

Yellow children are very sensitive and want to please their parents. Although they like to please, they also hate to be told what to do. Parents will frequently hear the word no from Yellow children. They can become extremely rebellious. (The "terrible twos" are merely a warm-up for Yellows' adolescence.) Typically, the parents discover that the form of discipline Yellow children most quickly respond to is physical punishment. This kind of punishment, however, can be very damaging to Yellows. These sensitive children are also physically affected when someone yells at them.

If parents tell Yellow children to clean a room, that is the last thing they will do. Parents will get better results by giving these children several choices and explaining the consequences that will follow each choice. For example, when asking a Yellow child to clean her room, the parent can allow her to pick up her toys, make her bed, or put away her clothes first. The choice belongs to the child. If she chooses none of the options, she must also know the consequences of that choice. Parents must learn to follow through with the consequences if they expect a child to learn about making responsible choices. Learning to give choices and follow up with natural consequences is a much healthier way to discipline Yellow children. They then learn that their choices make a difference and that the consequences are more positive when they make wise and responsible choices.

It is not advisable for parents to force Yellow children to sit still, grow up, or be more serious. Yellows' priorities are to play, have fun, be creative, and heal people. Forcing goals or priorities upon Yellows will hurt their feelings. They will close down, become depressed, and not believe in their own worth. The sensitive Yellows are insecure and fear people will not like them. Reassuring Yellow children they are liked and bring joy to people helps them open up and live their full potential. It helps them believe in themselves.

Yellow children are so sensitive that if their parents have an argument, they will be the first to sense the unhappiness and try to make everyone happy again. If they feel they cannot improve the situation, they will withdraw and hide or develop nervous and erratic behavior. All Yellows need to release anger and frustration physically — true for adults as well as for children. When Yellows are upset, they want to hit, kick, or break something. Yellows also cry easily. Parents should encourage Yellow children to release energy positively: to run, swim, ride a bicycle, or hit a punching bag. They should also help their children feel that it is safe to emotionally express their fear and sadness. If parents stifle children's need to release energy physically, these Yellows will eventually become depressed or self-destructive, turning the energy in on themselves. Yellows can typically turn to drugs or alcohol to numb pain, to avoid conflict, or to punish themselves.

Problem Solving

When in power, Yellows are creative problem solvers. They can create unique solutions, usually designed to make life easier. (It was probably a Yellow who first had the idea of remote control for television.) Yellows also enjoy reading books with such titles as *A Lazy Man's Guide to Enlightenment* or *The Trick to Money Is Having Some*. Often, Yellows' solutions are humorous. Their light-hearted optimism helps them keep their heads clear; therefore, problems are not seen as overwhelming or disastrous.

When Yellows are out of power or are living in fear, however, they become insecure about their abilities and afraid to take risks. They will ignore or run away from their problems. Running away can include physically leaving, sleeping, overeating, drinking, smoking, getting sick, watching too much television, hiding out with computer games, or constantly moving to different places. Out of power, they do not like to face responsibilities, hard work, or anything uncomfortable. When there are challenges, they prefer to take the easiest route, which is usually either escaping or doing nothing at all. When they realize that avoidance and procrastination usually stem from fear, they can learn to face their fears and move forward. After Yellows regain their center, they become relaxed and can once again develop creative solutions.

Money

Money is not a motivating factor for Yellows. It does not take much money to make Yellows happy, nor do they want to work that hard for it. Typically, Yellows are not very financially reliable. They tend to play with money or spend it irresponsibly. They are generous to a fault; money seems to disintegrate in their hands. They usually have no idea what happened to the money they earned. Yellows often become involved with get-rich-quick schemes because it is easier than working. (This is especially true for Yellow/Green combinations.) Making and managing money can feel like too much responsibility. Yellows need to know that working and managing their finances can be fun and creative. To create more money, Yellows should simply imagine how it would physically feel in their hands. This seems to be one method of attracting money to them.

Success

Yellows do not judge their success in terms of money or physical possessions, but by how much fun they are having, by how much freedom and flexibility they have, and by how many people like them. Feeling young and healthy is also important to them.

Occupations

Yellows must have fun in their careers. They seldom choose only one career in a lifetime (unless they are a Logical Tan/Yellow Combination Color); instead, they prefer a variety of careers. Life is like a candy store to Yellows. They need variety and choice. Yellows are commonly drawn to three basic fields: creative and artistic pursuits, health and healing, or physical labor and sports.

Most comedians have yellow in their auras. Bill Cosby (Yellow/Violet), George Burns (Yellow/Green), and Lucille Ball (Yellow/Green) are prime examples. Sports personalities also tend to have yellow auras. Wilt Chamberlain, Michael Jordan, and

John Elway are all Yellow/Violets. John Denver was a Yellow/Tan with Violet.

Some occupations Yellows are drawn to include the following:

Athlete	Comedian
Surfer	Artist
House painter	Musician (especially
Construction worker	drummer)
Laborer	Writer
Lifeguard	Chef
Firefighter	Interior decorator
Gardener	Healer
Bodybuilder	Doctor
Auto mechanic	Nutritionist
Designer	Veterinarian
Bartender	Physical therapist
Park ranger	Massage therapist
Waiter/waitress	Maintenance worker
Conservationist	Court jester for the world

For other occupations Combination Colors (Yellow/Logical Tan, Yellow/Violet, and Yellow/Green) are drawn to, see chapter 5.

Health

Yellows in power are some of the healthiest people on the planet. Healthy Yellows have very long life spans. Their positive, lighthearted attitude as well as their natural ability to channel life energy through their bodies helps them live longer and healthier lives. They usually look and feel younger than their actual age.

Physically, Yellows' primary weak areas are their backs and knees. When Yellows are out of power, holding back their feelings or being afraid to move forward in life will create injuries predominantly in these areas. Other potential health problems occur in their legs, feet, prostate, and liver. Yellows' sensitivity also makes them prime candidates for colds. A suppressed inner hurt or a need to cry can often cause a cold or other sinus problems. Out of power, Yellows can also develop drug- and alcohol-related health problems. Staying happy, optimistic, and physically active will help them avoid such problems. Spending time in nature is very therapeutic for Yellows.

Yellows typically have a sensitive sense of smell. They commonly smell everything before eating it, are uncomfortable in strange-smelling places, and are sensitive to body chemistries.

When they are young, energetic and rebellious Yellows tend to take a lot of physical risks — motorcycle riding, mountain climbing, racing, etc. But as they grow older, they tend to slow down, avoiding physical activities that are overly risky or dangerous because of a basic fear of pain.

Because Yellows channel so much healing energy through their bodies, they can usually heal their bodies quickly. Any time Yellows become ill, it is a sure sign they are experiencing inner fear or conflict. To become healthy again, Yellows must face their issues, moving through and beyond their fears.

Three activities can keep a Yellow healthy, happy, and balanced: exercise, refraining from negative addictive substances, and keeping a sense of humor.

CHAPTER THREE
mental life colors

Mental Life Colors comprise Logical Tan, Environmental Tan, Sensitive Tan, Abstract Tan, and Green. Each Tan has a tan-colored band that encircles the body; each has a variance, however, in the shade of tan and has a different-colored second band that accompanies the tan band. Each Tan has a unique emotional makeup that differentiates him from the others, although all are similar in that they tend to focus on details and are cautious, practical thinkers.

LOGICAL TAN

The Logical Tan has a light tan-colored band that encircles the body and is usually kept tightly drawn to it. This reflects Logical Tans' tendency to keep their feelings and thoughts to themselves. Logical Tans are very logical and analytical. They choose to process every step, from one through ten. Tans do not like to skip or miss anything. Their method of processing cannot be rushed. They need to analyze and comprehend the logic in each step before proceeding to the next. They like to establish a firm foundation and then slowly build brick by brick, step by step. Otherwise, they are afraid the entire project will collapse. Not being risk-takers, these methodical thinkers need to see all the data and all the facts before making any moves. Everything for Logical Tans is done in an orderly and sequential manner. Every detail is meticulously processed.

These security-conscious people are more comfortable repeating familiar patterns. They know what to do, what is expected of them, and what the results will be each time. Moving on to new patterns is not easy. New patterns pose an entirely different set of problems to deal with. Before leaping into another job or situation, they need to know all the details — exactly what they can expect with the salary, the hours, the job duties, the retirement benefits, the health plan, and the stability of the company. These Tans prefer each step to follow a consistent pattern.

Logical Tans typically form habitual patterns. They are more comfortable repeating the same duties day after day. They don't like their routines to be altered. Even rearranging the furniture in their homes can throw them off and cause them to feel awkward until they are able to adjust to the new situation. These Tans are the least flexible and adaptable personalities of the aura spectrum. Their sense of security is attached to sameness, reliability, and predictability. They can often get into ruts. A lifestyle others may consider boring Logical Tans may consider stable, secure, and comfortable.

Logical Tans will not usually believe in something unless they have been shown the evidence. E.S.P., channeling, and psychic phenomena are just mumbo-jumbo to them unless they can see the proof or discover that science has proven their validity. For these Tans, beliefs are based on seeing is believing. They prefer to stay grounded in reality. These practical personalities want to make sense out of the three-dimensional world. They enjoy analyzing and figuring things out.

Logical Tans have produced such technical achievements as computers, radios, televisions, and modern appliances. Few other

Life Colors have the patience or persistence to deal with the intricate, detailed components of these inventions. These Tans have the ability to accomplish tasks that others consider mundane or tedious.

Being detail oriented, Logical Tans also tend to express themselves slowly and methodically. Someone with a Green Life Color, who prefers to get straight to the point, can become impatient and frustrated listening to Tans' detailed accounts of the day's activities. Their stories can seem long and drawn out. Most Life Colors soon stop paying attention. The Green just wants to hear the punch line. The Blue just wants to know how the Tan felt about the incident. The Violet wants to hear about the bigger picture.

When Logical Tans are in power they are reliable and responsible. They are also some of the most dependable people in the world. They will accomplish tasks with thoroughness and efficiency, making sure every detail is handled. They can eventually develop the rational and practical proof to support many theories produced by others.

Logical Tans can have a calming and stabilizing effect on people. Their grounded and practical behavior can help others look at the logic behind a situation. If people are in a hurry to accomplish something, Logical Tans' slower methods may frustrate and irritate them, causing more stress and panic. But their behavior can also calm people by encouraging them to move more slowly and think rationally. "Haste makes waste" is a favorite expression for Logical Tans.

Logical Tans out of power can become stuck, narrow minded, and critical of things they do not understand. They can become stubborn when it comes to change, forward movement, or discussions involving theoretical ideas. Even with proof, they can be overly skeptical of new methods or of conclusions based on incomplete data. To regain their power, they need only to recognize their skepticism and evaluate whether it is realistic or perhaps is based on a fear of moving forward. After all, most scientific facts were once unknown. Exploring other unproven and uncharted areas will keep Logical Tans from becoming stagnant and judgmental. For them to move forward, they must learn to take some risks, to jump into the unknown without information or guarantees. They need to stay open to the possibility that today's unproven concepts may eventually be validated.

In their conversations, Logical Tans prefer to talk about how they think rather than how they feel. They do not choose to talk about their emotions. They keep such information to themselves. If someone does persuade them to discuss how they feel, they will usually talk about how they think they feel. Logical Tans are often not in touch with their feelings. If an emotional incident occurs, they will analyze the situation while keeping control of their feelings. They will emotionally shut down and withdraw, then calmly and rationally discuss the incident.

Relationships

Many aura colors are drawn to the stability and reliability of Logical Tans. These Tans are conscientious and consistent providers who are also willing to be in long-term, committed relationships. However, if people are looking for excitement, thrills, passion, and romance, Logical Tans are not the best candidates. They are much too practical and logical for such "unnecessary" frills. Many emotional aura colors are disappointed when they discover their Logical Tan mates are emotionally unavailable and unresponsive to them. Logical Tans are not the ones for open, emotional communication and deep bonding. For intellectual conversation, calm and rational thinking, stability, reliable behavior, and consistent financial support, Logical Tans are a good choice.

Sex

Logical Tans do not have a very strong sex drive. It's not that they don't enjoy sex, it's just not high on their list of priorities.

Frequently, these Tans will put aside sex to take care of practical responsibilities — paying bills, bringing work home from the office, or balancing the checkbook.

Being habitual by nature, Logical Tans can also fall into habitual patterns with sex, such as always having sex on the same day of the week, in the same location, and in the same position. As with other things in their lives, sex can become boring and predictable. Sex is not usually a passionate, lustful, physical experience for them. Rather it can become an obligation or tradition. These Tans are caring and considerate with their mates. Too often, however, they can become analytical and concerned more with technique than with experiencing wild, passionate sexual abandonment. (See chapter 5 to learn the sexual behavior of Violet/Tans and Yellow/Tans.)

Logical Tan Parents

Logical Tans will usually calculate the costs, consider the timing, evaluate the responsibilities, and list all the pros and cons before they will bring a child into the world. After all, children don't always abide by schedules, are costly, and can disrupt the established system.

These Tan parents are responsible and reliable providers. Their children will be fed and clothed to the best of these Tans' abilities. There will be no excess and no waste. Their children will not be spoiled. Logical Tans believe their children should learn the value of a dollar.

Logical Tan parents are disciplinarians. They want structure and obedience in their homes. They do not typically show their emotions or share openly with their children. (There are some exceptions with Combination Colors. See chapter 5 for Tan/Violet and Tan/Yellow characteristics.)

The challenge for Logical Tan parents is allowing their children to be children — to play and be irresponsible. Tans stress responsibility, consistency, accountability, and discipline. Logical

Tans need to communicate openly and with sensitivity if they expect to bond with their children. Otherwise, although the children will probably respect their Logical Tan parents, they will not feel that they really know them or that they connect emotionally with them.

Logical Tan Children

Logical Tan children seem to be introspective and often solemn. They, like their adult counterparts, process slowly, cautiously, and methodically. They often take things apart to see how they work, especially Yellow/Tan Color Combinations. They love to analyze, calculate, and see cause and effect relationships.

Because of Logical Tans' tendency toward detailed and methodical processing, these children are often thought of as being slow learners. They do not always develop quickly. Often, they do not grasp ideas as cunningly as some of their peers and may have to work longer and harder to complete a task. But the Logical Tan child will develop eventually. Parents should allow these Tan children to work at their own pace. They cannot be rushed; they must be allowed to comprehend each step before they proceed to the next one, otherwise the steps will not make any sense to them. They must build logically and sequentially upon all the data to come to a conclusion.

At school, these children are usually quiet and withdrawn. They are slow to make friends. This is not always the case, however, if they have another Life Color in their auras, for example, Violet/Logical Tan or Yellow/Logical Tan.

Logical Tan children, like their adult counterparts, do not usually show their emotions or share their feelings easily. Most tend to withdraw and then analyze the situation to see what has caused the problem and what the rational solution may be. To these Tans, emotional outbursts are illogical and usually don't accomplish anything. Their habit of closing down can frequently create concern for parents, who usually have no idea what is truly going on inside their heads. Parents will need to be patient and understanding with these children, allowing them to share what they are comfortable sharing, and then letting them figure out the rest for themselves. Parents can sometimes help by reviewing the facts with their children. This gives these Tan children more data and tools to come up with solutions.

Logical Tan children do not react to much, although changing their familiar environment by adding a new baby to the home or moving to a new location can cause them stress. These children, like Logical Tan adults, are upset by change.

To keep these Tan children from getting stuck in behavior patterns that may feed their fear of change and of taking risks, parents may want to occasionally introduce new ideas or activities into the children's lives. Maintaining a stable and reliable foundation for children is fine; all Tans need the security of knowing they can count on a few constants in their lives. What can be helpful, though, is to add new concepts, people, or objects to their stable foundations so they get used to the idea that change is a safe and normal part of life. Showing Logical Tan children other possibilities encourages personal development and creates trust in growth.

Problem Solving

Logical Tans typically exhibit good problem-solving abilities, provided they can remain open minded and receptive to many possibilities. Given enough time, they will eventually figure out practical and realistic solutions. When these Tans refuse to see any other choices but their usual, logical answers, they become closed and have difficulty arriving at alternative solutions. Not being risk-takers, they tend to choose solutions that are safe and have proven successful. Logical Tans prefer to preserve the status quo. These thinkers will carefully analyze a problem, incorporate every detail, and conclude with a rational, practical, and detailed solution.

Money

Security and stability are important to Logical Tans, who therefore tend to prefer a regular paycheck to the uncertainty and unpredictability of being self-employed. They want money, but they believe they must work long, hard, and consistently for it, then safely invest it in long-term, solid investments such as T-bills and life insurance policies. These security-minded Tans have the ability to work for the same company for years. Retirement benefits and pension plans are considered major assets to Logical Tans. These prudent spenders tend to be frugal with their money, buying the least expensive and most practical items. (Greens, who always want the best, classiest, and most expensive items, can become frustrated with Logical Tan's practical attitude. However, Greens, who also tend to spend beyond their means, can learn and benefit from a Logical Tan's practical spending behavior, and can help them stay out of financial debt.)

Success

Success for Logical Tans can be measured tangibly by how many accounts they have maintained in business, how well they have been able to provide financial security for themselves and their families, and how many of their investments have proven to be profitable. These Tans like to see how well they have been able to figure out life and to what degree they have been able to provide a secure and comfortable niche for themselves and their families.

Occupations

Logical Tans are most often drawn to safe, secure, analytical office jobs. They love to calculate numbers, analyze data, and work with details. They prefer secure, long-term positions with stable companies. It is rare to find Logical Tans in the unpredictable entertainment business. However, Harrison Ford and Kevin Costner are both Yellow/Logical Tan combinations with

Violet in their outer bands. The Yellow and Violet aspects enable them to flourish in this type of creative field.

Typical Logical Tan occupations include the following:

Engineer	Office clerk
Architect	Data processor
Bookkeeper	Factory assembly worker
Accountant	Librarian
Computer analyst	Court reporter
Researcher	Appliance repairperson
Scientist	Electrician
Technician	Computer operator
Mathematician	County surveyor

See chapter 5 for information on preferred occupations for Yellow/Tan and Tan/Violet combinations.

Health

The main health problems for Logical Tans tend to stem from long hours of detailed mental work. Many of these Tans have poor vision as a result of straining over computer work, financial ledgers, or legal papers. Because they usually do sedentary mental work, they often suffer from such maladies as hemorrhoids, headaches, excess weight, and weak muscles. They also tend to suppress their emotions, which can cause ulcers, stomach or digestive problems, constipation, and even impotence.

Logical Tans usually have an additional Life Color in their auras, which can cause a variety of other illnesses. For example, a Logical Tan/Violet combination is susceptible, more than any other Combination Color, to cancer, heart attack, and stroke because of the struggle to harmonize the conflict between the grounded logical Tan and the emotional, visionary Violet. To stay healthy, these Tans must worry less about the details. They need to rest their eyes occasionally to prevent strain (blinking the eyes frequently also helps the strain). They need to balance mental work with physical exercise (this also increases oxygen to the brain so they can think more clearly and effortlessly), and they need to express, not suppress, their feelings more often.

ENVIRONMENTAL TAN

The Environmental Tan Life Color is a deep tan-colored band layered with a forest green-colored band. Environmental Tans are the bridge between the physical family and the mental family. They experience their reality by physically touching their environment and then mentally analyzing it. (Occasionally, Yellow/Tan Combinations who have suppressed their free-spirited Yellow aspects believe themselves to be Environmental Tans. Yellow/Tans must find a way to reconnect with their Yellow aspects rather than live believing they are Environmental Tans.)

Like their Logical Tan and Sensitive Tan counterparts, Environmental Tans desire security, stability, logic, structure, and discipline. They operate best in a world of rules, boundaries, standards, and logical outcomes that follow basic laws of cause and effect. They process life in an orderly and sequential manner just as Logical Tans do, but they have the added ability to measure their environment from an inner perception. These amazing personalities can intuitively analyze spatial situations. They can sense the exact distance from one side of a room to the other just by looking at it. They can hold something in their hands and know exactly how much it weighs or look at a garage full of junk and know in how many and what size boxes it will all fit. Environmental Tans relate kinesthetically and mentally to their environment. They physically handle their surroundings and then internally and methodically process the information.

Environmental Tans are usually serious, self-controlled personalities. Life is not meant to be the playful, spontaneous creation that Yellows believe it to be. Rather, it is an orderly, well-planned universe that needs to be analyzed, categorized, and understood logically to provide the best opportunities for humankind. Environmental Tans' purpose for being here appears to be to analyze, understand, and learn from three-dimensional, physical reality, and they want the planet to be a place where modern technology fits in harmoniously with the physical environment. Many have an innate desire to help improve or rebalance that environment.

Environmental Tans demand reliability and dependability from their world — everything must have a logical and rational explanation. They make good scientists or military personnel because these fields have a solid foundation of order, cause and effect, and predictability — a natural hierarchy or chain of command. In power, Environmental Tans are adept at planning strategies based on logic, spatial measurements, and available resources. They meticulously calculate all the steps and details. Their physical and mental systems can often be overloaded with too much data and information, which can cause them physical and mental stress. They need to absorb information in an orderly manner. Too much happening at once means chaos. These systematic Tans prefer their environment to be neat, clean, and orderly. (Yellow/Tan Combinations are not usually neat and orderly.) They need quiet time alone to analyze all the information.

Environmental Tans are very intelligent people. However, they frequently have trouble expressing themselves, which makes them appear aloof and unresponsive. They tend to be quiet and shy on the outside while a great deal of information is being calculated and processed on the inside. They believe their personal lives, their thoughts, and their feelings are not anyone else's business. They relish their privacy and typically withdraw from crowds or social settings.

An unusual characteristic of Environmental Tans is that many are fascinated with airplanes, boats, submarines, and other vehicles that put them in contact with their environment. They love to sense their physical bodies in relation to altitude, velocity, and distance. Many own their own airplanes.

Environmental Tans see themselves according to where they fit into their environment. They are very aware of their physical positioning, even in their offices. They know how far from the wall their desks sit and where everything on their desks needs to be placed to ensure the easiest accessibility.

Life must be tangible, three-dimensional, and logical for Environmental Tans to pay much attention to it. They are adept at taking projects, naming and categorizing them, and giving them three-dimensional substance.

In power, Environmental Tans have a strong sense of responsibility. They are loyal and competent workers. Having a strong need to complete a task, they often overwork to accomplish a project. They take their agreements and commitments seriously.

Although Environmental Tans are independent and self-sufficient, they are not always secure or trusting of their abilities or of their environment. They are not always sure they have taken all the available information into consideration — maybe they miscalculated or maybe their physical environment isn't as safe and predictable as they have assessed it to be. Environmental Tans want their world to be dependable and reliable. They are not risk-takers, and stepping into the unknown can cause them anxiety. They prefer explainable and probable results.

Out of power, Environmental Tans are not very flexible regarding their understanding of reality. There are basic laws and standards in which they believe. Any changes are thoroughly researched and analyzed before given consideration. Needing logical proof at every stage can cause Environmental Tans to become obstinate and slow moving. Like Logical Tans, they can get stuck in a rut. By accepting only what has been proven in the past, Environmental Tans limit themselves and cannot see broader horizons or other alternatives.

To stay in power, Environmental Tans must be willing to step beyond what their mental and physical senses are showing them and consider other possibilities. They must also be willing to accept their feelings and learn to find a way to express them, at least to themselves. This will keep them from holding in the emotional stress that can eat them up inside.

One of the ways Environmental Tans can stay in power is to take long walks in a natural environment, especially one where they can experience the majesty and power of nature. Hiking and experiencing the peaceful strength of unspoiled forests and towering mountains inspires them to see life from a greater perspective. This seems to broaden their outlook and opens their minds to greater possibilities. (Some more sensitive and spiritual Environmental Tans receive intuitive information by being in the presence of trees.)

Relationships

Environmental Tans are slow to develop relationships. They are very cautious and selective even when they choose friends. When they do develop a significant relationship, they are extremely loyal and committed. They are very quiet and reserved. They do not openly share their feelings or thoughts with anyone, including their mates. They believe they have an inner understanding and an unspoken agreement with their partners. They assume their love is obviously known and accepted. They do not need to prove it, test it, or discuss it.

This attitude can frustrate those who are in relationships with Environmental Tans. They often feel they are not receiving the emotional sharing, open verbal communication, or demonstrative and affectionate behavior they desire. It is also, however, the Environmental Tans' strong and quiet Clint Eastwood-style mystique that many find attractive. (Clint Eastwood is, in fact, an Environmental Tan with some Violet.) Often people will pursue Environmental Tans for the challenge of capturing and conquering this elusive personality, only to be disappointed when discovering they will not be changed.

Those in relationship with Environmental Tans need to understand their nature in order to maintain harmony. They also need a strong sense of self-esteem. If mates confront Environmental Tans with emotional issues, these Tans' tendency is to shut down or disappear. They are, however, very responsible and reliable providers. Their partners can feel secure in knowing they will always be financially supported. Environmental Tans will always find a way to pay the bills.

Environmental Tans are not always physically available to their mates. Their work frequently requires that they travel for long periods. The archeological site may be miles away in an area unsuitable for wives and children, or the environmental research may take place at a polar ice station where conditions are too harsh and the location too remote for families. Most Environmental Tans are loners. Consequently, when their work brings them into isolated situations, they are not usually traumatized. They enjoy their privacy and their time alone.

Environmental Tans are independent mates. They prefer partners who are intelligent and can successfully hold their own in the real world. They do not want mates who are emotionally needy or unable to deal with the responsibility of maintaining a practical and secure lifestyle. They require mates who have the patience and understanding to allow them to figure out their lives in their own time and in their own way. Environmental Tans require a lot of time, space, and freedom.

Sex

Environmental Tans tend to be more sexual than their Logical Tan counterparts because they appreciate and operate more from their physical bodies. They relate more to their surroundings by touching first and then processing the data. However, they must be given ample time to process the information they have received through their physical senses.

Environmental Tans need to develop a sense of trust and

security with their partners before they can totally involve themselves sexually. They tend to be cautious and often inhibited until they learn that their partners are trustworthy and sincere. They frequently remain emotionally distant until a bond of closeness has been established. This can often take a long time for the methodical Environmental Tans. When security, understanding, and trust have developed, they can be dedicated and committed lovers.

Environmental Tan Parents

Environmental Tans, like Logical Tans, are disciplinarians. They want order, cleanliness, and structure in their homes. These practical people think logically and rationally when planning a family; first, a detailed cost analysis is carefully considered. Environmental Tans can be reliable and consistent providers for their children, saving for a college education while giving them adequate food, clothing, and shelter. Environmental Tans are not lavish spenders; they are prudent and economical. Consequently, they will buy sturdy and durable products for their children.

Emotionally bonding with their children isn't easy. Although they care deeply for their children, it is difficult for them to share their feelings or openly show affection toward their offspring. They often withdraw emotionally, which can cause their children to feel abandoned, rejected, or neglected. Environmental Tans believe that providing a secure and stable environment for their children and setting appropriate boundaries for their welfare should be adequate proof of their love.

The challenge for Environmental Tan parents is to open themselves and be emotionally available for their families, and to allow their children to be children before they are expected to be adults. These parents need to learn that providing emotional and mental support for their children is just as important as physical and financial support.

Environmental Tan Children

Environmental Tan children are more quiet and reticent than most of their peers. They don't usually laugh and play outside like typical children. Instead, they are more somber and serious. They tend to spend more time by themselves. They do not easily connect with others, but tend to stay withdrawn and removed. They are slow to make friends. However, when they have learned to trust other people, they are dedicated and loyal friends. Having an abundance of friends is not important to Environmental Tans. They prefer instead to have one or two close companions with whom they feel secure and accepted.

Frequently, their growth and development is slower than that of other children. To learn, these tactile children need to handle objects, to physically analyze things by touching them. Parents frequently worry about their Environmental Tan children because the children seem so isolated and disconsolate. If parents can allow these children to develop at their own rate, and refrain from forcing the children into uncomfortable social situations, they will eventually grow up to be well-balanced and stable citizens. However, if they are made to feel like social misfits, unacceptable by "normal" standards and misunderstood by their families, they tend to withdraw into themselves even more.

Environmental Tan children will eventually catch up with their peers. They are very intelligent children and will eventually prove their intellectual abilities if given the chance to develop in a safe, secure, and nonjudgmental environment.

Courses in school that appeal to Environmental Tans allow them to do hands-on experiments and research, measure the environmental impact of technology, study spatial components such as geometric shapes, work with mathematical equations that involve velocity, dimension, volume, and weight, and examine minerals, soils, and rock formations. Courses such as computer technology, science, geology, or botany can help them analyze and understand their physical environment.

As with all Environmental Tans, connecting with the natural environment is healing and centering for these children. Going for walks in the woods can be very therapeutic for most Environmental Tan children. It calms them and gives them a sense of grounded security.

Money

Money has tangible substance for Environmental Tans. Its purpose is to provide security for them and their families. Environmental Tans are loyal, dedicated workers who believe, like their Logical Tan counterparts, that people should work at long-term, stable jobs, earn decent wages, keep their money in secure money market accounts, and look forward to retirement benefits.

Environmental Tans are practical and cautious when spending or investing their money. They are not gamblers or risk-takers when it comes to deciding the fate of their hard-earned money. These pragmatic personalities believe they need to work for a long time to build a sturdy financial foundation. Using their money for physical investments such as land appeals to them because land has a tangible form they can touch. They can see their hard work translated into a physical reward that creates a sense of security for them.

Problem Solving

Because Environmental Tans relate strongly to the physicality of the world as well as to its mental and logical aspects, they solve problems most effectively by simultaneously collecting and scrutinizing the data and physically sensing the solution in their bodies. It's as if they have an internal sensing device that gives them technical readings and feedback. They can walk the grounds of an archeological site and not only logically figure out where another structure may be buried, but also locate the site through sensations in their bodies. Environmental Tans use a combination of mental and physical senses to figure out solutions. When planning military strategies, they move markers on maps to sense whether these maneuvers will be successful.

Environmental Tans are cautious decision-makers, weighing all the facts and possibilities before committing to a plan of action. When they are in power, they eventually are able to analyze enough data to draw a conclusion and recommend a solution. If they are out of power, they become stuck in their habitual past solutions. When the same methods are no longer appropriate or useful, confusion and mental dilemmas may result. To stay in power, they must figure out ways to introduce new variables into the equation.

Success

Environmental Tans consider themselves successful if they are able to develop a secure and stable lifestyle for themselves and their families and improve the environment through the combined use of intellect and technology. Environmental Tan farmers are satisfied when they are able to financially provide for their families while they work with the soil and provide quality food for people. Environmental Tan researchers are pleased when they are able to produce a system that replaces valuable nutrients in an exhausted and abused environment. Environmental Tan employees feel successful if they make intelligent, rational, and practical decisions that result in profits for their employers.

Occupations

Environmental Tans are often drawn to occupations that allow them to analyze, measure, and physically interact with their environment. These kinds of jobs enable them to sense where and how they fit into their physical world.

They are drawn to such occupations as the following:

Archeologist
Geologist
Environmental researcher
Botanist
Scientist
Explorer
Map maker
Forest ranger
Military personnel
Shipping and
    receiving clerk

Pilot
Purchase order clerk
City planner
Developer
Architect
Computer operator
Lab technician
Telephone repairman
Aerospace engineer
Electrician
Farmer

Because Environmental Tans and Yellow/Logical Tan Combination Colors both enjoy physical and mental work, they often share similar career interests.

Health

Even though Environmental Tans frequently work in dangerous outdoor environments, they are careful planners and cautious workers. They analyze situations before undertaking tasks, so they rarely encounter physical harm. Even if they are in telephone repair and must climb to the top of telephone poles, they are careful enough to secure all safety devices first.

Environmental Tans are more likely to experience health problems that are related to mental stress. They are dedicated, hard-working people who push their mental stamina to the limits, completing their assigned tasks no matter how many hours they must work.

To stay healthy, Environmental Tans must maintain balance with mental work, physical exercise, nutrition, and rest. Frequently, they become so involved in their work they forget about the rest of their lives. Quiet, meditative time in natural surroundings is the most effective rejuvenation process for Environmental Tans.

SENSITIVE TAN

Sensitive Tans are the bridge between the mental colors and the emotional colors. Their auras are a combination of a light tan color with a light blue band next to it that encircles the body. Their personalities are a subtle combination of the mental Tan qualities and the emotional Blue qualities.

Sensitive Tans combine the characteristics of mental, analytical logic with loving and intuitive compassion. These gentle personalities are quiet, sensitive, and supportive. They prefer, like Logical Tans, to maintain a rational, intellectual foundation while they analytically process data. They are more emotional and intuitive than Logical Tans, however, but they tend to keep their feelings to themselves. When a problem arises, Sensitive Tans will retreat inside to figure out the most practical solution.

Like their Logical Tan counterparts, Sensitive Tans desire security and stability. Their homes are important to them. They can become very attached to their possessions, to everything from their furniture to the family pictures on the wall. Although their families are the most important element in their lives, Sensitive Tans also love the comfort and security of knowing they have things around them.

These loving personalities, although sensitive and emotional, are not quite as emotional as Blues. When facing conflict, they tend to remain more rational and calm than Blues do. Blues tend to wear their emotions on their sleeves and can experience strong mood shifts between deep depression and euphoria; Sensitive Tans are less dramatic with their ups and downs. Sensitive Tans may lose their center momentarily, but they are quick to regain their composure. (Sensitive Tans may want to read in chapter 4 the section on Blues, but reduce the intensity and drama by at least fifty percent!) Nor is the mental-versus-emotional battle of Sensitive Tans as pronounced or as intense as that of the Blue/Green Combination Colors. Sensitive Tans' emotional waves are more like those in a pond or a lake than those in an ocean.

These serene people can be great secretaries and other support personnel because they love to calmly help people while taking care of details. They tend to be withdrawn and shy, so they prefer less conspicuous jobs. They feel the safest and calmest taking care of details in the office — bookkeeping, filing, typing, or answering the phone. (Some Sensitive Tans can be intimidated by the fast-paced pressure of a busy switchboard. Others, however, can be calm and patient, methodically handling each call without becoming traumatized.)

Sensitive Tans send quiet, nurturing energy to people. They have a calm sense about them when they are helping people. They can be very efficient therapists because they are sincere and patient listeners. They deduce answers based on data as well as on intuition. Sensitive Tans often put others' needs before their own. They are extraordinarily unselfish. They are delightfully modest hosts and hostesses. They do not overwhelm their guests with hospitality the way Blues frequently do. Their personalities are subtler. Sensitive Tans are so patient, understanding, and calm that they are typically compatible with everyone.

Sensitive Tans are service-oriented humanitarians. They love serving their communities and organizations dedicated to helping people. Their idea of God or of religion is essentially that people should be honest and good, love one another, and treat one another with compassion, patience, and understanding. By teaching these concepts, Sensitive Tans help people to create peace and harmony in their homes, their communities, and, therefore, the world.

Although Sensitive Tans are intuitive, much like Blues, they also want facts and data to support what they feel. Their ability to sometimes support their intuition with common sense and logic helps people trust them and feel secure with their advice. Together, their logic and intuition create a healthy balance.

However, these two aspects can also create conflict for Sensitive Tans. They may get a feeling or an intuitive sense of something and then analyze it to the point that they no longer trust their intuition. They can experience persistent arguments in their heads. Their Tan aspect leans toward accepting the apparent physical evidence; their Blue aspect feels that something may be true even when there is no data to support the feelings. As an example, a Sensitive Tan may see her employer arranging a business deal with a client. All the facts and figures are checked out. The transaction appears to be running according to the established system, but the Sensitive Tan has an odd feeling something is wrong. She doesn't have any data or facts to support her feelings, and just continues typing up the paperwork. Later, when the business deal falls through, she feels that if she had just trusted her instincts, she may have been able to search for and uncover the problem.

To stay in power, Sensitive Tans need to trust their intuition and not depend just on the apparent facts. Using both their inner and outer faculties will keep them balanced and enable them to make calm, clear decisions. To live their greatest potential, Sensitive Tans should attend to their own needs, not just the needs of others. Nurturing and supporting themselves will help them maintain their positive energy and keep them from being taken advantage of by other people.

Relationships

Sensitive Tans value love, commitment, dedication, patient understanding, and good communication in their relationships. This is exactly what Sensitive Tans give to their mates — therefore, they want the same consideration. They want someone who will listen as well as talk with them.

These loving souls want mates they can depend upon, who will be secure and stable providers as well as kind and considerate partners. They don't require partners who are powerful, charismatic, or driven to be the best in their fields. Such mates would intimidate them. They prefer practical, reliable, and devoted mates who will commit to a long-term relationship. Although

Sensitive Tans are intelligent, they prefer to work behind the scenes, supporting and nurturing their mates' dreams. But they want to know that in return they will be loved, honored, provided for, and appreciated by their mates.

Sensitive Tans will take care of more than their fair share of responsibilities and will be good providers themselves. These thoughtful individuals will also make sure their mates have comfortable, secure, and loving homes. Being very loyal, monogamous, and committed, they focus on maintaining sincerity and integrity in their relationships. They are usually calm and sensible when disagreements occur.

Sensitive Tans feel best when they are in secure, stable relationships, but they don't fall apart when this isn't the case. They aren't happy if the comfortable, established structure is upset — for example, divorce — but they are too practical and levelheaded to let a divorce destroy them.

Sex

Sensitive Tans are usually reserved, although loving and affectionate. Sex for them is not a wild, tempestuous, animalistic act. Rather it is to be experienced with sensitivity, sincerity, tenderness, and integrity. They are too gentle and caring to have wild affairs or one-night stands. They have more respect for themselves and others than to sexually use people. To them, making love shows that there is mutual affection and admiration between two people. Sex for them also fulfills the function of procreation.

Sensitive Tan Parents

Sensitive Tans' greatest priority is creating a traditional, stable, and loving family unit — mother, father, and happy, well-adjusted children. They will, however, be very practical when planning for a family. Taking into account all the potential liabilities, financial circumstances, quality of schools in the area and the ages of both parents, Sensitive Tans will consider all the possible consequences involved in their decision before taking action.

Sensitive Tans are usually calm and rational parents. Although they believe there must be a sense of order and discipline, they are usually not unreasonable regarding rules for their children. They believe in setting loving yet fair guidelines.

In power, Sensitive Tan parents can be understanding and supportive toward their children. They allow them room to grow and freedom to experience their childhood while still setting safe and realistic boundaries for them. They usually have more tolerance and patience for child rearing than many Life Colors, even preferring to stay home to raise the children. Although some aura colors feel a strong need to concentrate on careers, Sensitive Tans feel that providing a secure and supportive environment for their families is just as high a priority, if not higher. In power, Sensitive Tans will take an interest in their children's welfare as well as in the community that affects their children. To support their children, these parents will attend PTA meetings, make decorations for the class Christmas party, or carpool if it means supporting and staying involved with their children's lives. They want to make sure their children grow up well balanced and feeling loved.

Out of power, Sensitive Tans can be weak and ineffective parents. Wanting their children's love, they can frequently become too nice and too lenient. Children learn at an early age how to manipulate the Sensitive Tans' generosity and patient nature. They can also be too cautious and protective toward their children. None of the Tans are risk-takers; consequently, they usually want their children to play it safe, maintain the status quo, stay inside the "normal" boundaries, and perform at least moderately well in school.

To stay in power as parents, Sensitive Tans need to trust their intuition just as much as they analyze the facts. Because they tend to be cautious, they often take statistics too seriously. If they read that the leading cause of death among teenagers is drinking and driving, for example, they may place unwarranted restrictions on their children because of those statistics. If they can trust what they feel, they may see that their children are trustworthy and that they will be safe. If Sensitive Tan parents can balance their intuition with their mental deductions, they will survive parenthood very successfully.

Sensitive Tan Children

Sensitive Tan children are usually quiet, polite, practical, sensible, and responsible. Because they process information slowly and analytically, they are not always the quickest in class, but they are some of the most consistent and dependable students. Sensitive Tans seem to understand the value of education. They tend to do well in subjects in which analysis and attention to detail is required, like math, bookkeeping, and language.

The Blue aspect in their auras is revealed when they show a desire to help people on some level. They are frequently interested in subjects that relate to people, but that also have a practical application — subjects such as history, sociology, art theory, and literature.

Parents need to allow these quiet, reserved children to move at their own pace. Schoolwork may be slower for them, but they eventually will get it done. Efficiency and accuracy are important to Sensitive Tans.

Socially, Sensitive Tans tend to stay unnoticed. They may be late bloomers, if they bloom at all. They love people and want to be liked, but they are usually shy. They are uncomfortable at parties where a high level of interaction is expected. They prefer instead to be on the party's decorating or refreshment committee. They receive more pleasure from setting up everything in a festive array so other people can enjoy themselves. On Saturday nights, Sensitive Tans are frequently found studying in the library or reading a book at home. They strive to be nice, well-respected, caring, yet practical people.

Pushing these children into gregarious social functions will only cause them anxiety. Parents need to be understanding and patient. Sensitive Tan children will eventually find their roles in life. These gentle humanitarians are here to serve their communities by teaching compassion and integrity, not by being football stars, cheerleaders, or famous world leaders. They will live life in their own subtle and unassuming way.

Problem Solving

When solving problems, Sensitive Tans want to calmly review all the facts and then take everyone else's feelings and preferences into consideration before making a decision. As much as possible, Sensitive Tans want to make sure everyone is happy with the solution. They do not want to be rushed or forced into making snap decisions, preferring instead to have time to weigh all the facts and hear all sides of the problem.

Sensitive Tans will never force their opinions or advice upon anyone. They have an inherent trust that good will come of most situations. They believe that people are basically good and loving.

When in power, Sensitive Tans calmly and rationally come up with a solution that combines the most practical answer with the one that makes people feel the best. They have the ability to reason with everyone so that discussions don't escalate into emotionally heated fights. They are natural mediators and peacemakers. They make people around them feel as if they are all winners. Although sometimes frustrated by the slow pace of Sensitive Tans' decision-making processes, people usually trust their decisions and advice because they know everything has been well thought out before the conclusion was reached.

Out of power, Sensitive Tans can become so emotionally caught up in the situation that their common sense is blurred, causing them to be unable to make any decisions. Out of power, Sensitive Tans stop trusting their intuitive, inner knowing. Consequently, they stop using all their abilities to make a decision.

Money

Money is important to Sensitive Tans only because it provides them and their families with security and stability. Sensitive Tans want enough money to pay the bills, buy decent clothes for their children, buy moderately priced yet comfortable furniture for their homes, and occasionally go out to dinner.

Sensitive Tans are very cautious with their money. They want savings accounts and safe investments. Not being gamblers or risk-takers, they feel more secure when they know they have nest eggs. They want money tucked away for the children's college education or for family emergencies.

These Tans believe it takes time to build financial reserves. They don't usually have the abundant financial assets that Greens have, nor do they have the outrageous number of debts that Greens usually have. Greens can risk a lot of money to make a lot of money. Sensitive Tans prefer the quiet security of building their financial foundations slowly and steadily.

Sensitive Tans frequently take positions such as secretaries, bookkeepers, clerks, and receptionists — jobs in which the income can be steady, but not always high paying. Often Sensitive Tans have discontinued their education to raise families. When returning to the workforce, many take jobs that do not require a college education and typically do not pay well.

Success

Sensitive Tans' priorities are serving their families and their communities with love and integrity. They prefer to deal with life in a calm, rational, and sensitive manner. If they feel they are providing their families with love and security, teaching goodness and compassion to those around them, and contributing positively to society by serving their communities, they feel they are living successful lives.

Occupations

Sensitive Tans prefer jobs in which they have the security of regular paychecks. They like jobs that can be both helpful and analytical. They are dedicated employees who work well with others. They prefer low-stress, slow-paced jobs in which they can easily know what is expected of them every day. Their responsibilities must be well defined and consistent from day to day. Chaos, last-minute deadlines, and panic can cause undue stress for Sensitive Tans. They are happier when there are no surprises in the workplace — just a well-planned, efficient, and calm environment.

Sensitive Tans enjoy working on details, such as balancing the books or programming computers, as long as they also have interaction with people. They have more patience to deal with repetition and details than most Life Colors.

If they become therapists, Sensitive Tans prefer their clients to be scheduled for long-term, regular visits. They believe the therapeutic healing process has multiple stages and can take a long time. (In addition, Sensitive Tans prefer the economic security of knowing their clients have committed to a regular, long-term schedule.) Because Sensitive Tans like to be in service for the good of the community, they will take jobs that require analyzing the community's current situation and making plans to improve it — positions such as city planners or community service developers. Companies would do well to employ dedicated, hard-working Sensitive Tans, who are more than willing to take care of the mundane details of daily business.

Angela Lansbury portrayed a Sensitive Tan, Jessica Fletcher, in the television series *Murder She Wrote*. Writer Fletcher used research, as well as hunches and intuition, to solve crimes.

Occupations that appeal to Sensitive Tans are the following:

Bookkeeper	Arbitrator
Receptionist	Judge

Secretary	Dentist
Office personnel	Hygienist
Accountant	Welfare, social worker
Therapist	Teacher, educator
Counselor	Child care worker
City planner	Community service
School advisor	developer
Writer	Investigator
Career counselor	Public relations
School administrator	Principal
College recruiter	

Health

A common health problem for Sensitive Tans is with their eyesight. Like all Tans, they tend to focus on details, which can cause eyestrain. Sensitive Tans can take on the same health problems that affect Logical Tans and Blues. These composed individuals tend to stay healthier than the other Life Colors, however, because they have the sense to eat properly and stay calmer and consequently less stressed.

Like Blues, Sensitive Tans are not exercising fanatics. They do have the common sense, however, to know that the human body needs exercise, so they are more likely to exercise than Blues are. There is enough of the Blue aspect in their auras, however, to keep their exercise schedule erratic. They start out with a schedule, then shift into exercising only when they feel like it.

To remain healthy, Sensitive Tans need only to maintain their common sense, eat healthy foods, stay calm (without suppressing their emotions), and exercise regularly. They can also follow the advice given to Blues and Logical Tans.

ABSTRACT TAN

Abstract Tans have a light tan-colored band that is surrounded completely by a brilliant red band. This red is not the same as the Red Life Color or the Red Overlay. The Abstract Tans' personality traits are entirely different.

The bright and curious Abstract Tans are unique characters in the mental family. They are the most childlike of all the Tans. They are open, friendly, and outgoing. They have incredibly optimistic personalities. Though they frequently have high energy, it is also usually scattered. Although they see all the details and steps that need to be handled, they do not proceed in an orderly fashion. They have random thought processes. Rather than proceeding step-by-step, they attempt to work on all the steps simultaneously. They do not sense that any step is a priority — the first step is just another piece in the project, as is the last one. All other Tan personalities process information in a logical and sequential manner.

Abstract Tans see projects in much the same way as they see jigsaw puzzles. They see all the pieces laid out on the table, but are not sure where to begin to put the puzzle together. They will choose any piece of the puzzle and then jump over to another section of the puzzle for no apparent reason. Eventually, all the pieces are put in place and the puzzle is completed; in the process, however, they have probably driven everyone else crazy. Other people, who usually start with one piece of the puzzle and logically build onto it, can see no reason behind Abstract Tans' methods. Abstract Tans' world looks like an embodiment of confusion and chaos.

(Many Yellow/Violet and Blue/Yellow combinations believe they are Abstract Tans. These key elements will distinguish between the combinations and Abstract Tans, however. Even though both Abstract Tans and Violets can become quite scattered, Tans still prefer to work with the details. Violets do not like dealing with details. They have a sense that they are here to do something very big and very important. Typically, Tans do not feel that way. Abstract Tans prefer the security of a long-term, regular paycheck; Yellows do not want to work in the same place long term.

Reading the chapters thoroughly and seeing which job descriptions are most appealing to you will reveal whether you are an Abstract Tan, a Yellow/Violet, or a Blue/Yellow.)

Because their thinking is so random and illogical, Abstract Tans have trouble organizing their lives. They don't have any concept of establishing priorities or setting up schedules. They do not do first that which is the most important or the timeliest. Instead, their priority becomes whichever task they happen to focus upon. When Abstract Tans are preparing for a party, they may decorate the house, then clean the house and then bake the cake, not realizing that the cake could be baking while they clean the house. These scattered individuals are often late for their own parties because they do not schedule their preparation time accordingly. As usual, they see all steps that need to be taken, but take each step randomly.

Abstract Tans don't have a firm understanding of linear time. When they recount stories, the past, present, and future all seem to exist simultaneously. They remember all the facts, but not necessarily the order in which they occurred. People often consider Abstract Tans to be unreliable and even flaky because their thought processes — and therefore their behaviors — are so erratic. Abstract Tans' energy can be exuberant and eager, which often makes them appear to be nervous. When they talk, they frequently go off on tangents and randomly recapitulate the facts. People often have trouble following their conversations.

To others these sensitive individuals often appear scatter-brained. They consistently misplace or lose their possessions and usually can't remember where they put things. Their lives seem to be in a constant state of confusion and disorder. Their energy is so unfocused that people around them can become agitated trying to pin them down. Abstract Tans have energy similar to that of fireflies or hummingbirds. Their rapidly vibrating wings move a hundred times a second as they constantly change course in midair. People are amazed when the scattered Abstract Tans actually complete projects, because it usually appears that they do not know what they're doing. And yet, although their processes seem scrambled, they eventually put all the pieces together.

Abstract Tans are excited about new ideas. They love to immerse themselves in new projects and examine everything about them. They love to research and explore, collecting a multitude of data and then retaining only what is important to them. They love to learn from nature, because nature has a sense of order to it: chronological events, cause and effect, and patterns such as the cycle of seasons.

These inquisitive personalities love to attend social gatherings where they are able to talk with a wide variety of people. From them they are able to gather a lot of information and store their newly found knowledge in different parts of their mental computers. (Although Abstract Tans and Violets have many similar qualities, Abstract Tans can chitchat with anyone about anything. Violets prefer to talk about important social, political, or spiritual ideas. They do not like meaningless conversations.) Abstract Tans also have an unconditional love for humanity, loving people on a universal level. They have a broad acceptance of and a great curiosity about people's differences. They are interested in learning about other cultures, other languages, and other lifestyles.

Although Abstract Tans have a great love for people on an abstract level, they also have difficulty experiencing intimate relationships. These Tans are sensitive and childlike personalities who are eager to please and to be liked by others. Their feelings are easily hurt, however. Rather than risk being hurt, they tend to stay in their heads and theorize ideas rather than become deeply involved with others. They freely discuss concepts about how and why people feel, think, and act the way they do, but won't discuss their own emotions. Having been so misunderstood and unappreciated in childhood, they often have learned not to open up or be vulnerable. They detach themselves from their emotions. They feel safer being around a lot of people, learning and discussing ideas.

When Abstract Tans are in power, they are energetic, optimistic, bright, and cheerful. Their friendly and accepting nature makes them nonthreatening to other people. They have enough energy to handle many projects simultaneously and can be storehouses of information. Although they prefer the information to be intellectually and factually based, they are not afraid to explore for further information. They enjoy adding to ideas and concepts. Abstract Tans are much more open minded and flexible than the other Tan personalities. When they are in power, Abstract Tans feel an unconditional love and total acceptance for humanity. With this love and acceptance, they are able to teach people to accept themselves and to appreciate their differences.

Out of power, Abstract Tans can be scattered, forgetful, and ineffective. They tend to overcommit themselves and then cannot follow through with their promises. They are easily confused and distracted. Out of power, these sensitive individuals close themselves off emotionally from others. They slowly retreat inside their heads, which leaves them safe but lonely. Although these personalities are usually very sociable, when they are out of power they become more isolated, especially as they age.

To stay in power, Abstract Tans must learn to give themselves schedules and guidelines. Abstract Tans, unlike the other Tans, do not operate well within the confines of rigid, structured systems. They need more room to explore and research new ideas. They do need some structure, however, to keep their lives from scattering. They need calendars so they don't commit themselves to too many activities in one day. Being associated with people who can help them stay more structured and disciplined also helps. When they have a well-established and responsible foundation, these lively personalities are free to explore their alternative ideas and projects.

Relationships

Although the friendly Abstract Tans are liberal with their time, energy, and enthusiasm and are willing to be with other people, they have difficulty opening up to intimate relationships. They are not usually emotionally available to their mates.

Marriage is more like a port in a storm for these disorganized individuals. They want mates who can help to establish order in their chaotic lives. They want partners who are willing to provide a steady foundation and who will understand their theoretical discussions. They need partners who are stronger and more capable of taking care of them. Abstract Tans don't need deep emotional bonds. They prefer caretakers as well as playmates. Frequently, their mates become frustrated, feeling more like parents than partners.

Abstract Tans sometimes have difficulty even finding mates. Their energy is much too scattered and frenzied for most people to handle. Consequently, they tend to flit from person to person, having one encounter after another. They tend to have many casual relationships, but few intimate, meaningful connections. Their hectic lifestyles also keep them safe from having to be in intimate, committed relationships. They don't focus their energies long enough to be available for serious relationships. In addition, they tend to be attracted to people who are unavailable to them. Actually, what Abstract Tans want are companions. These friendly Tans can become depressed and lonely if they remain single for too long, but they tend to hide their feelings behind cheerful and energetic facades. Their dilemma is staying calm, unafraid, and focused long enough to be accessible to others.

Mates of Abstract Tans soon discover that these frenetic characters are not in one place for long. Abstract Tans are enthusiastic and cheerful, but they are also constantly busy. Their partners have trouble keeping track of them. People in this relationship must be stable, grounded, and patient. They must be willing to add structure and responsibility to the relationship.

Abstract Tans can bring a great deal of cheerful optimism and enthusiasm to a relationship. With their exuberant energy and wealth of information, relationships with Abstract Tans would never be boring.

Sex

Sex must be safe for Abstract Tans. They must feel a sense of security and trust for their partners. It is very challenging for Abstract Tans to completely trust anyone. They tend to live safely in their heads, even during lovemaking. They rarely abandon themselves to passion. Letting go makes them feel too vulnerable.

All Tans tend to be reserved and emotionally cautious with sex. Although they enjoy sex — especially with partners they trust — sex is not a priority in their lives.

Abstract Tan Parents

As parents, Abstract Tans are very warm, sensitive, and caring toward their children. They do not usually provide a disciplined structure, however. Because these Tans are usually so disorganized, their homes can be disheveled and chaotic. Clothes and possessions are often strewn everywhere. The children are frequently hustled from school to baseball practice to music lessons because their Abstract Tan parents have scheduled too many activities on one day. Abstract Tans have very good intentions, but they often fall through on their promises to their children because they overcommit themselves. Abstract Tans can experience difficulty organizing their children's lives because they cannot organize their own lives. They are like eager children themselves — children who need looking after.

Abstract Tan Children

These children are usually outgoing, cheerful, optimistic, and enthusiastic. However, they are often misunderstood because their thought processes are so scattered. They are eager for others to like them, but their chaotic energy often wears on people. These children have very sensitive feelings, and it is at this stage that they begin to lose trust in people. They fear being hurt or rejected by others who don't understand their erratic behavior.

They learn to slowly withdraw their feelings and ideas and retreat into their heads.

Abstract Tan children are often chastised for neglecting their possessions. Like their adult counterparts, they leave their clothes and toys everywhere. Possessions are not important to them. They are constantly losing or misplacing things. Parents can become frustrated by what appears to be the children's apathy and carelessness. Try as they might, it is a struggle for these children to stay organized. When they see they are constantly disappointing their parents and feel their lack of understanding and disapproval, Abstract Tan children learn to shut down. They learn to see themselves as misfits.

Parents must teach these energetic children how to focus their attention. They shouldn't restrict or confine them, but teach them to follow simple schedules. Parents need to learn patience with these abstract thinkers. In power, Abstract Tan children are not scatterbrained — they are just adept at seeing all the pieces at once. If they are not forced to follow the traditional, linear ways of accomplishing tasks and are given the freedom to do the tasks in any order, these children will succeed.

Abstract Tan children function better in nontraditional educational systems. They are curious and eager learners. They are drawn to subjects such as foreign languages or world cultures, but they need time to fully research or experience each subject. Jumping from one topic to another before they have completed the first one causes them to become even more scattered. With help, they can learn to better organize and channel their abundant energy.

Problem Solving

Abstract Tans, unlike the other Tans, are open to new ideas. They are willing to learn different approaches. They can see ideas from myriad perspectives and so believe problems can be solved from many angles. Although they are open to exploring alternatives and can easily see everyone's point of view, they tend to choose solutions that are most closely aligned with their current belief system. They prefer solutions that have intellectual and rational foundations. They prefer, as do all Tans, to see all the facts before making decisions.

Abstract Tans easily jump from one solution to another in midstream. Although this tends to confuse those around them, Abstract Tans can quickly and easily change direction. But by shifting from one solution to another, and then to still another, Abstract Tans often lose perspective of the original problem. Because they are able to present so many options to the group, however, someone is inevitably able to see at least one solution. Abstract Tans do not solve problems based on which problem is more important, but rather based upon which one happens to be in front of them at the time.

Although Abstract Tans are unsystematic thinkers, they are capable of finding many unique and feasible solutions to a given problem.

Money

Abstract Tans experience difficulty managing their money. Prioritizing financial obligations is a challenge for them. Their money is dispersed randomly — the bills that are paid change from month to month. They do not plan well; consequently, they do not always spend their money wisely. Often they buy items they already own because their lives are usually in such disarray that they either have misplaced the items or have forgotten they already own them.

Abstract Tans have trouble following budgets or financial plans. They are happier and their lives operate more smoothly when they employ others to keep track of their financial obligations.

Success

Abstract Tans are exuberant, childlike people who want to be liked. They are happy with their lives when they feel they are understood and accepted. They feel best when they have others around them who can provide a safe and secure foundation. They want the freedom to process life in the random, abstract manner that is natural for them, without being criticized. They do not want invasive, emotional demands placed on them. They are happy when they can bring all the pieces of a project together.

Occupations

Abstract Tans need jobs that involve a variety of tasks and that allow them to randomly juggle all their skills and talents. They need freedom to create their own schedules and plenty of room and time to complete assigned projects. They need free reign to accomplish all the necessary tasks in random order. They cannot feel confined or restricted by stringent boundaries.

Abstract Tans function better when they are employees. They are not organized enough to run their own businesses. However, they also cannot be limited to rigid structures. If they become teachers, for instance, they can be given a list of the school's required subjects to be covered, but they must have the freedom to bring the information together in their own random patterns. In a political science class, for example, rather than trace the history and development of politics, they should be free to choose a topic and randomly discuss related events.

Although their processes are often chaotic and without logical, sequential reasoning, Abstract Tans eventually put all the pieces together. They are happiest when they can work on all parts of the project simultaneously. They prefer their jobs to have an intellectual base, though they are not adept or organized enough to deal with a lot of paperwork. They prefer theorizing, reading, and discussing ideas.

Occupations that appeal to Abstract Tans include the following:

Teacher	Gardener
Consultant	Salesperson

City developer Computer programmer
Landscaper Designer
Health practitioner Interior decorator
Interpreter Graphic artist
Childcare worker Tour guide
Travel agent

Health

Abstract Tans commonly have frequent and various health complaints, though most of their illnesses are not serious. They have random patterns of internal illnesses. Health practitioners have difficulty tracking their illnesses because nothing stays still long enough to be treated — while the stomach is treated for viruses, for example, the illness may move to the intestines. Abstract Tans do not follow normal disease patterns. Because Abstract Tans do not experience normal illness patterns, health practitioners are more successful at finding cures if they treat Abstract Tans' mental and emotional conditions rather than the physical conditions.

Being forced to fit all the pieces together within tight time frames or within rigid structures can cause illness for Abstract Tans. Illness arises when they become overwhelmingly frustrated and fear they cannot pull it all together.

To remain healthy, the easily distracted Abstract Tans must learn to slow down and not take on too many commitments at once. Because they are inefficient at planning their time, they may want to find others who can help them plan realistic schedules. They need to include something every day that addresses their health. For example, on some days they can exercise or swim; on other days they can do yoga or stretching exercises. Or, they can relax or take a vacation. They can eat a variety of healthy foods every day. Their health care plan should be a complete package that has a variety of programs.

The most effective way for Abstract Tans to stay healthy is for them to maintain a sense of balance and freedom in their lives. They must be free to process their thoughts randomly. They should stay away from jobs or people who attempt to confine them to linear tasks. Allowing themselves to express their true nature — friendly, optimistic, curious, and bright — will also help them stay healthy.

GREEN

Greens are drawn to money, power, and business. They are some of the most powerful and intelligent people in the aura spectrum. They process information and ideas quickly, jumping from step one to ten because they do not like dealing with all the steps and details in between. Projects that are too detailed are tedious and boring for Greens. They prefer instead to deal with ideas and concepts — developing an idea, organizing a plan, and then delegating the details to someone else.

In power, these quick thinkers are organized and efficient. They write lists and check off items as they are completed. They recognize patterns and discover solutions very quickly. When they are in power, they can accomplish anything. They love to set goals and are determined to achieve them. Greens are movers and shakers when it comes to taking action.

Greens are highly competitive and enjoy challenges. They thrive on taking risks. Gambling is common for Greens, especially if there is potential for large winnings.

Being strong willed, these powerful personalities are determined to have their own way, which they usually feel is the right way. People rarely win arguments with Greens. Even if their opponents win the argument by proving their point with logic or statistics, Greens will rarely admit defeat. Greens hate to be wrong.

Greens also dislike taking orders. They usually believe they are more intelligent than other people are. They are quick learners who will listen to the facts and then arrange things their own way. They not only like to be in control, but they seem to need to be in control. If situations arise that appear to be out of their control, they become frustrated, worried, and stressed. They want to be in control of their emotions, environment, income, and relationships. They also have a need to understand everything.

Greens' life purpose is to experience as much as possible in this lifetime, to accomplish as much as they can, to grow and learn intellectually, and to empower others by example. (The behavior of Greens and Violets can be quite similar, especially when they are both out of power. Many Violets who read this chapter believe they are Greens. Read in chapter 4 the Violet section, especially about Violets' life purpose, to learn whether you are a Green or a Violet, or even a combination Violet/Green.)

When Greens are in power their motto could be where there's a will, there's a way. They love to be challenged mentally. After they have accomplished something, however, they want to move on to another challenge. They are hungry for knowledge and ask a lot of questions, especially "How?" "How did you start your own business?" "How did you become so successful?" "How did you earn your money?" Because they are such avid learners, Greens typically seek further education. They are the perennial students, always obtaining more licenses and degrees. Often they believe that a certificate, degree, or specialized training will prove to them and to the world that they are qualified for a particular job.

Greens are such quick learners that they can simply watch someone else do a job and figure out how to do it themselves, quite often doing it better (at least in their opinion). Despite this ability, however, they still believe they need official training and education to prove to the world they are qualified. In power, Greens are some of the wealthiest and most successful people in the world — for many of them it is despite their lack of formal education.

These ambitious personalities are driven to accomplish, and they become intense and serious when working toward their goals. They push themselves, always appearing to be in a hurry. Greens are the prime examples of workaholics.

These hard workers have a tendency to compare themselves to others, usually to people who are more accomplished rather than to those they have surpassed. Continuously competing and striving for greater accomplishments can keep Greens moving forward. However, their obsessive behavior may also create a constant feeling of unrest and dissatisfaction. They may perpetually judge themselves and their achievements as never being good enough.

Greens often have a fear of failure, although they rarely fail. Self-critical and demanding, Greens often judge themselves as failures, but if one were to compare Greens' accomplishments to others', Greens usually will have accomplished more. Greens are their own worst enemies. (No one else would even want the job.)

Greens do not usually have the patience to listen to the problems of others. If you turn to Greens with a problem, they will listen, give advice, and then expect you to act on the advice. If you return with the same problem, they will lose respect for you, judging you as weak, undisciplined, and unmotivated.

Greens usually have strikingly beautiful features. They take great pride in their appearance. They prefer to dress in sophisticated and classy styles. They cannot tolerate being overweight, looking upon it as a lack of self-discipline and willpower. If they gain a few pounds, they quickly lose respect for themselves. (If they have a Combination Color, such as a Blue/Green aura, weight can frequently become a problem.) Greens can become so concerned with their appearance that they can develop eating disorders such as anorexia. When Greens are out of power, no matter how much weight they may lose, it is never enough.

When Greens are out of power, others have a difficult time being around them. They are so aggressive and opinionated that they have a tendency to intimidate others. They can become judgmental, arrogant, and impatient. When they want something, they want it now. They are very demanding and expect high performance from others as well as from themselves. They are perfectionists, and their behavior often pushes people away.

Greens feel they accomplish more when they are alone, and often perform solo. These perfectionists frequently use the word *should* in their conversations: "I should have done it better, sooner, quicker." They tend to believe that life is hard work. Some words most commonly heard from out-of-power Greens are *hard, struggle, try, should, can't,* and *need.* Their lives would be easier if instead they use these words: *desire to, easy, effortless, will, can,* and *I am.* If Greens are not able to say "I desire to do this project" instead of "I have to do this project," they are probably out of power and are not enjoying life.

When Greens suppress their power or when they are blocked from having what they want, they become frustrated, bitter, and resentful. They are also quick to blame the cause of their problems on other people or on outside circumstances, frequently blaming employees, clients, friends, spouses, parents, lack of time, or lack of money. When they are upset, they release their frustrations verbally. They say exactly what they think, no matter how it sounds or whom it may affect, feeling this is the most effective way to change the situation. They can often become hurtful and mean. When they are out of power, nothing pleases them (although winning ten million in the lottery may placate them for awhile).

The only ones who can suppress Greens' incredible power are Greens themselves. Greens block their power by placing obstacles in their way. By blaming others, Greens give away their power. The quickest method for Greens to regain their center is to take responsibility for their lives. They must recognize where they are holding themselves back, make a list of everything they want, and then take action. By identifying what they want and taking action to obtain their desires, they will feel in control again. When Greens are back in power, they become so dynamic and powerful that they do not have time to blame anyone else for the problems in their lives.

Relationships

One of the greatest challenges for Greens, especially Green women, is finding mates. Greens need to find mates they can respect and who can stand up to their incredible power. Their partners must measure up to Greens' high standards. Greens need to feel respected by and respect for their partners. They need to feel that their partners are mentally stimulating and intelligent. They can quickly outgrow and become bored with mates who are not as ambitious and goal oriented as they are. They can run over most Life Colors. Greens also want to make sure that being in a relationship will not deter them from accomplishing their goals. Their high expectations and workaholic behavior often create isolation. Greens frequently build walls around themselves. They are very selective with both friends and mates.

This information is not meant to be discouraging for Greens. Some Life Colors can handle Greens' immense power and intelligence, provided they stay balanced and in power. Violets and Reds can both be competent mates for Greens. These colors are awed and inspired, rather than overwhelmed or intimidated, by the power and intelligence of Greens.

Sex

Before they will be sexually involved with others, Greens must first know they are admired and respected for their intelligence. They must also be able to respect and admire their partners. Greens do enjoy sex. When they become angry, however, the first thing they withhold from their partners is sex. They will refuse to be touched until the issue is resolved and they know their point of view is respected. A Green's mate can become well acquainted with the living room sofa or the spare bedroom.

For Greens who are out of power, sex can become an intense power play. They can use it to manipulate, control, or overpower their partners. They can become vindictive if hurt. Greens often derive more pleasure from accomplishing goals, negotiating business deals, or making large sums of money than they do from having sex — tough competition for their mates.

Green Parents

The decision to have children is a difficult one for Greens. They do not want to be deterred from their goals and ambitions. They do not usually even want pets. (It may have been a Yellow/Green who invented the pet rock.) Children and pets can demand a lot of time, energy, and money. These are valuable commodities for Greens, and they are not always willing to make the sacrifice, even to have children. If they do have children, they will want nannies to free them from domestic responsibilities. Greens are not parents who can sit at home for long. They need to be out challenging the business world, accomplishing something, and being respected.

Greens are organizational parents. They want the best for their children — the best education, the best training, and the best opportunities. They will organize the children as they lead them out the door, giving them lunch money and their schedules for music lessons. (Because time is money, giving the children lunch money is more efficient than spending time making peanut butter and jelly sandwiches.) Greens like their children to keep things well organized, neat, and clean. Everything has its place in their homes.

Green parents can be some of the most impatient and controlling parents in the aura spectrum. They must pay attention to overdemanding attitudes they may have toward their children. They must remember they are dealing with growing, developing children, not short adults. Teaching children to learn responsibility, respect, and discipline is admirable, as long as the means do not intimidate or frighten them, causing them to close down their real potential or unique personalities. Although Greens like discipline, conformity, and control, they may want to remember that they themselves are the first to challenge someone else's attempts to control them.

Green parents operate best when they stay centered and aware (not that it is easy for anyone to stay centered all the time). When Greens are centered, they empower and teach their children by example. If Greens are frustrated and are pushing someone else to change, the truth is that they are probably dissatisfied with their own lives. They need to clear their own fears, blockages, and frustrations before they can effectively relate to their children.

Greens who function well with order and discipline may want to schedule time with their children. They can use this time to teach them, to learn from them, or just to get to know them better.

If Greens make their relationships with their children as much of a priority as they do their businesses, they will be successful at both. However, raising children does not need to be, nor is it usually, Greens' priority. (See in chapter 5 the potential conflict arising within people with Green/Violet or Green/Blue auras when they are raising children.)

Green Children

Green children are very intelligent. They ask a lot of questions and learn quickly. These strong-willed, determined little people tend to develop strong goals at a very young age. They can be self-disciplined and self-controlled. Green children, however, can also be the first to challenge their parents' decisions. Greens do not like being told what to do, even as children. Instead, they become accustomed to giving orders. Green children seem more like adults than most adults do.

Green children want to be listened to and respected. They can become easily frustrated if things don't go their way, becoming vocal with their protests by screaming, interrupting conversations, and otherwise demanding attention.

For parents, dealing with obstinate and demanding Green children can be frustrating if they do not understand their children's priorities. When the children are frustrated, parents can work with them to develop plans on how the children can accomplish their goals. Can the children earn the toys they want by doing chores? Can they solve the puzzle another way, rather than tenaciously putting the piece in the wrong spaces? Is there a more appropriate way of getting the parent's attention than screaming and interrupting?

These children are quick to understand when their parents discuss situations logically with them. Green children can argue, challenge, and resent authority with the best of them. However, they are also inspiring to watch as they develop understanding, strength, determination, self-reliance, and independence. Parents of Green children do not usually have to worry about their children being successful. These children will usually come home with high grades, achievement awards, and success stories.

Parents should be sure to praise Green children for their accomplishments. Respect and admiration are extremely important to them. It is beneficial for parents to encourage their Green children to go after any goal they desire and not to fear failure. Because all Greens tend to demand perfection from themselves, if parents see their Green children being too hard on themselves or emphasizing their own shortcomings, they can instead remind their children of all their accomplishments. This will help Green children learn to stay balanced and to appreciate themselves.

Problem Solving

When solving problems, Greens analyze the situation and develop solutions so quickly that they leave others behind. They are valuable assets to anyone's business. However, when Greens are out of power, they can be stubborn and tenacious. They can beat their heads against the wall, thinking that if they are just persistent enough they will break through. Often, their persistence eventually pays off. Clear thinking and exploring other options, however, will usually be the quicker, more efficient way. Because they do not like to be wrong or admit they have made a mistake, it is often difficult for them to change their course or their tactics.

Money

Money is extremely important to Greens. They like wealth: nice clothes, nice furniture, nice homes, and nice cars. Having very high standards, they want the best. They are not happy or satisfied when they compromise. If they buy something that is not exactly what they want, they will never appreciate it or use it. When Greens are out of power, no amount of money is enough for them. They continue to strive, plan, and push for more and more. They also tend to overspend, getting themselves deeper and deeper into debt. When Greens are unhappy, they think that more money and more possessions will solve all their problems.

When Greens are in power and are thinking clearly, their strong desire for achieving abundance and prosperity has created in them the ability to manifest money easily and quickly. Greens are traditionally some of the wealthiest people on the planet. (Violets, their wealthy counterparts, also manifest money easily. However, while Greens can work purely for money, Violets cannot. Violets need to believe in what they are doing, enjoy doing it, and feel that there is a higher purpose involved. Greens pride themselves on being able to sell anything to anyone, and can build oil platforms in places where it may not be beneficial to the environment. Violets would usually protest such actions.)

When Greens do a job, they want to be well compensated for their efforts. Money represents power, status, and control to them. (See in chapter 5 their potential inner conflicts regarding money.)

Success

Greens judge their success by how much money they have, how much they have accomplished, and how much they are admired and respected for their accomplishments.

Occupations

These ambitious entrepreneurs prefer and even need to be self-employed or at least in top management. They have effective, efficient, and sharp minds for finance and business. Greens like to be in charge and relish telling other people what to do, preferring to delegate tasks and responsibilities. However, they tend to be perfectionists and often feel that others do not live up to their high standards. They can offend people with their controlling, critical, and domineering attitudes.

Because Greens can accomplish anything they put their minds to, they are in almost any kind of occupation. However, they prefer occupations that enable them to be in charge, challenge their mental skills, and offer a great deal of money. They need to be well compensated, mentally challenged, and treated with respect.

Well-known Greens include Bill Gates (Green/Violet), Donald Trump (Green/Yellow), Bette Davis, Fred Astaire, Arnold Schwarzenegger (Yellow/Green), Queen Elizabeth, and Ross Perot.

Occupations that appeal to Greens include the following:

- Corporate executive
- Real estate agent
- Business entrepreneur
- Banker
- Stockbroker
- Producer
- Fundraiser
- Office manager
- Financial and investment advisor
- Salesperson (especially sales involving expensive items such as cars, gems, insurance, and homes)
- Organizer
- Business manager and agent

| Marketing and | King (or at least "owner" |
| advertising coordinator | of the world) |

See Green/Violet, Green/Yellow, Green/Tan, and Green/Blue for other occupations.

Health

When they are in power, Greens are strong, powerful, and healthy. Out of power, however, Greens often become neurotic about their health. Their main problem areas are the stomach and internal organs. They worry so much that they have a tendency to develop ulcers, stomachaches, colitis, and intestinal problems. Because of this it is advisable that Greens stay away from coffee or other stimulating substances. Although Greens like the energy stimulation of caffeine, it can be devastating to their nervous systems as well as to their stomachs. It is usually their only addiction. They can get more work done after they have coffee. As the effects wear off, however, they become irritable and agitated, causing them to think less clearly. (Greens often enjoy drinking alcoholic beverages because, at the end of the day, using alcohol is the only way they can shut off their incredibly active minds.)

A major problem for Greens is learning to relax. They do not seem to know how to relax, to take time off, or to take vacations. They have the highest suicide rate as well as a greater frequency of heart attacks. These workaholics tend to take life and their financial problems too seriously. Having a tense body is common for Green perfectionists. With work and stress, they frequently experience a tight neck and shoulders. They often become so worried and anxious that they forget to breathe deeply. Another frequent problem area for Greens is the throat. If Greens suppress what they want to say, their throats can become tight and irritated.

To keep from experiencing health problems Greens must learn to relax, but the only time they do relax is when they feel they are in control of their lives. It is helpful for Greens to keep a list of things they want to accomplish so they feel organized and in control rather than overwhelmed. They should also schedule time to do things they enjoy rather than work-related tasks (although Greens usually enjoy doing these tasks, overworking can cause stress). Many Greens enjoy themselves on golf courses, at the racetrack, or in casinos.

Greens must learn to appreciate their accomplishments rather than focus on the hundreds of yet uncompleted tasks. Being extremely busy makes Greens feel important, but it also causes stress-related health problems. Greens can ask themselves how important it really is that they have control over every situation. They can evaluate the severity of each situation to see if it really requires worry and concern. They must learn that it may not be possible or even necessary to control every aspect of life. If they can learn to trust the process of life more often, life can prove to be more cooperative than they had imagined. One of the most important pieces of advice for Greens is to remember to breathe. People can think more clearly and rationally (and live longer) when they breathe more deeply more often.

CHAPTER FOUR

emotional life colors

BLUE

Blues are some of the most loving, nurturing, and supportive personalities of the Life Colors. They live from their hearts and emotions. Their purpose for being on the planet is to give love, to teach love, and to learn they are loved. Their priorities are love, relationships, and spirituality.

Blues are traditionally teachers, counselors, and nurses — the loving nurturers and caretakers on the planet. Blues are constantly helping others. They want to make sure everyone feels loved and accepted. People always turn to Blues for comfort and counsel because Blues will always be there for them. They consistently provide a shoulder for others to cry on.

Blues are the most emotional personalities in the aura spectrum. They can cry at the drop of a hat — when they are happy, hurt, angry, sad, or for no apparent reason. Even watching a sentimental commercial on television can bring tears. People with other Life Colors may have difficulty understanding Blues' intense emotional personality. It is their capacity for such emotional depth, however, that makes Blues so warm, compassionate,

117

and caring. They are capable of deeply understanding the feelings of others. Seeing another person cry can often cause Blues to cry in empathy. (During a group therapy session, if one Blue starts to cry, every Blue will automatically start to cry.)

Blues' greatest talents are their ability to give unconditional love and their intuition. People love being around Blues who are in power because then Blues radiate love, acceptance, and forgiveness. These compassionate beings will even befriend those whom others find unlovable. Blues look for the good in people. They will give everyone many second chances. No matter what mistakes people make, Blues will love and forgive them. This behavior often earns them the reputation of being doormats. They are often accused of being too nice. People can easily take advantage of their unselfish and endlessly giving nature. One of their hardest lessons is learning to say no. They are afraid that if they do say no, other people will feel unloved and rejected or will not love them in return. Blues must learn that saying no to people does not mean Blues do not love them.

Blues are some of the most intuitive personalities in the aura spectrum. They know things. There are often no facts or reasons to support what they know; they just feel it to be true. They can meet someone and sense if that person is upset or unhappy. They can feel when something is about to happen. They can think about someone they have not seen in a long time and that person will call a few minutes later. When Blues have a question, whether it is regarding relationships (usually their biggest challenge), business, health, or other matters, they need only become quiet and ask themselves the question. They will hear the answer inside. The challenge for Blues is learning to trust what they hear inside and not overanalyze it.

Although all of us have the capability of receiving intuitive information, Blues seem to operate primarily through their intuition. They operate so much from their feelings that they often speak in those terms, using such phrases as "It just feels right," "I feel that my friend needs help," or "I feel something big is about to happen."

In addition to being helpers, givers, and teachers, Blues are highly spiritual. Blues believe there is a God, a Higher Power, a Universal Intelligence, or All That Is. They have had experiences as children of seeing or talking with God. Their lives are often spiritual quests to learn more about God and to serve. They are very loyal to their religious or spiritual organizations as long as they feel those organizations teach what they believe to be the truth. Otherwise, they go from one church or religion to another in search of more spiritual knowledge to explain and validate what they feel inside. Living a loving and spiritual life is a strong priority for them.

When Blues are in power, people trust them. They know Blues would never do anything to hurt anyone and that their intentions are always loving and sincere. Because of their loving integrity and dedication to high moral standards, Blues can do something only when they believe in it. Then they are some of the world's greatest promoters. If they discover something they enjoy or that has helped them, whether it is a movie, a book, a restaurant, or a religion, they want to share their discovery with all their friends.

The loving Blues usually have an abundance of friends. Their loved ones are a high priority in their lives. They will give up their valuable time and energy to help friends in need. These sensitive, caring individuals are also the perfect hosts. They will consistently cater to their guests' needs, offering food, drink, or whatever else is needed for comfort. During conversations, Blues will also make sure everyone feels included. They can become overly concerned, at times, with everyone else's well-being. They can become so caught up in their friends' dramas that they frequently end up feeling more distressed and emotionally burdened than their friends feel. A challenge for Blues is to not worry about everyone else's problems. They are the ultimate rescuers on the planet. (Yellows also tend to help and rescue people, but they usually focus on using their sense of humor to cheer them up.)

Blues are good givers, but not good receivers. They even have trouble receiving compliments. Because they do not want to bother or inconvenience anyone, they feel guilty asking for or receiving help. They also have trouble delegating authority. Consequently, they become incredibly overworked and overwhelmed with responsibilities and with volunteering all their time. Blues are the ultimate doers — they feel people love them because they buy them gifts or work hard for them, rather than because they are themselves lovable people. One of Blues' greatest lessons is to learn they are loved just the way they are, not for what they do.

Blues want deeply to be loved, though they often doubt they are loved. They frequently doubt their self-worth. They can hear a hundred times that they are beautiful and loved, and yet if one negative thing is said, it is the negative they will remember. Blues even test people (especially their mates) to see if they really love them. "If he really loved me, he would run after me if I left him." "He would remember my birthday since I did so many wonderful things for him on his birthday." "He would worry about me if I appeared to be unhappy."

Blues want to be loved, but don't believe they should have to ask for it. Because Blues are the loving and intuitive rescuers, they want to be loved and rescued when they are depressed, overworked, or overwhelmed. Because Blues know when someone else is upset and needs love, they expect that others know when they are upset. However, not all the other Life Colors are as intuitive as are the Blues. Nor do they all feel a need to rescue people. Although Blues retreat into the bedroom and wait for someone to comfort and rescue them, others do not understand and can even resent being manipulated by Blues' guilt-inducing behavior. It is when Blues don't receive the love they want, or when they don't recognize or accept the love given to them, that they can become overly dramatic and consumed with self-pity. Then they become victims and martyrs. Out of power, they use guilt to manipulate others, hoping that if people start feeling guilty enough, they will give Blues more love and attention. Blues just want to feel loved and appreciated.

Blues can become so emotional and depressed that they sometimes contemplate suicide, though they will not usually go through with it for fear of hurting the people they love. They then imagine being at their own funerals to see how many people would attend (just another test to see if they are loved). Many out-of-power Blues will hit bottom before they will accept help from others. They will become overworked, overwhelmed, ill, or devastated over relationship problems. Usually hitting bottom is the only time Blues will give themselves permission to stop rescuing everyone else and take care of their own needs for awhile.

Blues also hold onto the past and onto guilt more than the other colors do. Far into their adult lives, they continue to feel guilty about things they did as children. (It is very common for Blues to have issues with their mothers. Yellows typically have issues with their fathers.) They usually blame themselves when things go wrong. They are habitually apologizing for their behavior. "I'm Sorry" could be the Blue's theme song. If you step on a Blue's foot, the Blue will apologize for being in the way. Blues also tend to take things personally. It's difficult for them to be around angry people. They see others' anger as a personal rejection.

To become centered again, Blues must learn to love themselves, which is their greatest challenge and biggest life lesson. But they are typically afraid that if they love themselves, no one else will. Their greatest fear is being alone, abandoned and unloved. To help them love themselves, Blues need to understand that all their actions are always based on one of two motives: to give love or to be loved. If they can realize that both are benevolent and altruistic motives, then they can begin to be more gentle and understanding with themselves. They also need to realize they chose to serve and to give to others. No one has forced them. Blues achieve satisfaction and fulfillment from loving and giving to others.

To regain their power, they also need to calm down and reconnect with their inner knowing. They need to trust that they are loved. If they become deeply depressed, their quickest cure is to do something nice for someone else. As soon as they focus on helping someone else, they forget about their own problems and become less depressed. When Blues regain their balance, they return to their natural loving and generous nature. (Helping others should be only a temporary solution, however, because Blues can become overly involved in the lives of others to avoid facing their own fears and challenges.)

Relationships

The two most important priorities in a Blue's life are spirituality and relationships. More than anything in the world, the devoted Blues want to be in loving, committed, and emotionally connected relationships. Blues can be the most loyal and supportive mates of all Life Colors. (See in chapter 5 the conflict that frequently arises with Blue Combination Colors.) Blues are happiest when they are in good relationships. They are the most unfulfilled and depressed when they are alone or are in bad relationships.

Because relationships are so important to them, Blues can give themselves away or change themselves just to be loved. They often feel they are not good enough as they are. They will change their hairstyles, the way they dress, or their behaviors in an attempt to become the people they think their mates want them to be.

Out of power, Blues tend to choose mates who need rescuing or who emotionally abuse them. In addition, despite everyone else's opinions and advice, Blues will hold on to these unhealthy relationships, feeling that if they love their partners enough, the relationship will work out. They are afraid of being alone. They are also afraid of abandoning and therefore hurting their mates.

Blues have a difficult time letting go. To Blues, to let go means to stop loving. Because love is a necessary element in their lives, it devastates Blues to feel they should stop loving anyone. Even if they are miserable and unfulfilled in their relationships, Blues do not deal well with the guilt, sadness, fear, loss, or the pain of ending relationships. When they do end a relationship, they need to give themselves permission to continue to love that person, but also to expand outward to love another.

When Blues love, especially their mates, they want to be around them all the time. When another Life Color needs time alone, a Blue will take it personally, believing the other person does not love her as much. Blues have so much love to give that they can often overwhelm non-Blues. (See in the Relationships chapters how Blues relate to each Life Color.)

Sex

To Blues, love, trust, and affection are more important than sex. They love to be held, hugged, and cuddled. Being very moral, Blues grow up feeling they need to be "good," sleeping only with someone they love. Meaningless sex is difficult for Blues, often considered by these virtuous souls to be unspiritual or unclean. (Blue/Yellows can experience conflict with their morality because Yellows like sex so much.) Blues can have difficulty experiencing sexual satisfaction unless they completely trust their partners and feel devoted love from them. While making love, Blues often cry in moments of passion (which can thoroughly confuse their carefree Yellow partners, who are usually laughing and joking while making love). Making love is a deeply emotional experience for Blues. It expresses their love and commitment to their partners.

Blue Parents

Being natural mothers, most Blues want children (unless they are burnt out because they have mothered everyone else; also,

Blue/Yellow and Blue/Violet combinations often struggle with the issue of having children). They want to bond emotionally with their children. They love to read them stories, hug them, and be involved with their lives. They are usually loving, generous, and compassionate parents. If they choose not to have children, they may share their homes with cats instead. Cats are drawn to the intuitive Blues.

Out of power, Blues can often smother their children in the name of love. They tend to sacrifice their own lives, goals, and ambitions by living their lives for their children. When their children are learning to ride their bikes, Blue parents want to hold onto the handlebars so they don't fall and hurt themselves. Blues believe this is the best way to show they care. Through such actions, however, they may be giving their children the impression that they do not believe in them, that they are incapable of succeeding without them. The children become insecure regarding their own abilities and then become dependent upon the protective parents. Blue parents need to realize that the most loving attitude is to believe in their children and help them believe in themselves. They need to release the handlebars and show their children love by inspiring and empowering them, not by creating dependency.

Out of power, Blue parents can be good at tying apron strings to their children, who then may feel guilty "abandoning" their Blue parents when it is time for them to leave the nest. Blues love to feel needed by their families, but they should remember that there are plenty of other people for them to help. They do not need to channel all their energy and attention onto their children.

Children need to realize that their Blue parents only want to know they are loved and appreciated. When Blues are in power, they intuitively know how much their children love them. They are truly giving and nurturing parents who are devoted to caring for their children.

Blue Children

Blue children are very loving and emotional. They try very hard to please their parents so they will be loved. They want to be good helpers. Not wanting to upset or disappoint anyone, Blue children are usually well behaved and well mannered. Being emotional and sensitive, they are similar to Yellow children. Blue children will sit indoors, however, calmly combing their doll's hair or playing with toy ovens while Yellow children run around outdoors, climbing trees and playing sports.

At a young age, the sensitive Blue children want to show love and take care of everyone. They are very aware of and compassionate toward the underdog at school. They feel sorry for anyone who seems lonely. They want everyone to feel loved and accepted. Blue children can even feel responsible for their parents' happiness and well-being, and can sacrifice their own happiness to support their parents. Blue children are often afraid to "abandon" one or both parents, especially if the parents are experiencing unhappiness in their marriage. Parents should teach their Blue children that they do not need to sacrifice their lives for their parents. Let them know they are loved and encourage them to live happy lives of their own.

Blues usually develop an early interest in having relationships. Blue children have an idealistic picture of some day being in loving marriages. It is very easy for them to develop many romantic crushes in school. Because of their sensitivity and lack of self-worth, however, Blues can experience many traumatic experiences of unrequited love. They take rejection personally. (Although the optimistic and flirtatious Blue/Yellows may quickly move onto a new crush, the deep and intense Blue/Violets tend to become more guarded and isolated. Blue/Violets may become overly involved in school projects to avoid facing future disappointments in love.)

Usually, Blue children are loved by their peers. A Blue/Yellow or Blue/Violet combination can be one of the most popular cheerleaders or class leaders in school. Even though Blue children have an abundance of friends who care about them, when they are out of power they often feel unloved, unworthy, and lonely. They, like their adult counterparts, do not always comprehend what it means to be loved by others. They often have low self-esteem. It is important to help Blue children develop a sense of self-worth and self-appreciation, to help them recognize their loving, compassionate, and giving nature.

(Yellow and Violet children are quite similar to Blues. They are all sensitive and emotional. However, Blues are the most emotional of the three; Yellows are the most energetic and active or shy; Violets are the most powerful, authoritative, and independent. If dance, music, creativity, sports, freedom, or independence are important to the child, chances are the child is a Yellow/Violet, a Yellow/Blue, or a Blue/Violet combination aura.)

Problem Solving

Prayer and meditation are the most common tools Blues use to solve challenges. When Blues are centered, they pray or ask their inner selves for answers. They must learn to listen and trust the answers they receive, however. Trusting is their biggest challenge. When Blues have questions, whether about relationships, business, or even what to eat, they only need to become quiet and centered, ask themselves the questions, and hear the solution inside.

When Blues are out of power, their method of solving problems involves sitting in their homes and crying to be rescued. They often pray for help, but are not always listening inside when the answers come. Blues' quiet intuition, trust, and knowing will give them the answers they need and solve their challenges every time.

Money

People and relationships are more important to Blues than money, so they often struggle financially, choosing low-paying, service-oriented jobs. Because money is not a priority, Blues are usually fearful of not having enough, especially when they have families to support. In addition, it is easier for them to complain, suffer, and dramatize their hard work and sacrifices than it is for them to ask for a raise. (See in chapter 5 the Blue/Green's conflict regarding money.)

Because Blues are very good givers but not very good receivers, one challenge for them is learning to receive money. They usually feel that their services should come from the heart, not from a desire for money. They commonly feel that being spiritual means being opposed to having material wealth. Even though Blues are happy being givers, they need to learn how to receive. By never learning to receive, they are cheating others out of the joy of giving and are, to a certain extent, looking down on them. They are, in a sense, saying, "I am wonderful and prosperous enough to give to you. You, however, are not prosperous or powerful enough to give to me." The most loving and empowering gesture a Blue can make is to allow others to feel prosperous, generous, and capable of giving. This empowers others to feel good about their capabilities.

Blues can also feel guilty having more than their friends or families have. They subconsciously feel they must suffer with everyone else by not being prosperous or in harmonious, satisfying relationships. If friends are suffering financially, Blues will either empathize and complain about their similar financial situations or give them money to help them out. Blues will also try to help everyone first before they will help themselves. They feel that sacrificing their needs and putting others first show how loving they are. They often fear being unloved and alone or of being seen as selfish if they succeed.

As long as Blues feel they must help everyone else first, they are destined to suffer. Their bravest and most loving action is to first live their own dreams of abundance, love, health, and happiness, which will inspire others to live their dreams, too. (What motivates Blues is discovering that their actions will help others.) Blues also need to learn that love, happiness, prosperity, and spirituality can all be connected.

Success

Blues define their success by how many people love them and by how many people they have been able to help. The quantity and quality of friends, the length and quality of their marriages, the depth of their compassion and loyalty to those they love, and their dedication to their spirituality are what they consider to be most important.

Occupations

Because Blues are here to be in service, they are usually drawn to the helping professions such as teaching, counseling, and nursing. They work best one-on-one and heart-to-heart with people. (Although Violets are also drawn toward helping people, they work more often with groups rather than with individuals.) Because Blues feel that love and money do not mix, they have created some of the lowest paid positions in the professional fields. (Most service organizations are also nonprofit organizations.) Blues do not believe they should profit from helping others. Learning that prosperity, love, and spirituality can coexist harmoniously is a major lesson for them.

Any occupation that allows them to help other people appeals to Blues. Also, they appreciate the opportunity to spend time at home creating a loving, cozy, and nurturing environment.

Occupations that appeal to Blues include the following:

Teacher, educator	Volunteer
Marriage and family counselor	Religious or church helper
	Clergy
Nurse	Nun or priest
Childcare worker	Homemaker

Assistant or director at nonprofit organizations	Parent
	Housekeeper
	Waiter or Waitress
Secretary	Social worker
Astrologer	Psychologist
Psychic	Spiritual adviser

See in chapter 5 regarding occupations for Blue/Yellow, Blue/Green, and Blue/Violet auras.

Health

Blues do not focus much energy on their physical bodies; therefore, they are not motivated to exercise. Walking to the mailbox is usually the extent of their exercise program. They rationalize a thousand reasons why they do not have time to exercise. Because they rarely send energy to their bodies, Blues usually have cold hands and feet. (See in chapter 5 the inner conflict created with a Blue/Yellow aura. Yellows need to exercise to feel happy and healthy.)

One physical weak spot for Blues is the throat area. Throat problems are created by years of choking back hurt and swallowing tears. Blue women can also experience problems with their breasts and reproductive systems. They create challenges such as vaginal infections, cramps, cysts, and ovarian or breast cancer because they typically carry feelings of guilt, anger, shame, or inadequacy regarding themselves, their relationships, or sex. Obesity is also common among Blues, who often doubt they are attractive or sexy. When they fear not being loved, Blues will often put on layers of fat for protection, particularly below the waist to protect their sexuality. Extra weight also keeps Blues grounded and in their bodies.

Walking, breathing, and meditating are healthy activities for Blues. Releasing past guilt and the fear of not being loved will also keep them healthy. When Blues learn to give themselves as much love as they give to everyone else, it will be easier for them to keep themselves healthy.

VIOLET

Violets are the inspirational visionaries, leaders, and teachers who are here to help save the planet. Most Violets feel drawn to educate the masses, to inspire higher ideals, to improve the quality of life on the planet, or to help save people, animals, and the environment. Violets have an inner sense that they are here to do something important, that their destiny is greater than that of the average person. Most have felt this way since childhood, when they imagined becoming famous or traveling the planet, possibly joining humanitarian causes such the peace corps. Many of these charismatic personalities take on roles as leaders and teachers; others prefer to reach people through music, film, or other art forms.

Being visionaries, Violets can literally see the future in their mind's eye. They process life through their third eye or inner vision. They often speak in visual terms, using such words as "I see," "I picture," "I envision," or "I have a dream." They can see a work of art completed before they begin creating it, a house built before they design it, and the results of a project before they start working on it. They can see the future results of anything they focus upon — from fashion trends to music trends to the fate of the world. Violets who are in power and in touch with their vision can see what must happen to ensure the survival of the planet, and they have a message to pass along to humanity. When they are not yet in touch with what that message is, it is because they are not centered or quiet enough inside to hear it.

Because this era is currently the Violet age, Violets who are not accomplishing what they came here to do are experiencing an inner push — even an inner earthquake. Inner forces seem to be shaking them up and pushing them to move into action, to fulfill their life purpose. Violets know they are here to do something significant. However, they aren't always sure what that something is or how to accomplish it. Many Violets were taught as children that their dreams and aspirations were unrealistic, so they have lost touch with their original visions. It's important for Violets to reconnect with their life purpose and vision and to take action. Otherwise they will always feel unfulfilled. They will always sense something is missing from their lives. They need to slow down long enough to listen to their inner voice and to connect with their higher vision.

Violets are older souls. They seem to have an innate intelligence or common sense that goes beyond any formal education they may have received. They just know things. They believe that what they see is common sense. They do not understand why everyone can't see what they see. To most Life Colors, what Violets see is beyond their comprehension or limited sight. To those who need to understand all the facts and data in order to consider some futuristic possibility, Violets' visions and ideas can seem unrealistic and impractical.

These visionary Violets, in their attempt to improve the quality of life on the planet, can upset those people who prefer their lives remain the same — predictable and familiar. Not everyone wants life to change. Many people feel safer with the status quo. It can appear to them that Violets are threatening their current, familiar way of life. However, Violets are here to inspire and create change. They are the communicators on the planet, and they feel their voices must be heard.

The Violet age began in the mid-sixties, definitely a time of social change and upheaval. Violets such as John F. Kennedy, Robert Kennedy, and Martin Luther King, Jr. so challenged the status quo that those who were upset by their visionary and radical ideals wanted them silenced. Violets haven't always felt safe to express themselves around those with limited vision.

Many Violets felt isolated and misunderstood even when they were children. They often felt that they didn't fit in or that they didn't belong here. As adults, many Violets continue to feel this way. They sense concepts and ideas that don't exist yet. Even though they have few role models because their thinking tends to be ahead of the masses, it's helpful for Violets to find mentors who can inspire them to accomplish their visions.

Violets often feel, or have felt in their younger years, that it's difficult to be on the planet. The energy here can feel dense and slow to them. Violets are not known for their patience when they are out of power. They want to accomplish their dreams and visions now. Frequently, they even want to finish people's sentences for them. Until they learn to see the bigger picture and trust that their visions will manifest, Violets can experience a great deal of frustration.

Violets' lives can sometimes be more intense, dramatic, and challenging than other aura colors. It is quite common for Violets — although not all Violets — to have been raised in dysfunctional or troubled households. Because Violets are here to help save or educate the masses, many seem to have begun their lives in a way that could help them understand and empathize with other people's pain and fear. This way, after they have grown and overcome their own initial challenges, they can help others through their problems. Having been through the same pain, these Violets are now credible and understanding helpers and teachers.

Violets seem to take on bigger challenges than the average person does. However, when a Violet's life is finally fulfilled, the payoffs are also usually bigger or more profound than the average person's.

Violets have extraordinary depth and compassion. Their compassion tends to extend worldwide. Watching a program about starving children in Africa can overwhelm them emotionally, often inspiring them to become involved and to make changes. Violets in power are very passionate about the causes they believe in.

Violets are also passionate about music, which can move

them to ecstasy or to tears. It is best for these musical connoisseurs to listen to — or create — positive, empowering, and inspiring music or calming and centering music. If the lyrics are angry and negative or the music nerve-shattering, they will become irritable, fragmented, and confused. Violets' energy and moods are greatly affected by music. Violets are the communicators on the planet, and for them music is the universal language, but they need to be aware of the messages they are hearing or sending through music.

These visionaries also love to travel. (Since Violets are here to save the planet, they need to see and understand the planet they are here to save.) Their careers and lifestyles must afford them the freedom to travel or they will become frustrated and feel limited and unfulfilled. Traveling the world and exploring other cultures broadens their horizons and expands their understanding. (Yellows travel to escape and have fun. Violets travel to learn and to be inspired.)

Although some Life Colors process mentally and analytically, needing to understand every step in the process as they go, Violets see the bigger picture. They see step one to step fifty without necessarily seeing all the steps in between. If they trust their vision, Violets know that step fifty will occur, though they don't always know what it will take to accomplish it.

What Violets want to accomplish often seems too big, too grandiose, too unrealistic. If they can stay focused and in power, however, they will inspire and earn the respect of those around them when their dreams actually manifest. To begin the process of creating their dreams, Violets just need to listen to their inner guidance and take whatever steps they do know how to take. It is then that the next steps will appear or be revealed to them. When Violets are in power, many coincidences and synchronicities seem to occur in their lives. People are often amazed at the seemingly magical circumstances that can occur for Violets. Violets need to accomplish their life mission here or they will experience deep regrets, always wondering what their lives could have been if only they had taken chances.

Violets are very affected by their environment. If they are around people who have a limited perception of life, Violets can start believing in and living that kind of life. If Violets dream of developing a new career, it is helpful for them to start associating with others who are involved in that kind of work. This way their dreams will seem more realistic. In other words, if Violets want to be artists or writers, they need to attend art or writing classes, associate with artists and writers, attend writers' conferences or art gallery openings, go to places where they will be inspired by others' art and writings. They need to move beyond their limited experience of life in the office, the bank, etc.

Violets have charismatic and magnetic energy, and people are drawn to them. Violets also love to be the center of attention. They are natural performers. (If they also have Yellow, Blue, or Tan in their auras, they may experience conflict regarding being the center of attention. Because Yellows, Blues, and Tans tend be more quiet or shy than Violets, they often prefer to stay in the background.) When Violets write, speak, or perform, energy and information literally channel through them. The information seems to come from a higher source, touching and inspiring anyone who hears it. Afterward, Violets feel larger than life, full of energy and power.

Even though Violets can appear to be quite social and gregarious at times, they prefer to have intelligent conversations with people rather than meaningless gossip or chatter about the weather. Violets do not need hundreds of friends who could take up their valuable time. Instead, they prefer a few quality friends who inspire and connect with them on a deeper level.

When Violets are out of power, they can become narcissistic, arrogant, and judgmental, thinking that they are better than everyone else is. They can become impatient and critical of other people's apparent lack of vision and intelligence. They can also develop tyrannical personalities and love to be idolized by their "subjects." Out of power, Violets have domineering and controlling qualities similar to those of out-of-power Greens. It is difficult for people to be in the presence of such self-important Violets.

When Violets are in power, they are much more accepting and compassionate toward others. They allow others to follow their own paths while they follow theirs, knowing that everyone has a direction and life purpose. Violets in power tend to "allow." To stay centered, Violets need to keep a clear perspective of their roles in the larger universal scheme. They need to remember that they are a part of the whole, that everyone has an important and valuable role to play, and that everyone is here for a unique experience. Not everyone is here to accomplish the same mission as the Violets'. If they can realize that everyone is part of the same greatness, that awareness can help prevent them from becoming critical, arrogant, and self-absorbed.

If Violets can stay focused and trust their vision, it will guide them forward. Out of power, however, Violets can become scattered and overwhelmed. When they don't trust their vision, they see too many possibilities. Either they will then attempt to accomplish all of them at once, taking on ten projects simultaneously, or they will become mentally paralyzed, unable to do any. Violets cannot be told to limit their visions, but they can be encouraged to focus on no more than two or three projects at a time. This focus enables them to be more effective. Focused Violets are powerful and inspiring. When Violets do not trust their vision, they can lose touch with it and become lost and confused again.

Taking time to focus and meditate will help Violets get in touch with their vision. Listening to empowering or beautiful music, mentally surrounding themselves with the color violet, and meditating are valuable tools for keeping Violets centered and in power. The most imperative of these tools is meditation, which can be as simple as quiet, reflective time.

The Universe will support Violets on their path by almost magically and effortlessly opening all doors for them. Violets know that this is the way the Universe naturally operates. Although many Life Colors cling to the belief that life is hard work and struggle, Violets in power can teach us to trust the universal flow and guidance.

The Violet age, which began in the mid-sixties, will continue until 2000–2014, at which time the planet will begin its transition into the Indigo age. Violets are here to lead us into the Indigo age, an era of global unity, compassion, and understanding in which we learn to live in harmony with one another and with our environment.

Relationships

Violets want relationships, but ultimately, accomplishing their missions takes precedence. They tend to be more independent and less reliant on relationships than most aura colors. Because Violets are here to have an impact on the planet, they want partners who will create their visions with them and share similar paths. Violets want equality, inspiration, passion, and communication in their relationships. They want mates who are willing to travel with them or at least understand and support their need to travel.

Violets are passionate. They are willing to bond emotionally, physically, and spiritually with their mates. In power, Violets tend to be very understanding and accepting and can usually get along with most aura colors. Blues feel free to cry with the deep and compassionate Violets. Greens are allowed to be strong willed, temperamental, and even controlling. Violets will listen to and respect Greens, and then they choose what they (Violets) want anyway.

Because Violets often feel different from other people, it can take them awhile to find mates who are equals, who understand them, and who are not intimidated by their power, vision, and independence. It is common for Violets to marry late in life or to outgrow their mates if they married at a young age. Violets often connect with partners who they believe will fulfill the supportive role by staying home with the children or by bringing home the regular paycheck. In this way Violets assume they will have the freedom to pursue their visions. Unfortunately, what typically occurs is that Violets eventually become bored with partners who are not inspirational to them. Their partners find themselves left for those who are passionate and vibrant, those who travel along-side and share the Violets' dreams.

When Violets are afraid to focus on their higher purpose, or if they doubt they will be able to accomplish their dreams, they often create distractions, such as affairs or other dramas, in their relationships. With the Violets' strong sexual appetites and their desire to be the center of attention, they can be prime candidates for extramarital affairs. They see that there are many options available. Violets have a charismatic and sexual chemistry, and they are strongly attractive to others. Violets who do not keep a loving and focused perspective can hurt their relationships by desiring too much attention for their ego satisfaction. When Violets stay focused and see the bigger picture, they realize they can create passion and fulfillment in their current relationships. When they realize they may be running away from the larger issue, mainly that of fulfilling their mission on the planet, they can stop creating relationship dramas and other distractions.

Sex

Violets, Yellows, and Reds are the most sexual of the aura colors. Violets love sex and are extremely passionate. During love-making, Violets often sense the universal connection of every-thing. Making love can be a cosmic experience for them. Although Yellows are sensitive to their partners, when they finish making love they are ready to jump up and play. Violets can stay next to their partners in a bonding embrace until the encounter has naturally and fully concluded (unless they have too many other projects demanding their attention).

If Violets go too long without sex, they become increasingly frustrated. Often, this is when affairs occur. Affairs can also occur when Violets are afraid to move forward to their next stage of development or on to their greater visionary projects. Channeling energy into sex or relationships can be a strong, seductive diversion.

Violet Parents

Violets love children and will bond with them emotionally. They see the potential in children and willingly share in the responsibility of raising them.

In power, Violet parents can be very accepting, seeing the bigger picture and allowing children to be children. These loving parents usually teach best by leading the way, being examples, and believing in and living their own dreams. This teaches their children that they also have permission to live their dreams.

Out of power, Violet parents can become dictators, insisting that their rules must be obeyed. They will not listen to opposing arguments or other viewpoints. They can also become so scattered and busy that they don't have time for their children.

Occasionally, Violets will stay at home with the children during their early formative years, but they soon feel the need to become involved again in the real world. Violets cannot just sit at home and be parents. As much as they love their children, they have too much to do in this lifetime. They need to have a positive impact upon the planet.

Violet Children

Violet children, like their adult counterparts, are powerful, charismatic, and wise leaders. Other children are drawn to follow them. Violets can appear to be taken with themselves at times. However, if parents teach these children to have compassion toward others, they will learn not to abuse their power. Parents can help their Violet children by encouraging them to become involved in humanitarian causes or projects. These children need to channel their energy into outlets and projects that are bigger than they are. Otherwise, Violet children can become self-obsessed and dramatic or they can become deeply depressed and confused. These advanced beings tend to be very serious (unless they have Yellow in their aura, which will make them either shy or comedic). Violet children tend to feel different from their peers. They typically have interests that are beyond that of other children their age. Finding older mentors who can inspire and support them can be beneficial.

Violet children seem to have advanced wisdom. It's common for these older souls to give advice to their parents and to intuitively know information that is well beyond their years. Instead of becoming intimidated and overwhelmed by their children's powerful and independent nature, parents need to encourage and support them to believe in themselves. These children have big dreams and need all the support they can get.

Violet children tend to be very sexually oriented, often experimenting at a young age with their bodies and sex. This seems natural to Violets, and so parents need to deal with the topic in a mature and nonjudgmental way. Otherwise the children grow up believing there is something wrong with expressing their natural passion through sex. (Unfortunately, because these children often emit a sexual charisma, they can be prime targets for sexual abuse.)

These visual Violet children usually love artwork and reading, putting their own pictures to the stories they hear. They also love music. Playing soothing music is a good way for parents to calm their intense Violet children.

Violet children see a lot of options and want to explore them all. They will often have several piles of toys out at the same time. (This could irritate Green parents, who want order, cleanliness, and discipline.) Parents of Violet children need to teach them to focus, but not limit, their attention.

Because Violet children have such a unique visual perception, they are often able to see energies others have long since learned not to see. Violets are the first to see auras, spirits, angels, other dimensions, or energy waves. Violets often have premonitions. If Violet children say they see or sense something, it is better for the parents to encourage them to describe what they see than to belittle their active imaginations. By denying or demeaning their visual experiences, parents will teach the children to mistrust their own visions. This will cause them to become scattered and unclear of their direction later in life. Many Violet adults learned at a young age to shut down or fear their amazing visionary or clairvoyant abilities.

Problem Solving

When facing challenges, Violets in power have the ability to visually project themselves into the future and see past the problem. By seeing the future, they know how the problem can be solved. Violets out of power cannot see past their four walls. They are confused regarding solutions, and they can become disoriented and overwhelmed. Violets must learn to trust their visions and to act on what they see. Asking Violets what they see (not what they think) encourages them to use their inner vision, which is their strength in solving problems

If Violets don't trust their visions while they are awake, the information will appear in their dreams. Violets receive these messages more than the other aura personalities do. It's helpful for Violets to keep dream journals so they can keep track of the information.

Money

The wealthiest people on the planet are Greens and Violets. The difference between them is that Greens can take jobs just for the money and they can sell anything to anyone, but Violets (in power) cannot. Violets must believe in what they are doing, enjoy it, and know there is a higher purpose involved. When Violets are in power, the money flows in. Greens want money for the things it will buy — expensive clothes, cars, homes, and furniture. Although Violets also enjoy those items, they instead prefer to have money for the freedom it gives them to accomplish their missions. When Violets have money, they travel and become philanthropists.

Visualization is a powerful tool for Violets. If they desire more money, visualizing it in their lives will help attract it to them. Because Violets often criticize the destructive power of money, however, they fear that having wealth could make them appear less spiritual and humanitarian. This judgment can limit Violets' ability to make money. They need to realize that being prosperous can enable them to accomplish their missions here and that money is not inherently evil.

Success

Violets judge their success by how much freedom they experience, the quality of their performances, and how effective they have been in reaching their audiences. Violets have a statement to make. They feel fulfilled when they know they have reached people with their messages and have inspired change. Violets need to know they have done their part in making the planet a better place to live.

Occupations

Violets are most fulfilled when they work for themselves or are as independent as possible. They have difficulty working for anyone else because they see too far ahead of others to be limited by people who are narrow minded or shortsighted. Occasionally they can work for organizations, but they need to feel they are team members and able to be part of the decision-making process, not just employees. Also, Violets can outgrow their jobs quickly or become easily bored. Although some aura colors prefer security and stability, Violets need to experience growth, innovation, and expansion in their work.

Because Violets are here to inspire change on the planet and are charismatic in front of audiences, they are usually drawn to one (or all three) of the following categories.

The first is communications or the media. Violets are the performers and the communicators on the planet. The media is a perfect vehicle for Violets to reach the masses, as is performing on stage or in front of a camera, singing, dancing, acting, playing music, or modeling. Violets can also reach the masses through the Internet or off-camera by directing, producing, writing, painting, designing, marketing, advertising, or photography. Paul McCartney, Elvis Presley, George Lucas, Steven Spielberg, Cher, Sting, Barbra Streisand, and Oprah Winfrey all have violet as one of their Life Colors.

The second area is teaching or psychology. Violets enjoy teaching workshops, seminars, and classes. Because they are spiritual leaders, they may also teach and inspire as ministers. Violets seem to have an intuitive understanding of human behavior, which makes them natural counselors. The only way Violets can tolerate being psychologists or therapists, however, is if they lead frequent group sessions, write books, or interact with the media. Focusing on individual clients day after day is too tedious and limiting. They need to feel they are effectively reaching the world on a greater scale.

The third area is law, politics, or causes. Because Yellows and Blues typically do not like politics, Violets with these Combination Colors tend to veer away from law and politics. Blue/Violet and Yellow/Violet Combination Colors will frequently become involved in causes, however. They will usually choose environmental causes such as saving the whales and the rain forests, or humanitarian causes such as helping starving children and the homeless.

Violets are natural mediators. They want people to listen to one another, communicate openly, and discuss matters in a calm and fair manner. Abraham Lincoln, Martin Luther King, Jr., John and Robert Kennedy, Gandhi, the Dalai Lama, Mikhail Gorbachev, and Nelson Mandela are examples of Violet leaders. (Note what happened to some Violets who became leaders before the Violet age was fully empowered. Some of their ideas were too far ahead of the times, and, out of fear, they were eliminated from their leadership positions. Now that the Violet age has reached full power, the once-radical ideas of Violets are becoming accepted.) Typically, more Violets are in the Democratic Party and more Greens in the Republican Party. Bill Clinton is a Violet/Yellow combination. Jacqueline Kennedy Onassis, Eleanor Roosevelt, Al Gore, Jesse Jackson, and Ronald Reagan (who began his career as a Democrat) have Violet auras. Harry S. Truman, George Bush, Boris Yeltsin (Green and Yellow), Nancy Reagan (Green and Violet), Donald Trump (Green and Yellow), and Ross Perot are all Greens.

Other areas to which Violets are drawn include philosophy, religious studies, world travel, the humanities, interior decorating, and advanced computer technology.

Typical Violet occupations include the following:

Performer	Psychologist
Actor	Social worker
Singer	Activist
Musician	Consultant
Artist	Lecturer
Writer	Politician
Designer	Lawyer
Producer	Company president
Director	Business owner
Camera operator	Developer
Photographer	Investment broker

Teacher, educator	Leader
Minister	Astronaut
Travel agent	Futurist
Mediator	Quantum physicist

Health

Eyesight challenges are common for Violets. Because Violets can see the future better than most people, many have misunderstood or felt threatened by them. To feel accepted by others, Violets often shorten their vision and start wearing glasses. To improve their eyesight, Violets need to give themselves permission to "see," even if it means upsetting others.

Violets often gain excessive weight because they feel a need for protection; they are unfulfilled; they suppress their dynamic power causing it to expand their bodies; or they feel a need to become larger in order to be seen. Many Violets never feel understood for who they really are. To lose the weight, they need to see, acknowledge, and accept themselves. They also need to stop suppressing their powerful energy and start accomplishing their missions. When Violets are confused and unhappy, they can also develop eating disorders such as anorexia or bulimia.

With the scattered tendencies of out-of-power Violets, health problems can be varied and unpredictable. To maintain good health, Violets need to focus their attention on a few projects, not scatter their energies by becoming too busy. Meditation has a calming influence and can help Violets stay centered, which in turn keeps them healthy.

LAVENDER

Fantasy, enchantment, dreams, myths, spiritual beings, angels, and fairies are all concepts that fill Lavenders' minds. Lavenders tend to live in fantasy worlds. They prefer to spend their time out of their bodies, where life is pretty and enchanting. It is challenging for these airy beings to live in three-dimensional reality. They prefer imaginary pictures of the world, seeing butterflies, flowers, and wood nymphs rather than dirt, concrete, and large cities. Physical reality seems cold and harsh to them.

These sensitive creatures are fragile and frail, and their physical appearance is often weak and pale. Their skin is often alabaster because they don't like being outdoors, unless it is to be surrounded by beautiful flowers and gardens. These childlike personalities are sensitive and simple. They would rather spend time watching clouds float by or daydreaming. They prefer to escape this reality with all its demands and responsibilities.

The Lavenders' behavior tends to frustrate others who may expect them to be dependable. They have no understanding of what it means to hold a responsible job or to earn money. They are more familiar with other dimensions and imagined realities. Lavenders even have a difficult time relating to or connecting with the concepts of time, space, and physical matter. They tend to experience events in their imagination, but they are not usually grounded enough in physical reality to accomplish anything tangible. Because they have a hard time differentiating fantasy from reality, they tend to be spacey and forgetful; they are not sure if they actually told someone they would attend a party or if they just imagined it. The Lavenders' innate ability to use their imagination makes them extraordinarily creative. They are also highly intuitive. Using common sense, logic, and reason, however, is not easy for these gifted spirits.

At first, people are fascinated by the Lavenders' creative imagination, but after talking with them for awhile, people wonder if anyone is "at home." The Lavenders' eyes can appear glazed, almost as if they are under the influence of mind-altering substances. They have a tendency to leave their bodies during conversations. Their concentration tends to drift into other worlds. Their seemingly uninterested behavior can irritate and insult people.

At the same time, Lavenders can be very entertaining and educational. They can take us beyond our limited reality into a world filled with possibilities. They believe that other worlds exist. They enjoy playing in other dimensions and in other realities. Although they can fully experience the other worlds, they often have difficulty explaining their experiences to others. They can become lost, agitated, or even angry if they are expected to explain what they have seen because their experiences do not necessarily make sense in three-dimensional reality.

Lavenders' visions and ideas seem unrealistic and illusionary to others. (Although Violets are also accused of being unrealistic dreamers, their visions have at least the potential to be actualized. In addition, Violets are dynamic and powerful enough to fulfill their visions.) Lavenders dream and fantasize, but don't usually follow through with their ideas. They need to be with people who can see the potential in their ideas and are capable of forming plans and taking action.

After Lavenders experience something in their imagination, they feel it is too much effort to recreate their vision in tangible form. If they create stories, they do not necessarily feel drawn to write them. They have already received the emotional effects from the experience, and that's all that matters to them. Lavenders don't feel obligated to share their experiences with the world. They can experience all they need in their inner worlds where they prefer to live because the outside world often can't compare.

Because of their creative talents, Lavenders make excellent artists and writers. They are especially adept at writing poetry or children's fiction. Painting pictures of castles in the sky or writing about mythological characters appeals to these whimsical beings. Through their visual and imaginative styles, they have a unique ability to take people into a fantasy world that is alive with feelings, sensations, and sounds.

Lavenders can perceive energies through their unique inner sense. Frequently, they are able to see other dimensions, hear colors, feel sounds, and experience other realities. Being forced to stay in their bodies can be physically painful for them. They need to escape into their dreamworlds for the same reason people need to sleep. It helps them relax and recuperate from the stress of the real world.

In power, Lavenders can use their creative talents to show people the possibilities of other realms. In power, Lavenders have the ability to transform their visions into works of art, thereby enhancing the lives of others. Lewis Carroll, the author of *Alice's Adventures in Wonderland,* is a perfect example of the creative Lavender who has inspired the imagination of people around the world.

Out of power, Lavenders have difficulty functioning in the real world. They cannot hold jobs or pay bills, and frequently require others to support them. Out of power, they can be much like timid little rabbits that when frightened run down the rabbit hole and into another dimension.

To stay in power, Lavenders need to be brave enough to face the real world and to stay in their bodies long enough to be a useful and functioning part of society. They can allow themselves to explore their imagination, but they also need to be responsible adults. Escaping into other realities is fine, but Lavenders must remember to come back. They must be willing to apply the information they learn from those experiences in the three-dimensional world.

Lavenders are gentle and free spirits who are not attached to following rules or being limited by systems that dictate how they should live. They live by their feelings and intuition, rather than by their intellect. They want to be free to move in whatever direction feels right at the time, and their directions change as often as the clouds do. Lavenders are not here to make a social statement, change the planet, or rescue others. They just want to be free to explore their imagination and experience other realities.

Even their spirituality is not easily defined. Lavenders have the feeling of a Presence, but not the limited description of the typical anthropomorphic God. These fantasy-oriented personalities enjoy soft music, wind chimes, candles, incense, meditation, and the rhythmic sounds of chanting. They enjoy any sound, color, or texture that can inspire their imagination, help them float out of their bodies, or take them into an ethereal state.

Lavenders see life as a magical world of adventure filled with fairies, spirits, and angels. They are here to explore other realities and then describe them to us. They are here to stimulate our imagination, to inspire our sense of wonder, and to keep the idea of magic alive in us all.

Relationships

At first, people are attracted to and fascinated by the imaginative Lavenders. They soon learn, however, that they are living with fragile butterflies who are sometimes present and sometimes not. Although these sensitive personalities are gentle and good natured, they are not always willing to be equal partners in relationships that require intellectual communication or the sharing of responsibilities. Because Lavenders are not grounded, they have a hard time offering stability to a relationship. They are often not available to their mates because they live so much in their own inner worlds. They do not like the serious nature of commitment because it carries with it a sense of responsibility and a requirement to focus on physical reality.

Usually, their mates will need to financially support the bewildered Lavenders, unless some of the Lavenders' creative ideas make money. Otherwise, Lavenders cannot be bothered with — nor can they even comprehend — the concepts of jobs, budgets, bills, or household chores. Their mates quickly learn not to depend on them.

Although Lavenders want to be supportive and loving mates, and their intentions are good, their follow-through is poor. Because they don't usually act on their intentions, they can appear to be inconsiderate and uncaring toward their mates. Seeing disappointment in their loved ones' eyes can devastate the sensitive Lavenders. They have a fear of disappointing others and of not being loved. If Lavenders feel they have failed, they withdraw more and more into a fantasy world. They do not know how to deal with rejection. Their tendency to withdraw when situations become uncomfortable usually irritates their mates even more, who feel left to solve the dilemmas by themselves.

It takes very loving and patient people to understand and maintain relationships with Lavenders. Because Lavenders are so naive and childlike, their mates may at times feel more like parents than spouses. However, if treated with gentleness and kindness, these loving Lavenders will be gracious, sensitive, appreciative, and dedicated mates. Their loved ones can eventually find the Lavenders' innocence and creative imaginations endearing and lovable.

Sex

Lavenders love to fantasize during sex. They love to be experimental and creative, allowing their imagination to take them anywhere. As long as they remain physically safe in their explorations, Lavenders will play. Sex can be either a gentle or an exotic experience for them. During lovemaking, Lavenders commonly leave their bodies to drift in and out of other dimensions. This can add a level of excitement and fascination for Lavenders' partners, or it can leave them wondering if they are even a necessary element in the experience.

Lavenders do not enjoy sex as much if it leads to serious attachments and commitments. At the same time, they must feel safe and trusting of their partners if they are to lose themselves in the experience at all. Lavenders do not want any demands placed upon them. They do best with partners who are sensitive, caring, playful, trustworthy, and free.

Lavender Parents

Lavenders are fascinated with children, relating wonderfully to their free imagination. Together, Lavender parents and their children enjoy reading stories, going to movies, decorating their rooms, designing art projects, or writing stories. Having parents who help them design Halloween costumes or create birthday party decorations can be fun for children. However, Lavender parents are not always there for their children. They can be irresponsible and unreliable parents. They are frequently scattered and forgetful, and they don't always follow through on their promises.

If their children are in serious need of help or require counseling, Lavenders typically withdraw or "float away." They do not feel capable of dealing with intense emotional situations. Their guidance usually comes in the form of stories in which the children take imaginary journeys. The stories often include lessons the children can learn from. Lavenders will talk of helpful fairies and protective angels to calm the children and show them they have nothing to fear. Although there is no reason to doubt the existence of such helpful entities, this information doesn't always help children prepare for the realities of school, peers, and adults in positions of authority.

Usually, Lavender parents will not be the disciplinarians or the providers in the family. However, they will teach their children to believe in magic, dreams, spirits, creativity, and the possibility of other realities. Children of Lavender parents learn not to expect much from these fragile adults. They learn to turn to the other parent for answers or grow up quickly on their own.

Lavender Children

Lavender children, like Lavender adults, spend most of their time in fantasy worlds. They are fragile children who often seem afraid of the real world. These gentle and sensitive souls often have difficulty relating to other children, preferring instead to play with imaginary friends.

These children spend quite a bit of time daydreaming and

often experience trouble in school because they do not pay attention. They are not troublemakers looking for attention; usually they are just unaware of where they are. They drift easily in and out of other realities.

Lavender children are very creative, and relate best to subjects that allow them to explore their imagination and creativity. Courses such as art, creative writing, and design help them exercise their natural skills. Subjects that involve mental calculations, logic, memorization, or communication skills intimidate Lavender children. Usually they become lost in excessive data. When they are overwhelmed, they withdraw into their own worlds and hesitate to return to the real one.

Parents can become easily frustrated by Lavenders' irresponsible behavior. No matter how much parents talk to them, Lavender children aren't listening — they have drifted off into another world. They can be adept at making it look like they're listening when in fact they're not. (Just because children do not listen to their parents, it does not mean they are Lavenders, however. Every child stops listening at one time or another.) Parents must learn how to gently coax these escape artists back into physical reality. When Lavender children see a disapproving or angry look on a parent's face, their first response is to withdraw and hide. Yelling at them only increases their fear of being in this reality. But if they feel this world is a safe and pleasant place to be, they are more willing to spend time here.

All Lavenders, children included, just want to be free to use their imagination. They do not cope well with responsibilities, which can be quite a challenge for parents. Parents can help by calmly teaching these children a basic sense of responsibility and how to be productive with their creativity. Parents must be patient, sensitive, and not overly demanding. Otherwise, these timid Lavender children will retreat into their inner worlds, possibly never to emerge again.

Problem Solving

Typically, these ungrounded personalities do not like problems. Dealing with conflict forces them to pay attention to physical reality. It also makes them see the unpleasant side of life. Lavenders are not usually practical enough to be efficient problem solvers. In power, however, they can be very creative and inventive. Although their solutions are not always rational, they occasionally are so creative that someone else is able to find a practical solution in the midst of their ideas.

Being highly imaginative, Lavenders can create games or stories that enable people to solve problems, overcome management conflicts, or solve personnel difficulties. Their inventive style of turning problems into games can be less threatening for people who tend to become emotionally attached to the problem. However, because Lavenders are so illogical and ungrounded, people often have trouble trusting the Lavenders' solutions. They rarely appear to be realistic. Lavenders are also quiet and unassuming, so usually people do not pay attention to them or to their ideas.

When Lavenders are out of power, they do not want to face challenges. They are easily distracted by their imagination and love to daydream. Analyzing problems can overload the Lavenders' sensitive systems very quickly. Lavenders can benefit by finding people who can gently and patiently help them find rational solutions to their problems.

Money

Lavenders have a difficult time understanding money. Financial obligations are not only burdensome, but are too much a part of physical reality. Money is also physically dirty and unappealing to them. These childish personalities prefer to escape into other realities where everything they want is easily manifested.

Lavenders feel that if money is to exist at all, it should be used to obtain pretty clothes, crystals, ornamental jewelry, or other fanciful items. They resent having to put their energy into working hard at jobs they dislike just to pay for such basics as rent and car payments. The kinds of lives in which people must struggle just to have money is not worth living for Lavenders.

Because Lavenders don't understand such complicated concepts as budgets, investments, or financial planning, they can easily get into financial trouble. They spend money as fast as they get it; consequently, they can become overwhelmed with debts. Lavenders need to either find a fun and imaginative way to learn how to effectively manage their money or find someone who can manage it for them.

Success

Lavenders want the freedom to live the way they want and where they want, whether that means living in or out of their bodies, in physical reality, or in other dimensions. They prefer to live out of the reach of critical, nonaccepting realists who try to force them to live in a three-dimensional world, preferring a simple and fanciful world where they can freely roam with their imagination. Their ultimate joy is to be financially supported so they have the freedom to be creative dreamers. Although other colors such as Greens prefer to work, to be mentally challenged, and to accomplish, Lavenders prefer the opposite. They enjoy relaxing so that they are free to dream.

Occupations

Lavenders are pleasant and friendly, but they work best in quiet, low-stress environments that allow them plenty of time to daydream and create. Working regular office jobs is painful for them because too much mental concentration is required. Lavenders do not like calculating or analyzing details, nor can they be expected to organize anything. They are too forgetful and scattered. They even have trouble remembering their customers' orders in restaurants. Lavenders do not like to be burdened by too many responsibilities. They will not be rushed or pressured.

Careers in art or theater appeal to Lavenders because they have the opportunity to explore their imagination and creativity. These free spirits will frequently create through many art forms.

Occupations that are attractive to Lavenders include the following:

Storyteller	Dancer
Artist (especially fantasy art)	Actor
	Costume designer
Writer (especially children's books)	Interior decorator
	Set designer
Mime	Teacher, educator

Health

Because Lavenders spend little time in their bodies, they can have frequent and varied health problems. Because they do not always send life energy through their bodies, everything from their skeletal structures to their organs can suffer. Lavenders are not very attached to their physical bodies. If they feel pain or discomfort, they merely leave their bodies rather than deal with whatever warning signs they are receiving. They are not always aware of the benefits of good nutrition, exercise, or preventive medicine.

There are no specific areas in which Lavenders commonly experience health problems. But a lack of life energy can cause the entire body to slowly deteriorate. If Lavenders stay in power and spend more time focused in their bodies, however, they have a remarkable ability to heal their bodies by using their imagination. Lavenders are adept at imagining the "dragons" (cancer cells) being killed by the "white knights" (white blood cells) in their bodies. By focusing their imagination on healing, Lavenders can effectively cure their ailments. To stay healthy, Lavenders must remember they have physical bodies and they should take realistic, tangible steps to take care of them. Eating healthy foods and exercising are good beginning steps.

Floating in and out of their bodies can be beneficial for Lavenders. Leaving their bodies relaxes them and reduces stress. Spending too much time in physical reality can create stress-related problems. Lavenders need to occasionally focus on their bodies, however, to take care of them. Balance is important for Lavenders.

CRYSTAL

Crystal is a rare Life Color. Crystals have clear auras and are known as the "aura chameleons." Like chameleons, their auras will change colors to match those of the people they are connecting with at the time. They then take on the characteristics, emotions, and thoughts of that color. Consequently, in power Crystals can get along quite well with almost anyone. Yellows, for example, feel they can relate to Crystals who, when they are with them, act and think like Yellows. Later, when the same Crystals spend time with Sensitive Tans, the Tans feel as if they have found kindred spirits. However, Crystals' inconsistencies can also confuse people. One minute Crystals think and behave like Greens. Later they can act like Blues. The more they bond with others, the more their personalities change. Because Crystals tend to absorb the colors of other people's auras, people can, at times, feel an energy drain when they are in the presence of Crystals.

In power, Crystals can be clear channels for healing energy. Being natural healers, Crystals' gift is to help their clients clear blockages, thereby enabling their clients' natural healing processes to take place. While healing, balanced Crystals are able to keep their thoughts and emotions out of the way, making the healing more pure. Crystals do not always understand their healing abilities. Their abilities can often frighten and confuse them or cause them to feel overwhelmed. These rare souls are often physically fragile. Because of their unusual sensitivity, they can heal only one person at a time. They then need to go to a peaceful place to cleanse their auras. Working with too many people can short-circuit their systems.

Crystals like everything to be pretty, clean, and gentle — like a fairytale. Because they like simplicity and cleanliness, their environments tend to be quiet and orderly. They require a lot of time and space alone to meditate, reflect, nurture, and balance themselves. It is healing for Crystals to surround themselves with nature. Growing flowers or planting gardens can be very therapeutic. It gives them a chance to connect with their spirituality in peace and serenity.

Though they tend to be very quiet, Crystals are also quick thinkers and learners. They love to read books, watch movies, attend the theater — anything of social significance or that inspires them to ponder the meaning of life. They usually spend time alone, however, rather than with others, contemplating life and spirituality. They live their lives by intuition. If they don't follow what they know and feel inside, they become depressed and confused. They lose touch with themselves and their purpose.

Crystals tend to avoid people or environments that are harsh. The world often seems cold, heartless, insensitive, and dirty to them. They can become easily disillusioned with those around them. They typically feel uncomfortable in crowds. Being sensitive and easily overwhelmed, they retreat inside where it is safe. They can easily become disoriented and depressed. When they are out of power, they seem to forget why they came to the planet. They have no idea what they are supposed to do or what is expected of them. They watch others to see what is socially acceptable and appropriate. They don't act from what they know to be true, but from learning behaviors and responses from others. They are constantly looking for reassurance and guidance. They are often insecure about making decisions and can become dependent on others to run their lives. As they look to others for answers, they can become too attached to or overly involved in other people's affairs. Out of power, Crystals can become energy-draining and meddlesome friends. Being too involved in others' lives distracts them from having to deal with their own lives or finding their own answers.

To stay in power, Crystals must learn to regularly go within and to commune with nature, their spirituality, or their source. They must constantly retreat to their own environment to clean their auras of others' chaotic influences. This will help them remain centered and open channels for the healing work they came here to do.

Crystals' life purpose is to be a clear and willing channel for healing energy. They need to be quiet inside so that a pure understanding and a true connection with God can be made. When they allow themselves to do this work, they have a sense of inner peace and harmony. Even if they are not working in the healing fields, their peaceful energy can heal those around them. Their quiet and sensitive nature can appeal to everyone. Crystals are quiet, well-meaning souls. They vibrate at a very high spiritual level, which can create a very clear channel for healing energy.

Relationships

Those in relationships with Crystals must understand their quiet nature and allow their need for solitude. The Crystals' tendency to withdraw does not mean they are cold or conceited. Rather, peace and quiet are necessary for them to remain balanced and clear. Crystals can too easily pick up the frustrations, attitudes, and behaviors of their mates, causing these fragile personalities to become overwhelmed and fragmented. Giving themselves time for quiet meditation allows them to clear their auras and cleanse their energies.

In power, Crystals can have a calming, healing effect on their mates, which helps keep their relationships loving and harmonious. Out-of-power Crystals may have such low self-esteem that they withdraw inside for protection, leaving their partners feeling empty and disconnected.

Crystals are not aggressive, ambitious, driven personalities. They do not like to be the center of attention; they prefer instead to remain in the background where it is safe. These simple children do not strive to be leaders or decision makers. They are too easily overwhelmed and confused by information, emotions, and opinions. Therefore, they need mates who are willing to be decision makers and powerful protectors. Their partners must also be patient, allowing, and quiet, so that Crystals are not frightened or intimidated by them. Crystals need safety and calm in their relationships.

Sex

Crystals enjoy sex, but it can frequently be a traumatic experience for them. Because they interact with the other's aura so intensely during lovemaking, it is often painful for them to disconnect emotionally afterward. Fear of the resulting pain can cause them either to withdraw physically and emotionally from the other person or to remain distant for protection, which makes them appear unfeeling or frigid. Crystals can remain single or celibate for long periods because of the potential emotional and physical trauma involved in intimacy. They may prefer to live alone because it is easier and quieter. Their behavior is not a result of childhood problems; it is, by nature, their choice.

Crystal Parents

Crystal parents can relate to children because of their simple, unfettered natures. They are like children in many ways. Both are naive and fragile. Both prefer a simple existence. However, they can easily be overwhelmed by the energy of excited children. Crystal parents need to retreat to the solitude of the bedroom or the bathtub much more often than other parents do.

Crystals are loving, sensitive, and gentle parents who have a low threshold for confusion and noise. They are not disciplinarians, nor do they take charge of most situations. They usually depend on their mates to raise the children.

Crystal Children

Crystal children are much like their adult counterparts. They need a lot of time alone for solitude. They are incredibly fragile and easily fragmented, and they frequently display low self-esteem. They are overwhelmed by the confusion at school and are often uncomfortable with their peers. They tend to be shy and withdrawn, although they are also very loving and gentle. Parents of Crystal children need to allow them a lot of time to spend alone. Parents need to be gentle, accepting, understanding, and patient with their Crystal children. Crystals will never outgrow their need for solitude. If parents understand this need and allow them time to stay quiet and balanced, Crystal children can at least develop positive self-esteem.

In power, Crystal children are intelligent and can excel in most of their courses. Communication, drama, or speech classes can frighten them, however. They do not like expressing themselves in public or being the center of attention. Instead, they enjoy classes that help them explore the beauty or the meaning of life, classes such as art, philosophy, or music appreciation. (Yellow and Tan children can also be quiet and withdrawn. Read the list of occupations for Crystals, Yellows, and Tans to see which seems to fit most closely with the personality of your child.)

Problem Solving

Crystals are cautious when solving problems, leaning toward using solutions that have been previously successful. They are very good at summing up the thoughts and feelings of everyone involved and giving an objective summary, but are not usually brave enough to suggest solutions. They do not volunteer their ideas; they wait until they are asked. Crystals prefer solutions that are simple, clear, uncomplicated, and low risk. They are definitely not executive decision makers.

Money

Money provides security for Crystals and is handled with care. It is a complicated concept for Crystals, but they are conscientious and responsible with it. They would never think of shirking their responsibilities or not paying their bills. They do not like to take risks or get into trouble. They keep their lives as easy and simple as possible. They can make enough money to pay their bills, but usually have no concept of how to invest it. They prefer to let someone else handle the financial responsibilities while they focus on the peaceful and spiritual aspects of life.

Success

Crystals judge their success by how calm and peaceful they feel, and by how clear and effective their healing abilities are. Having a sense of inner serenity and a connection to God or some higher power is life itself for Crystals.

Occupations

Crystals are at their best in clean, quiet, low-key environments such as libraries or doctors' and church offices. They are dedicated and efficient employees, doing particularly well when there is structure and where details are important. No matter how repetitious a job may be, Crystals are patient and calm enough to take care of the details. They prefer the security of working for others. They are not usually powerful or ambitious enough to start their own businesses, and they prefer jobs where they can work quietly and alone.

Because they love beauty, Crystals are drawn to the arts. Because they have an ability to intensify energy in their bodies and create an outward flow, they are also drawn to the healing professions, such as massage, physical therapy, and medicine (especially holistic medicine). Healing is the field in which Crystals experience their greatest power. When clear and centered, they have an unusual and powerful ability to amplify healing energies from the Universe and transfer that energy to those who need it.

Crystals are drawn to occupations that are healing, artistic, creative, natural, quiet, simple, or reflective, such as the following:

Librarian	Interior decorator
Secretary	Florist
Receptionist	Herb grower
Massage therapist	Artist
Healer, doctor	Nun
Dental assistant	Monk
Physical therapist	Writer

Health

Because Crystals are emotionally sensitive and easily shattered, their physical bodies are fragile as well. Health problems can become a major concern. Almost anything can go wrong with Crystals. They can even take on the health problems of their companions. For example, if Crystals spend time with Greens, they can end up with the same health challenges as Greens have in areas such as the stomach, internal organs, or neck and shoulders. The Crystals' vibration resonates at such a high frequency and is so sensitive and vulnerable that they must spend time in solitude and quiet meditation to clear any negative energy influences they may have absorbed.

INDIGO

Indigo is the most recent aura color to arrive on the planet. Indigos are ushering in a new energy, a new consciousness, a new age of peace and harmony. Whereas Violets feel driven to help save the planet, educate the masses, and improve life, Indigos are here to live as examples of a new higher awareness. At this writing, most Indigos are children, although a few Indigos came as forerunners years ago. The words used to describe Indigos include honest, aware, highly intuitive, psychic, independent, fearless, strong willed, and sensitive. Indigos are old souls who know who they are and where they came from. They are so unusual and spiritually advanced that some people find it difficult to know how to deal with them. Some consider Indigos bizarre.

Indigos are born with their spiritual memories intact. Many parents report that their Indigo children regale them with vivid details of past lives or recent encounters with spiritual beings. They also report that these children can read their minds and seem to have amazing psychic abilities. The awareness and wisdom of these advanced young children is beyond rational explanation. Often, Indigos are able to speak in complete sentences long before other children have learned their first words. Indigo children seem to have an inherent understanding of technology. Most are highly adept at using computers at a very early age. Parents are often at a loss as to how to raise these amazing little beings.

An unusual characteristic of Indigos is that they frequently appear androgynous. It is often difficult to know if Indigos are male or female or homosexual, heterosexual, bisexual, or asexual. It's as if Indigos have both the yin and yang, male and female qualities within them. Their sexuality is not their primary concern, however; their spirituality is.

Indigos are typically very beautiful. Looking into their eyes, one may sense that these beings came from another world or that they know something far beyond what is known on earth.

In power, Indigos are aware, bright, creative, intuitive, and independent individuals. They live life from higher principles. They feel that all life should be honored and treated with integrity, compassion, and love. They follow their inner knowing and abide by higher truths. They understand spiritual and advanced concepts more easily than most do.

These souls sense that we are all divine beings, not merely physical beings, and that who we really are goes beyond what we see. They seem to know that matter and physical reality are illusions, that life is really composed of energy or living consciousness. They know that everything in the universe is somehow connected — that time, space, and form are not separate entities. There is no separation except in the human mind.

Although Indigos are honest and independent, in power they are also compassionate and accepting. They intuitively know when someone needs love and comfort. Their compassion knows no boundaries. They also show no fear. When love is called for, they are not shy showing their concern for others. They intuitively know when a stranger needs a gentle touch or a warm smile.

Indigos are intrinsically nonjudgmental. They treasure all life and see that every soul has value. They understand that male is not better than female, heterosexual is not better than homosexual, white is not better than black, people are not superior to animals, and so on.

Although Indigos are very sensitive and deeply compassionate, they are also very independent. Although they love people, they don't seem to need a lot of interaction with them and seem quite content to be alone at times.

These incredibly gifted and sensitive individuals are constantly questioning and searching for verification to support what they know inside. They are more interested in understanding the truth and higher life principles than in learning about society's out-dated rules, old beliefs, or limited versions of reality. Indigos will not be limited by antiquated ideals or by restrictive beliefs.

With their clarity and awareness, Indigos are extraordinarily truthful. Much to the dismay of parents and society in general,

Indigos are honest, forthright, and unwilling to be cajoled or forced into any mold. Indigos cannot be coerced into doing anything they do not believe in. Indigos will not accept direction unless they feel that others share the same ethical beliefs and the same inherent understanding of the truth. No amount of social pressure will force them to compromise. Indigos must live their lives in accordance with the highest principles they understand. Selling out causes them to become depressed, anxious, and self-destructive; it goes against their basic nature. They cannot be manipulated by peer pressure or by promises of acceptance and love from others. They do not believe in the concepts of guilt or punishment, so neither can be used effectively to persuade them to go against their basic beliefs. They lose respect for people who try to manipulate them by using such medieval tactics. When Indigos lose respect for their parents, teachers, or others from whom they expect love, truth, guidance, and support, they can become frustrated. They can react by becoming physically abusive, hyperactive, withdrawn, or self-destructive.

Indigos demand complete honesty from those around them. They need to know that they are being listened to, treated with respect, and loved unconditionally. They expect love, honesty, and respect from adults, which they are also willing to give.

The Indigo age will begin sometime between 2000 and 2014. Many Indigo children are being born on the planet at this time, which is an indication that we are preparing for this Indigo age.

When we move into a new era, we may feel confused or even threatened by the new consciousness that accompanies it. For example, when we moved from the Blue age into the Violet age, people were upset by the values Violets introduced. The Blue age was strongest during the 1950s — a time when mom stayed home, baked cookies, and "father knew best." The Violet age began in the 1960s — a time of peace demonstrations, civil rights movements, hippies, the original Woodstock concert, and the Beatles. Blues, being very moral and monogamous, did not like the Violets' passion for free sexual expression. The Tans did not appreciate the Violets' rebellious attitude toward their nine-to-five, traditional lifestyles. And big-business Greens — who like power and control, who held the perception that might made right and that wars were good for the economy — did not believe in the Violets' vision of global peace. When the Violets attempted to change the values held by the masses, they upset quite a few people. However, now that the Violet age is more empowered, people are finally turning to Violets for leadership. Global peace treaties, the demise of the Berlin Wall, the sexual revolution, global communication (the Internet), and environmental causes are all evidence of the Violet age.

Just as Violets upset people at the beginning of the Violet age, Indigos are now challenging the current belief system and are upsetting many people. The only Indigo currently in the public eye is Michael Jackson, although he also has Violet in his aura.

Some Violet readers may believe they are Indigos. What is happening, however, is that because Violets are visionaries and tend to see ahead of the masses, many are beginning to add Indigo to their auras. Some of these Violets are sensing the Indigo qualities emerging in themselves. If you feel you may be Indigo, you may be Violet, a Violet/Yellow combination, or a Violet/Blue combination instead. People with these aura colors also tend to feel highly spiritual, deeply sensitive, and different from others.

To find out whether you are an Indigo or one of the Violet combinations, ask yourself what you feel your life purpose is. If you feel you have a message to give, if you feel drawn to help change the planet, to save the environment, or to become famous, you are most likely a Violet combination. Usually, Indigos do not feel driven to save the planet or to be famous. They just want to live their higher ideals in peace, with their creativity, integrity, power, and life energy intact. Because many people — especially Violets — are beginning to add Indigo to their auras, perhaps this information will help them understand how to live harmoniously with the new energy.

Often Indigos have difficulty adjusting to their bodies because they don't seem to totally comprehend living in the physical world. Indigos are not always sure how to operate their bodies, which often feel like foreign space suits. In addition, their inner sense seems to be attuned to very high frequencies. Even their physical senses seem to be more refined, much like a dog's sensitive sense of hearing. This sensitivity can cause them to be easily overwhelmed, and they may withdraw inside for protection or react with hyperactivity. They can even be highly sensitive to foods, able to eat only foods that are organically grown.

With this highly developed system, Indigos seem to detect energies, spirits, auras, or other dimensions. They have the ability, on an inner level, to commune with animals, children, plants, and nature in general. Because Indigos often talk with imaginary friends, they are accused of having an active imagination or even of being psychologically unbalanced. People frequently have trouble understanding the Indigos' unique ability to comprehend other realities — for example, the idea that earth is a living entity, that trees can literally cry in pain, and that we are all connected in consciousness.

Indigos also have knowledge at a very young age that life is a continuous process and that death is a part of that process. These gentle souls feel connected to everything, and anything they own becomes a part of them, like an appendage, which then takes on their energy. It can be painful for Indigos to lose something they own. It is not that they are concerned with physical possessions. They see these objects as having a living energy they are able to connect with, just like most people connect with their pets.

Even though Indigos are honest, intuitive, outspoken, and wise beyond their years, they sometimes have difficulty putting concepts they intrinsically understand as truth into words. There is not always the vocabulary to explain what they know. In addition, Indigos feel that putting such expansive concepts into linear language limits the holographic picture of what life truly is. They do not separate their lives into categories of work, play, relationships, and education. Rather, they see that all these aspects fit together as a whole experience. If they have understanding and patient adults supporting them, Indigos can be powerful communicators, sharing advanced ideas that are beyond what many currently comprehend.

Although Indigos can be powerful and self-confident, they are also very sensitive beings. Out of power they can become frightened and disoriented. They lose touch with their inner knowing and then do not understand life. Because the current state of the planet is not in harmony with their belief system, many Indigos are having difficulty understanding what's happening here. The world doesn't look or behave the way they feel it should. War, violence, dishonesty, poverty, and starvation are alien concepts to Indigos. They don't understand how human beings could create such aberrations: Because we are all one, how can we commit such atrocities toward ourselves?

Because Indigos are just now starting to show up on the planet, they do not have much reinforcement or many teachers who can explain what is happening here. Few people are living what Indigos feel to be the truth. The current traditional educational system typically falls short of teaching what Indigos need to know. They need to study subjects that relate to life, not merely memorize useless data.

To hide from their confusion and quiet their inner voice, Indigos often turn to drugs or alcohol, or they become obsessed with computer games. Hiding out causes them to sink even further into alienation, confusion, and despair. Because they do not always have the words to express their feelings, communication becomes difficult and sometimes impossible when they are in this bewildered state. These sensitive and misunderstood souls will often end up in institutions where professionals will try to analyze, "reform," and mold them into socially acceptable people with traditional values and perceptions. It is quite common for Indigos to be diagnosed with ADD (Attention Deficit Disorder), ADHD (Attention Deficit Hyperactive Disorder), or learning disabilities. (Not all Indigos have ADD. Nor are those diagnosed with ADD necessarily Indigos. In fact, many children who are considered ADD have Yellow auras.) Many professionals do not understand the advanced and unusual perceptions of Indigos, so traditional therapy can intensify Indigos' inner conflict.

To stay in power, Indigos must trust as truth what they feel inside. They must remember that they came to the planet with all the knowledge they need to live life with joy, fulfillment, and harmony. They need to stay committed to the belief that love and truth will ultimately show life for what it really is — a beautiful and creative expression of All That Is. By being a living example of these principles, Indigos will eventually show people how to create a peaceful and harmonious world.

Out-of-power, Indigos can sometimes feel isolated and misunderstood. In power, they seem to be aware that life surrounds and encompasses them, and this gives them an inner knowledge that they are never really alone. Meditation and prayer are useful tools to help Indigos stay balanced and in touch with their spiritual understanding.

Indigos are sensitive human beings who believe there is more to us as beings than is physically apparent. They understand energy and consciousness. In power, they live from integrity, high principles, love, compassion, and a greater knowing. They are aware that all of life is connected. Although humanity seems to be only now uncovering evidence regarding the true nature of reality — information known by the ancient mystics — Indigos already possess that knowledge.

Indigos are here to usher in a new era, to show us how to live from higher consciousness and higher principles so that we can create peace, love, and harmony in the world. They are the new spirit, the new energy, and the new consciousness on the planet. What they intuitively know, all humanity will know in the coming era. They know that in the future, we will be living in cooperation with the environment and with one another. There will no longer be disrespect for life.

Relationships

Indigos are selective. They need to be with mates who are trustworthy and who will allow them to operate from their unique belief system. They need mates who can support their spiritually advanced way of thinking, mates who will be nurturing, dedicated, and understanding while allowing them their independence and curiosity. Indigos are very gentle and committed partners who prefer their spouses first be best friends and companions, then lovers. These unique beings relate on a soul-to-soul basis with their partners.

Indigos are very loyal and monogamous partners. Their principles do not allow them to be unfaithful. They are, however, very sensitive souls who can be hurt quite easily if their loved ones show anger or disappointment toward them. They understand the essence of commitment, and this allows for deeper levels of bonding.

Sex

Sex for Indigos is a deeply spiritual, bonding experience between two souls, not merely a physical function. Indigos do not have sex unless they feel a deep sense of love for the other person. They do not comprehend, for example, a Red's belief that sex is for purely physical pleasure. Because Indigos have incorporated the male and female aspects within themselves, they do not need sex to feel a sense of completion or wholeness. Sex is cosmic union. Indigos become emotionally and spiritually absorbed in the experience, often not even aware there are physical bodies involved.

Indigo Parents

Because Indigos are fairly new on the planet, there are few Indigo parents at this time. Indigos, although being powerful, are also a lot like sensitive children themselves. They believe that we are souls experiencing creative, physical reality on the planet. They also have a sense that, through their physical bodies other souls are allowed passage onto the planet. Although Indigos can feel protective toward their children, they don't feel a sense of ownership. They have a sense that they are here to teach and guide the young souls until they are able to develop understanding and a life of their own.

Because Indigos have a natural, intrinsic understanding of right and wrong, they expect the same of their children. They are shocked if their children do not behave with these standards in mind and have a difficult time teaching them how to adapt to the world. Their teaching comes from a higher awareness of the way the world should be. Indigo parents do not relate to physical punishment. When teaching their children, they tend to emphasize love, compassion, and honoring people as divine beings.

Indigo Children

Even as babies, Indigos are unusually bright, aware and inquisitive about their surroundings. Indigo children seem to have strong psychic abilities. Because they are so psychic, they seem to inspire that natural ability in others as well. They are also extremely sensitive and tend to cry easily. Their senses are highly developed, so they can be easily disturbed, frightened, or overwhelmed. These advanced souls require very little sleep, even as infants. They need only enough sleep to rejuvenate the physical body, and then they are ready to explore this physical, three-dimensional creation we call earth.

Indigo children tend to be loners because they are rarely understood or accepted by their peers. They also cannot be forced to do something that they don't understand or that doesn't feel right to them. Threats of punishment, pleading, rationalizing, or physical force cannot make Indigo children go against their inner beliefs. Adults attempting to force these children to operate against their values — for example, by asking them to pick flowers when they believe that flowers are living entities with souls of their own — will create confusion and anxiety in them. They have such an inner awareness of the difference between right and wrong that they do not necessarily need discipline. It is when adults don't allow Indigo children to act according to their beliefs that resistance is created in these children.

Often, Indigo children are more aware and mature than their parents are. Adults need to learn how to give these children truth, guidance, and reasonable boundaries that do not limit or suppress their awareness. While treating them with consideration and respect, adults must also demonstrate self-respect. They cannot let their Indigo children take advantage of them.

Indigo children are very inquisitive. They will not, however, accept simple answers just because those have been the traditional ones. Answers must feel like the truth or they will reject them and continue to search. This can frustrate parents as well as teachers. Indigo children have difficulty relating to most traditional subjects taught in school. They don't understand the relationship between these subjects and a spiritual life. They are not rebellious or angry children; they are merely hungry for truth. When they finally do get answers that resonate with higher principles, there is no further conflict.

Problem Solving

When in power, Indigos solve problems according to higher principles. The solutions must be ethical, loving, and humanitarian. They will not accept answers that lack integrity just because they are quick or convenient. In power, Indigos will never cheat, lie, or steal, so others can always count on these loving souls. When in power, Indigos trust their inner sense to tell them the right thing to do.

Out-of-power Indigos can become fearful, lost in a world alien to what they know to be true. They lose touch with their inner knowing. These sensitive individuals can become confused and mistrustful of their own solutions. When out of power, Indigos don't understand how their cosmic awareness fits into worldly reality. With their unusually sensitive physical and emotional systems, they can become withdrawn, which causes them to feel isolated and misunderstood. They can also become quite anxious or self-destructive. They have a hard time explaining their belief systems to others, so they feel out of place.

To regain their center again, Indigos need to go within and trust what they inherently feel are higher truths, or they can find others who support them by reminding them of these higher principles.

Money

Sacrificing life, love, health, or freedom for bits of silver or pieces of paper is not something Indigos comprehend. Because of their integrity, however, Indigos are not irresponsible. They will support themselves. In power, they can develop ideas and make money quickly. They can become quite the entrepreneurs. But they see money as an energy form that facilitates experiences and provides the necessities in a three-dimensional world. They do not need a lot of money to survive on the planet. They seem to know other methods of manifesting what they want in life. Money is only one form of created energy. Out of power, Indigos find working to make money becomes just another painful chore.

Like their spiritual counterparts — Blues and Violets — Indigos cannot work just for the money. They will not do anything that exploits people, harms the environment, endangers animals, or goes against their belief that life is sacred. Making money is not a reason to forsake principles.

to express themselves physically, often even explosively, intimidates the Crystals. Crystals, if they express themselves at all, do so through gentleness, touch, and sensitivity. Reds involve themselves in all things Crystals abhor. The physical realities that Reds enjoy — getting their hands dirty, changing the oil in the truck, butchering meat — are too grotesque for Crystals. Sex with the robust, lustful Red would also be too intense for the Crystal.

The Red could help ground a Crystal, but that grounding would probably be too severe for the delicate Crystal. The Crystal could absorb some of the Red's aura color; however, she probably couldn't maintain that Red energy for long. The Red would eventually tire of having to hold back his energy.

Red and Indigo Relationship

See Indigo and Red Relationship.

ORANGE

Orange and Red Relationship

See Red and Orange Relationship.

Orange and Orange Relationship

Because Oranges don't seek long-term committed relationships, neither partner would initiate a marriage. Rather than marriage partners, these two would make better adventure companions. The solitary Orange usually prefers to go mountain climbing or skydiving by himself. He loves the freedom and independence of challenging the environment on his own. However, Oranges do befriend other Oranges because they frequent the same environments. In many ways Oranges are compatible, but compatible as friends, not as mates. Neither would be interested in having intimate conversations, sharing feelings, or bonding emotionally. There wouldn't be much basis or need for marriage because neither needs the commitment.

Few other friends are willing to venture into the areas where Oranges love to go. Spending time with other Oranges may be their only chance for companionship. In addition because they both enjoy planning and strategizing, working on ideas together could be exciting. (They must learn the art of cooperation first, however. The Orange is used to being independent and alone.) They understand the other's need for personal freedom and space, and so don't have the needy or over-protective attitudes associated with some other Life Colors.

Both Oranges relate to the desire to challenge the environment, to experiment with danger, and to live life on the edge. However, there is the possibility these two could become so competitive that they would end up killing themselves by pushing too far.

Neither Orange wants to take on the mundane responsibilities of running a home, so home is not where either of them would spend much time. Because Oranges are so independent and self-sufficient, when the two partners disagreed they could merely go their own ways without emotionally damaging each other. One of the Oranges' greatest challenges is going within. Emotion is their most frightening frontier. It is easier for them to become angry at their mates and leave rather than face themselves and find out they may be part of the problem. Oranges do not typically work out emotional or relationship difficulties. With neither partner invested in a long-term commitment, a relationship between two Oranges may be short term. However, this relationship suits Oranges just fine. Their similarities can fulfill many of their mutual needs.

Orange and Magenta Relationship

The Orange and the Magenta would probably have only short-term relationships, if they were to have them at all. These two are compatible at first, because the Orange's daredevil behavior excites and fascinates the Magenta. The Magenta also appreciates that the Orange is independent. The Orange doesn't smother or depend on the Magenta, which allows the Magenta the freedom to go out and have a good time. However, because neither is interested in long-term committed relationships, they eventually drift apart.

With the Magenta's zany creativity, and the Orange's cunning ability to strategize and materialize ideas, a good working relationship is possible with this pair. If the Orange wanted to jump over the Grand Canyon, for example, the Magenta might be able to create a new invention to help him accomplish the feat.

As a rule, however, these two are too different to be in a relationship. An Orange is usually too serious for the fun-loving Magenta. While the Orange is away exploring, the Magenta is attending as many social events as she can. They don't even make good roommates. When the Orange wants to get a good night's sleep before going off to climb a mountain, the Magenta wants to stay up late and entertain friends. The Magenta's wild antics can disrupt the Orange's lifestyle, usually causing bad feelings between them.

Although Oranges and Magentas are both independent risk-takers and love to go beyond established limitations, they do not have much else in common. Each respects the other's daring and boldness, but neither can relate to the other's style. The Magenta feels that the Orange's need for physical danger is foolish and self-indulgent. The solitary Orange, who relishes his privacy, cannot relate to the Magenta's bizarre behavior or need to attract attention. While an Orange prefers a physical challenge and is cunning in the face of danger, the Magenta prefers a social challenge and is outrageous and defiant in the face of accepted social standards.

The Magenta and the Orange are seldom in the same environment. The possibility of these two meeting in the first place is rare. Even though they are fascinated by each other's independent and unique lifestyles, in time they find their differences too extreme and eventually go their own ways.

Orange and Yellow Relationship

See Yellow and Orange Relationship.

Orange and Logical Tan Relationship

See Logical Tan and Orange Relationship.

Orange and Environmental Tan Relationship

Both Oranges and Environmental Tans enjoy working with the environment. They also have a healthy respect for the power of nature. An Environmental Tan can be fascinated with and have respect for the physical challenges that an Orange is able to overcome. After awhile, however, the Environmental Tan often becomes uninterested in the Orange's relentless need to challenge the environment. The Environmental Tan feels the Orange is taking too many unnecessary, life-threatening risks. This Tan sees more value in researching the environment with sensible tactics. Although they are both interested in planning and organizing their tasks, they each have different reasons for their calculations. An Environmental Tan sees the value in research to better the environment. An Orange calculates the risks involved in the task to ensure personal survival. If an Orange and an Environmental Tan were to set off on an adventure together, the Orange would eventually want to leave the Environmental Tan behind. The Environmental Tan is too cautious for the daring Orange. The Environmental Tan, like the Logical Tan, can be too conscientious, security minded, and stable for the adventurous Orange.

These personalities do not deal well with emotions. They tend to keep intimate thoughts and feelings to themselves. In this relationship, verbal and emotional communication tend to be sparse — neither one usually instigates conversation. Sex would be somewhat of a convenience with these two. Neither sees sex as a focus or priority. Both understand the need for physical release at times, but then they prefer to move on to more important matters.

Because both tend to be isolated thinkers and loners, these two make better roommates than marriage partners. In marriage intimacy, emotions, and communication would be lacking, because neither chooses to deal with such issues.

Orange and Sensitive Tan Relationship

See Sensitive Tan and Orange Relationship.

Orange and Abstract Tan Relationship

An Orange and an Abstract Tan are not compatible. They have nothing in common. An Orange tends to be a loner and does not need companionship; an Abstract Tan loves people and enjoys socializing. Because the Orange is not usually emotionally or physically available to the Abstract Tan, this Tan begins to spend more and more time alone. This pattern continues until both the Orange and the Abstract Tan are living separate and isolated lives.

The childlike Abstract Tan needs someone who will communicate with her and take care of her. An Orange is indifferent to the Tan's theoretical concepts and tends to be a private, independent person who is not interested in being responsible for the childlike and dependent Abstract Tan. This gentle yet scattered Tan prefers to observe others and philosophize about life rather than to share in any of the Orange's daring physical exploits. The Orange doesn't have the time or the interest to untangle the Abstract Tan's thoughts and ideas. He is more interested in planning his next adventure.

These two are happier with more like-minded companions.

Orange and Green Relationship

See Green and Orange Relationship.

Orange and Blue Relationship

See Blue and Orange Relationship.

Orange and Violet Relationship

Although an Orange and a Violet would probably respect each other's independence and power, they would have different views about the purpose of life. An Orange is trying to challenge the world; the Violet is trying to save it. The visionary Violet believes there is a higher purpose for living on the planet, which involves inspiring and saving humanity. The brash Orange doesn't have the time or inclination to save the world. He prefers to be alone and adventurous.

Although an Orange admires a Violet's leadership ability, he resents the Violet if she attempts to lead him. An Orange does not respect the Violet's visions, feeling instead that she is an impractical and unrealistic dreamer. To an Orange, saving the world is too high an ideal. An Orange respects the environment and wants to see it protected, but does not usually choose to be involved in political battles. A Violet feels that the Orange is missing the greater purpose of life, which is helping humanity. Both personalities are powerful, independent, and courageous in their areas of expertise, but they disagree on the definition of courage and the purpose of life.

The Violet is a natural performer who prefers to have an audience; the Orange couldn't care less if people admire his spectacular feats of daring. Both the Violet and the Orange love to travel, but they have different reasons for traveling. The Violet loves to explore the planet to learn about people and cultures. The Orange tends to be drawn to places where people rarely dare to venture. The Violet is fascinated as the Orange tells of his adventures of climbing the highest mountain or jumping from a plane. She is able to live vicariously through the Orange's stories. But as long-term mates, these two have very little in common. The spiritual or humanitarian causes to which the Violet feels drawn do not interest the Orange; to the Violet, the Orange's daring exploits seem to be an unproductive use of time.

Orange and Lavender Relationship

See Lavender and Orange Relationship.

Orange and Crystal Relationship

This relationship isn't very compatible. A Crystal is much too sensitive and delicate to be consorting with the rough, rugged, and challenging Orange. An Orange wants to be outdoors confronting nature, exploring, climbing mountains, and taking on the challenges of the physical world. The sensitive Crystal prefers to be in the quiet, gentle solitude of nature. An Orange is too brash for this fragile, soft-spoken personality. Being around an Orange too long can overwhelm the Crystal's delicate system.

An Orange's lifestyle goes against a Crystal's way of life and her belief system. This loving being communes with nature. She doesn't challenge or conquer it. The esoteric Crystal needs someone she can relate to on a sensitive, spiritual basis. An Orange has no desire to discuss spiritual topics.

The Orange is also too independent to meet the Crystal's needs. He is rarely home, which would eventually upset the Crystal. Even though the Crystal needs a lot of time alone, the Orange would be gone far too much for the Crystal's well-being. The Orange would find the Crystal's need for quiet unappealing and unchallenging. The Orange craves excitement, adventure, and challenges. These two individuals would have absolutely nothing in common.

Orange and Indigo Relationship

This is another couple who would have nothing to talk about and nothing in common. The Indigo's concepts about the universe appear to be too strange and foreign to an Orange, who likes physical reality, excitement, and adventure. The Indigo prefers to deal with spirituality, love, and ideas about consciousness. An Orange has little or no interest in these topics. The Indigo may admire the Orange's courage and daring and respect her desire to go beyond accepted limitations, but would find her too brash, independent, and egocentric to be much of a companion.

An Orange tends to be a loner. The Indigo, although also enjoying time alone, usually enjoys quiet time with intimate friends. An Indigo would be bewildered by an Orange's need to conquer physical reality because the Indigo believes that physical reality is just an illusion. An Orange lives too much in her body for the Indigo to relate to her. The Indigo treasures life, believing that life has deep spiritual meaning. An Orange sees life as a physical challenge, an opponent to be conquered. The Indigo would love to be at the top of a mountain pondering the beauty of life. This is not why an Orange goes to the top of a mountain. An Orange prefers to conquer life, not to appreciate it. These two would find very little on which to base a meaningful relationship.

MAGENTA

Magenta and Red Relationship

Typically, this relationship would have major problems. Reds usually like everything to be practical, down-to-earth, and realistic. Magentas do not want anything practical, down-to-earth, or realistic. They want their lives to be outrageous. Magentas like to shock people, which Reds find totally embarrassing, unnecessary, and ridiculous.

These colors would have absolutely nothing in common. The Magenta loves to constantly try new, interesting, and bizarre things. She wants to go to parties and be outrageous. A Red does not need to try anything new. His life is solid and down-to-earth. This relationship is comparable to a tractor driver going out with a punk-rock star with purple hair. The Red's common sense and practical accountability would completely bore the Magenta. With the Red's stubbornness and unwillingness to change, the Magenta — who loves to try wild and crazy antics all the time —

would feel stifled. The Red's interest in sex, physical endurance, and strength does not interest the Magenta. These two usually have nothing in common.

The Red may occasionally want to express more of the wild and rowdy aspects of his personality, and in this case will join the Magenta in attending social gatherings. However, when a Red's behavior becomes outrageous or uncontrollable, it is usually because of his temper or his sexuality, which could intimidate the fun-loving Magenta and cause her to recoil. The Magenta usually shakes up people's traditional rules to make a social statement about nonconformity. A Red often causes a scene through sex or anger.

Although these two could enjoy attending wild parties together for awhile, a typical Magenta and a rambunctious Red would probably eventually start annoying each other.

Magenta and Orange Relationship

See Orange and Magenta Relationship.

Magenta and Magenta Relationship

Although these people would probably have a great time together at first, they would eventually try to see which could be more bizarre. This combination is not very practical. Neither has the desire to be responsible for the home or to support a relationship. Because Magentas tend to move from relationship to relationship very quickly, these two could have an interesting but brief experience together.

This pair would probably enjoy creating a bizarre, artistic work or invention together. They could have a great time shocking people by walking down the street wildly dressed with their hair different colors and shapes. They would enjoy attending parties together. Seeing a home that two Magentas had decorated would be an incredible experience. But two outrageous Magentas together would probably be too intense for their friends to handle. The more Magentas are around one other, the more bizarre and outrageous their behavior becomes. They tend to feed off each other.

This relationship would be interesting and fun for both for a short time. However, because neither would be a stable influence in the relationship, it would probably soon fall apart. Neither would want to pay bills, take care of details, or make a living. This couple would make great friends or roommates for awhile, but soon they would want to move on to yet another adventure.

Magenta and Yellow Relationship

These two could be great playmates. The Magenta would constantly be entertaining the Yellow, who is always looking for fun, entertainment, and excitement. They both love going to parties. They would have a great time together, as long as their goal is just to have a good time. However, when it comes to being responsible, taking care of the home, and going to work, they could encounter problems.

A Yellow would respect a Magenta's ability to make money without conforming to society's standards because the Yellow is also looking for the freedom to express himself creatively outside the restrictive nine-to-five job. Because both colors are so creative, they could create wild, artistic, innovative inventions together. A Yellow, who loves to laugh, would enjoy watching Magenta's antics. Because neither is interested in a committed relationship, they would give each other the freedom to come and go, to see other people, and to have a good time.

Sex for a Yellow is a very playful experience. For the Magenta it is a sensual experiment, so these two could enjoy playing with sex together.

Neither of these colors likes to be manipulated or told what to do, so they would allow each other the freedom to make their own choices. The main problem is that neither wants to be the responsible one at home. This couple would most likely be child-less because of the commitment involved in having children.

The childlike exuberance of a Yellow is fun for awhile, but the Magenta does not appreciate being around children for long. The Magenta would eventually want to experiment with a different, more challenging or outrageous mate. Although these two are great friends and playmates, they usually do not end up as long-term, committed partners.

Magenta and Logical Tan Relationship

This would be an unlikely pair. The Magenta's bizarre behavior would be too outrageous for a Logical Tan, who likes stability, reliability, and security. All these qualities go against the Magenta's beliefs and behaviors. A Logical Tan would become easily embarrassed by the Magenta's antisocial behavior. The open-minded and uninhibited Magenta could open up a Logical Tan's practical way of looking at life. And a Logical Tan could be a stabilizing and grounding force for a Magenta, who has a ten-dency not to pay bills, keep a steady job, or even keep a house-hold together.

Eventually, however, the Logical Tan would most likely become frustrated with the Magenta's unreliability and strange behavior. A Logical Tan desires logical, analytical, and sensible behavior. It is precisely those strict standards and disciplines that the Magenta loves to challenge. Everything that the Logical Tan finds sacred, the Magenta disrupts. Even the most open-minded Logical Tan would find these challenges exhausting after awhile.

This combination could provide an interesting balance for a short time, but this is not a very realistic or practical long-term relationship.

Magenta and Environmental Tan Relationship

See Environmental Tan and Magenta Relationship.

Magenta and Sensitive Tan Relationship

See Sensitive Tan and Magenta Relationship.

Magenta and Abstract Tan Relationship

Although there are many reasons, the main reason this relationship would not work is that the Magenta does not want to take care of the dependent Abstract Tan. Even though the Magenta enjoys unusual people, an Abstract Tan's energy is too scattered and chaotic for him. He eventually becomes annoyed and bothered by her inconsistencies. The Abstract Tan spends too much time in her head for the likes of the Magenta, who instead prefers to experiment and play with physical reality. When the Abstract Tan expresses her thoughts, they shoot out in all directions like fireworks. Trying to understand this Tan can be unnerving for the Magenta. Although the Magenta's behavior is bizarre, he feels there is purpose behind his madness. He wants to wake up people and keep them from becoming complacent. He cannot see any purpose or justification behind the Abstract Tan's rambling philosophical discussions. He can't understand how they apply to his life.

Both individuals enjoy social gatherings. Neither wants to be responsible for taking care of business. Their home is frequently cluttered and unkempt. In their own way, these two are both overgrown children who want someone else to pay their bills for them.

Neither cares to have strongly committed or deeply emotional relationships, though the Abstract Tan does want someone who can provide interesting conversations as well as a secure and supportive environment for her. The Magenta is too independent and wild to provide stability for this Tan. If the Abstract Tan tried to depend on the Magenta, the Magenta would rebel and leave. If the Abstract Tan attempted to communicate her hypotheses and notions to the Magenta in her typical shotgun style, he would become perplexed, then annoyed, and then apathetic.

The Abstract Tan could develop theories regarding the Magenta's behavior, but the Magenta is not interested in being analyzed. (He wouldn't understand this Tan's explanations anyway.) These two would typically end up going in their own directions.

Magenta and Green Relationship

See Green and Magenta Relationship.

Magenta and Blue Relationship

See Blue and Magenta Relationship.

Magenta and Violet Relationship

See Violet and Magenta Relationship.

Magenta and Lavender Relationship

Magentas and Lavenders both tend to live in their own worlds. The Magenta's world is outgoing, adventurous, and bizarre; the Lavender lives in a fantasy world and is more soft spoken, intuitive, and sensitive. They each tend to be the unusual personality in their color family. People have a hard time relating to either color; the Magenta and the Lavender would have a hard time relating to each other as well. The Lavender wants a partner she can relate to in a loving and gentle manner. The Magenta is too brash, independent, and outspoken for her. They would probably leave each other alone. Neither would insist that the partner follow the other's belief system.

Because these two live so much in their own worlds, it would be very rare for them to cross paths. They wouldn't have anything in common other than their unique ways of looking at the world and at life. Even though they would be fascinated by their differences for awhile, this pair would not be comfortable in each other's company for very long.

life colors

Magenta and Crystal Relationship

See Crystal and Magenta Relationship.

Magenta and Indigo Relationship

Magentas and Indigos are the avant-garde personalities of the aura spectrum. The Magenta is much too outrageous for the Indigo, however. The Indigo tends to be spiritual, quiet, intuitive, and sensitive. They both challenge the traditional but accepted belief systems. The Magenta challenges them because she loves having the freedom to express herself. She believes people should be able to experience life in their unique ways.

The Indigo questions the accepted beliefs because he believes they are limiting to the soul. He believes we are fully actualized God-beings, here to experience life through our creativity and spirituality. He questions belief systems because they are usually of lower consciousness or from a limited concept of reality.

The Magenta does not relate to the Indigo's spiritual ideas, which seem too esoteric and unrealistic. The Magenta prefers to express herself creatively and physically. The Indigo does not always understand the physical aspect of our being. The body is foreign to him. The Magenta is free sexually, experimenting with one person after another for fun and variety. To the Indigo, sex is something much more personal and spiritual. It is a soul-to-soul experience. The Magenta's sexual behavior would totally confuse and bewilder the Indigo.

The Magenta likes to be around people and attend social gatherings, but ends up being a loner because most people cannot relate to her bizarre behavior. The Indigo loves people, but finds very few he can relate to or trust. His spiritual ideas and height-ened sensitivity are so advanced that most people cannot communicate with him. Both the Magenta and the Indigo can feel like outcasts.

The Magenta doesn't seem to take life as seriously as the

Indigo does. The Magenta is not as sensitive. An Indigo out of power can become so confused and lost in this physical environment that he withdraws into drugs or alcohol. The Magenta will withdraw for awhile from society, but it is usually very short lived. She can become a loner, but it does not seem to bother her as much as it does the Indigo. Both tend to be the black sheep in society and so experience compassion for each other.

These individuals probably would not be in a relationship. They would respect each other's need for independence; they would be fascinated by each other's belief systems and how they relate to other people. But they would be unable to relate to or live with each other's approach to life. The Indigo would be intimidated by the Magenta's bizarre behavior. The Indigo wants confirmation that what he intuitively feels is the intrinsic truth about life. The Magenta would not be able to provide realistic answers to this inquisitive and gentle soul. In the presence of the Indigo's serious and sensitive spiritual nature, the Magenta would not feel free to express herself outrageously.

YELLOW

Yellow and Red Relationship

Even though both colors are in the physical family, the Yellow's energy is much too sensitive for a Red's power and strength. The Red would have a tendency to crush the carefree Yellow.

On the positive side, a Red could probably provide stability in the Yellow's life. The Yellow is so childlike that the Red often plays the role of the responsible parent.

Both love physical work, moving things around, and tactile sensation. Yellows are fond of being outdoors, connecting with nature, or working with their hands. They frequently take jobs as gardeners, electricians, plumbers, athletes, or other physically active work. Reds also enjoy working with their bodies and with the physical environment. Consequently, Reds and Yellows often choose the same environments and occupations.

Reds have an intense emotional side. They release anger and frustration abruptly. Yellows tend to run away from anger. The Red's power, strength, and explosive nature would probably intimidate the Yellow; the Red would definitely be the dominating partner in this relationship.

Both personalities understand what it means to live in the moment. They both enjoy physical pleasure and immediate gratification. Combining the Red's passion and sexual appetite with the Yellow's sexual playfulness and willingness could create a great physical relationship.

A Red tends to be much more grounded and responsible than a Yellow. A Yellow, however, can add playful and lighthearted fun to the life of the serious and intense Red. The Red would have to maintain patience and self-control so that he wouldn't intimidate or scare away the Yellow. The Yellow would have to stay in power to withstand the Red's intensity and temper. A Red would not approve of a lazy or irresponsible Yellow. He takes his work and responsibilities very seriously. He could become quite frustrated with the Yellow's easygoing attitude.

If both the Yellow and the Red stayed in power, this couple could provide a good balance for each other. Both enjoy physical activities, living and working with their bodies, and being in their physical environment. However, if either the Yellow or the Red slipped out of power, the Yellow would tend to feel like an abused child. Intimidated by the Red's volatile temper and overwhelming power, the Yellow would want to run away. The Red tends to be too strong, heavy, and overbearing for the sensitive and childlike Yellow.

Yellow and Orange Relationship

Both the Yellow and the Orange enjoy playing in their physical environments and in their physical bodies. These two often share some interests, but they do not have the same emotional needs. The Yellow is frequently fascinated by the Orange's feats and skills and often participates in similar activities. These two can be compatible if the Orange does not expect the Yellow to accompany him on all his dangerous exploits. The Yellow would eventually become insecure and frightened of the physical danger the Orange continuously faces. A Yellow fears the possibility of experiencing physical pain. The Yellow, being carefree and independent, is happy to play with other people while the Orange experiences the challenge of extreme skydiving.

Problems can arise in this relationship when the Orange becomes too aloof. The Yellow needs to be around people more than the Orange does. The Orange is such a loner that he is not always physically or emotionally available to the sensitive Yellow, causing her to feel abandoned. Frequently, the Orange is also too powerful and intense for the childlike Yellow. The daring Orange wants to challenge life and conquer the environment while the Yellow just wants to have a good time and play in it. An Orange takes his dangerous work very seriously. The Yellow rarely takes anything seriously. The Yellow also loves sex. An Orange is sexual, but sex is not one of his priorities. He is much more interested in going on an adventure.

This couple can have a good time together when they share physical activities. However, in the long run this relationship will most likely drift apart, with the carefree Yellow not finding the sensitivity and playfulness she requires in a mate and the Orange becoming bored with the responsibility of a relationship. Neither wants to pay the bills or take care of the domestic chores — they are much too concerned with having fun or going off on adventures.

Yellow and Magenta Relationship

See Magenta and Yellow Relationship.

Yellow and Yellow Relationship

Yellows play well together. A marriage between Yellows will often feel like children playing house. These two have a great deal in common. They understand each other's need for fun, freedom, and time and space to be alone. They both enjoy being physically active, being outdoors, laughing, playing, and generally enjoying life. Healthy, balanced Yellows can experience a joyful, energetic, and fulfilling life together. Unbalanced or out-of-power Yellows, however, may experience problems regarding financial instability, complications arising from negative addictions, or emotional insecurities because of the unwillingness to commit.

If one partner delves into a negative addiction, such as drugs or alcohol, it will probably cause problems for the other as well. Yellows have very little self-discipline when it comes to addictive substances. It will be twice as hard for one Yellow to stop if the other does not stop at the same time. And if one continues the addictive behavior without the other, the playmates will not be playing the same game, which will cause disconnection and hurt feelings between them.

Great financial wealth will probably not be a part of this couple's lives unless they are lucky enough to get it the easy way — through the lottery, inheritance, or a creative idea that happens in the right place at the right time. Usually, Yellows struggle with money.

What is most certainly guaranteed with this couple, however, is that their sex life (and many other parts of their life) will be fun and compatible.

Examples of Yellows in relationship: Goldie Hawn (Blue/Yellow with Violet) and Kurt Russell (Yellow/Logical Tan with Violet); Meg Ryan (Blue/Yellow) and Dennis Quaid (Yellow/Violet); George Burns (Yellow/Green) and Gracie Allen (Yellow/Violet).

Yellow and Logical Tan Relationship

See Logical Tan and Yellow Relationship.

Yellow and Environmental Tan Relationship

Even though the Yellow and the Environmental Tan enjoy many of the same physical activities, they are not the most compatible mates. The Yellow is too irresponsible and immature for the solemn and practical Environmental Tan. Although he enjoys the fun, lighthearted spirit of the Yellow, the Environmental Tan is eventually worn out and frustrated by her careless behavior. The Yellow needs a playmate, someone who can laugh, be silly, and enjoy life with her. The Environmental Tan doesn't really know how to play. His life is often burdened with responsibilities. Although the Environmental Tan can add stability and security to the Yellow's life, his seriousness can eventually become too heavy and burdensome for her. She can suffocate under the weight.

These individuals both enjoy experiencing the physical environment. They are often in similar locations enjoying the same activities. If they are in a relationship with each other, they can at least share some of these hobbies. However, the fun-loving Yellow is usually more reckless and free than the cautious Environmental Tan. They do not enjoy their sports with the same zest and enthusiasm.

If the Environmental Tan agrees to be the responsible and rational partner who takes care of all the details and pays the bills, then the Yellow has the freedom to bring fun and joy into the relationship. Both can benefit from this arrangement. The Yellow can bring light and hope into an Environmental Tan's often serious and grim life; the Environmental Tan can offer financial stability and order to the Yellow's chaotic and frequently impoverished lifestyle.

Although these two can provide elements missing in each other's lives, they are usually too different to enjoy each other's company for an extended period. The Environmental Tan is too regimented for the childlike Yellow. The Yellow does not want to abide by the Environmental Tan's rules and expectations. She prefers a mate who loves spontaneity and creativity. The Environmental Tan's personality does not allow him such frivolities. The Environmental Tan prefers a mate who is rational and responsible. He wants a companion who is an intellectual equal as well as a reliable and dependable partner.

These two are happier and more satisfied with mates who have personalities more similar to their own.

Yellow and Sensitive Tan Relationship

A Yellow and Sensitive Tan provide a gentle balance for each other. The Sensitive Tan's warmth and gentleness is safe and comforting for the childlike Yellow. A Sensitive Tan is understanding and accepting of the Yellow's playful behavior. Rather than judging or criticizing the Yellow, the Sensitive Tan's Blue aspect tends to mother and nurture him. (Yellows tend to attract mothering personalities.)

These two enjoy helping people. They are both caring, thoughtful, and likeable individuals. They tend to be sensitive and considerate toward each other. The Sensitive Tan provides a loving and secure environment for the disorderly Yellow; the Yellow brings lightness and joy to the more serious Sensitive Tan.

There are potential problems with this combination, however. Although the Sensitive Tan appreciates the Yellow's kindness, sensitivity, and willingness to help others, like the other Tans she prefers a mate to be dependable, prudent, and rational. She also values commitment. A Yellow usually has a fear of commitment and responsibility. A Sensitive Tan can occasionally feel frustrated by the Yellow's irresponsible and unreliable behavior. She finds herself being the stable, financial provider for the family while the jovial Yellow is off somewhere being creative or playful. The Sensitive Tan quickly discovers that the Yellow is better spending money than earning it.

Reacting to the Yellow's irresponsibility, the Sensitive Tan can easily develop a mothering attitude. She feels that she must take care of the Yellow or everything will fall apart. At first, the Yellow enjoys someone taking care of all of his responsibilities. However, he eventually can become resentful of living with a mother instead of with a playmate. Although the Sensitive Tan is usually forced into the role of caretaker by the Yellow's unreliable behavior, neither partner is ultimately happy with that situation. To create a harmonious relationship, either the Sensitive Tan must learn to accept her role as the practical partner (without becoming the Yellow's mother) or the Yellow must learn to become more responsible and reliable.

If these goals can be achieved, these two can make an excellent couple. Because the Sensitive Tan is such a patient person, she is tolerant of the Yellow's actions. She is the kind of partner who can live peacefully with a Yellow.

Yellow and Abstract Tan Relationship

See Abstract Tan and Yellow Relationship.

Yellow and Green Relationship

See Green and Yellow Relationship.

Yellow and Blue Relationship

A relationship between a Yellow and a Blue is very common. The two personalities are attracted to each other: The mothering Blue tends to be drawn to the childlike Yellow. Their relationship usually starts off well. The Yellow's needs are more than met by the loving, nurturing Blue, who likes to take care of everyone. Her nurturing often includes taking care of the Yellow financially. A Blue is well known for rescuing a lost, down, and upset Yellow, only to find that when she nurtures him onto his feet he flees the nest. Yellow-Blue relationships have potential for success, provided the Blue does not smother the Yellow and provided the Yellow can take commitment seriously.

Problems can occur between a Yellow and a Blue. When a Blue is in love with someone, she wants to be around him all the time. A Yellow needs time and space to be alone. When the Yellow chooses to be alone, the Blue takes this as a personal rejection. She retreats, feeling unloved and rejected. The sensitive Yellow, not wanting to hurt anyone and wanting to avoid conflict at all costs, will usually run away. A Yellow also hates being manipulated by guilt, which is a Blue's most common weapon.

Yellows and Blues both love to help people. Both are sensitive and giving. They will tend to be a pleasant couple, provided they make it to couple status at all. The priority for a Blue is a loving, committed relationship; one of the Yellow's greatest fears is commitment. The long-suffering, loyal, monogamous Blue may have to wait years to hear the words she longs to hear from a Yellow — and wait she usually does.

A Yellow-Blue union is compatible when the Blue, who will do anything for a loved one, will laugh at the Yellow's jokes, allow him his freedom and time alone, and learn how to receive gifts from him. (Yellows love to bring home little gifts.) A Yellow needs to allow a Blue to cry or talk about the relationship. He needs to not run away. A Blue never tries to hurt anyone. She just wants to know she is loved.

A Blue must love the Yellow enough to help him believe in himself rather than to create a dependency. A Blue must learn to allow the Yellow to be around her because he loves her, not because he needs her. A Blue must learn to release her need to be needed.

A Yellow must learn that commitment is not a confinement, but, rather, that it is a tool that promotes growth and deeper understanding. A Yellow needs to see that telling a Blue she is loved and appreciated brings her joy. He does not have to see her need for love as a maneuver to trap and smother him.

While Yellows came to the planet to bring joy and to heal people, Blues came to bring love. They can be a wonderful team if they can understand and support each other's goals, needs, and priorities.

Examples of Yellow-Blue relationships: Goldie Hawn (Blue/Yellow with Violet) and Kurt Russell (Yellow/Logical Tan with Violet); Meg Ryan (Blue/Yellow) and Dennis Quaid (Yellow/Violet).

Yellow and Violet Relationship

A Yellow and a Violet can be a fun, creative, and inspiring team. Together, the Violet's vision and the Yellow's creativity can produce some fascinating results. These two are comfortable playing together. A Violet is one who does not judge the Yellow's need to play.

Both personalities love people. Even though the Yellow may be shy until she gets to know people, both the Violet and Yellow enjoy socializing.

These two also enjoy sex. They are two of the most sexual Life Colors in the spectrum. Although the Yellow tends to be playful while the Violet prefers to be passionate, they can experience a good balance of energies together.

The Violet usually assumes the role of leader in the relationship. He takes his purpose on the planet much more seriously than the Yellow does. The only real problem that can arise with this couple is if the Yellow becomes consistently lazy or irresponsible. The Violet, who has a strong need to move forward and accomplish his goals and visions, can become frustrated and disappointed with the Yellow's tendency to procrastinate. A Yellow is frequently insecure and afraid to take risks. She prefers instead to be spontaneous and live in the moment rather than set goals and make plans. The Violet tends to be the dynamic force in the relationship. The Yellow adds lightness, fun, and creativity. Frequently, the Yellow prefers to ride the Violet's coattails, which means less work and responsibilities for the easygoing Yellow. This can cause the Violet to lose respect for her. It is usually the Violet who is more capable of making money. However, if the Violet is scattered and out of power, both the Yellow and the Violet can experience financial difficulties.

These two usually share many interests — music, entertainment, physical exercise, sex, people, and traveling. Although they have different purposes behind these interests, they tend to enjoy experiencing them together.

A Violet with a Yellow is typically a harmonious couple. They usually enrich each other's lives. As long as the Yellow doesn't become lazy, fearful, or irresponsible, she can inspire the Violet with humor and creativity. As long as the Violet does not become too arrogant or serious, and as long as he takes time out to play with the childlike Yellow, he can inspire the Yellow to reach greater levels of creative or healing abilities. He can teach her to take risks and experience more of her potential.

A Violet is here to help save the planet and change it for the better. A Yellow is a natural healer and is here to lighten up and bring joy to the planet. Together, these two can be an inspirational, creative team who can reach audiences through such mediums as film, art, and music, or they can travel the world, touching the masses together as healers. In power, they are a dynamic team.

The following are examples of Yellow-Violet relationships: Sonny and Cher (both Yellow/Violets), the Beatles (all Yellow/Violets), Elizabeth Taylor (Blue/Violet) and Richard Burton (Yellow/Green), Katherine Hepburn (Violet/Yellow and Green) and Spencer Tracy (Yellow/Green), John F. Kennedy (Violet/Yellow) and Jacqueline Kennedy (Violet), and Paul and Linda McCartney (both Yellow/Violets).

Yellow and Lavender Relationship

Yellows and Lavenders play well together, but a marriage between them would be like two kids playing house. Yellows are like children; Lavenders tend to live in fantasy worlds. Neither is driven to accomplish anything, though the Yellow often enjoys fixing things around the house. The fact that a Yellow tends to live more in his physical body can help the Lavender by keeping her in her body more often. They can physically play together. A Yellow can help keep the Lavender grounded, and the Lavender can tell great fairy tales to entertain him. However, in the meantime neither is paying bills, taking care of business, or making money.

Because both are sensitive and caring, neither wants to hurt the other's feelings. Both when threatened with conflict tend to run away. Neither is usually grounded enough to carry on an adult relationship with the other. This couple is similar to ice cream with chocolate syrup on top. It's beautiful to look at, it tastes good, but it's probably not the healthiest combination in the world.

A positive aspect of this relationship may occur when the Yellow's creativity is combined with the Lavender's fantastic imagination. The two can create wonderful children's books or toys. They will, however, probably need to find someone else to carry out the details.

Because neither manages money well, they tend to use it up quickly. Unless they are independently wealthy, they would be better off marrying responsible mates who can take care of them. They are a great creative duo, but not very practical marriage partners.

Yellow and Crystal Relationship

See Crystal and Yellow Relationship.

Yellow and Indigo Relationship

See Indigo and Yellow Relationship.

CHAPTER SEVEN

relationships with the
mental life colors

LOGICAL TAN

Logical Tan and Red Relationship

See Red and Logical Tan Relationship.

Logical Tan and Orange Relationship

These colors do not understand each other very well. An Orange usually finds a Logical Tan to be too safe and complacent. A Logical Tan usually thinks an Orange takes unnecessary risks. A Logical Tan enjoys calm, rational, mental tasks; an Orange needs to be physically active while challenging life. A Logical Tan does not see the logic or purpose behind an Orange's behavior. A Logical Tan prefers to settle down in the suburbs, have a stable nine-to-five job, and commit to her family for the rest of her life. An Orange finds a Logical Tan's way of life to be synonymous with a slow, boring, torturous death. This daredevil does not want the encumbrance of a relationship, the responsibility of a family, or the tedium of a nine-to-five job.

A Logical Tan does not usually respect or admire the Orange's risk-taking actions. She judges them to be self-indulgent, impractical, dangerous, and illogical. What these individuals do have in common, however, is that they both like to plan every detail. A Logical Tan can be impressed and fascinated by the Orange's cunning mind and organizational skills; the Orange can call on the detail-oriented Logical Tan to help him research all the facts and figures involved in the feat. They do not, however, enjoy the same lifestyles, hobbies, or challenges.

Logical Tan and Yellow Relationship

This relationship can either resemble that of a disciplinarian parent and an irresponsible child or provide balance for each partner. Commonly, the Logical Tan tries to encourage the Yellow to grow up and become more responsible. The Yellow will often respond by either rebelling against the Logical Tan's authoritative expectations or by shrinking away in fear of disapproval or rejection. The childlike Yellow frequently feels inadequate under the Logical Tan's scrutiny.

A Logical Tan prefers a mate who is reliable, practical, and responsible (traits that do not describe a Yellow). A Yellow, on the other hand, prefers a partner who can be playful, spontaneous, and physically adventurous. A Logical Tan finds it difficult to lose himself in carefree abandonment on any level — physical, mental, or emotional.

If these two can understand and accept each other's qualities, they can create a balanced relationship. The Logical Tan can provide a secure and stable environment in which the Yellow can feel free to create. The Yellow can lighten and add spontaneity to the Tan's predictable world. The Tan is practical enough to bring substance to the Yellow's creative ideas. The Yellow's easygoing attitude can help the serious Logical Tan learn to relax and enjoy life a little more.

The long-term success of this relationship depends upon the ability of each partner to recognize the other's complementary qualities and to allow the other's differences. The Yellow needs to see that following guidelines and analyzing data create a sense of security for this Tan and be grateful for his responsible behavior. The Logical Tan needs to allow the sensitive Yellow to be playful and carefree. He may want to appreciate the Yellow's enthusiastic and childlike qualities rather than criticize and suppress them.

Logical Tan and Magenta Relationship

See Magenta and Logical Tan Relationship.

Logical Tan and Logical Tan Relationship

This relationship has great potential for compatibility. Both are grounded, reliable, and methodical personalities. They share the same priorities. Both work, have secure jobs, and enjoy discussing intellectual topics.

Predictability can become a potential problem in this relationship. Logical Tans frequently work at the same jobs, live in the same home, and follow the same patterns their entire lives. There is no adventure in their lives. They have no motivation to change. This couple can become habitual, doing the same thing over and over again. However, they can also be content with their lifestyle. Growth takes place at a pace they find comfortable. It is safe and reliable.

Both understand the other's need to see all the data and proof. Both appreciate the other's dependability. What may be missing in this relationship, however, is emotional expression and passion. Both tend to keep their feelings to themselves. However, having a mate who doesn't demand emotional intimacy is comforting and safe for Logical Tans.

Logical Tan and Environmental Tan Relationship

This relationship is similar to one between two Logical Tans. This couple is very compatible, the only difference being that an

Environmental Tan is more connected with the physical environment. He wants to work with the environment and is more interested in physical activity than a Logical Tan is. If an Environmental Tan decides he wants to go diving to investigate part of the ocean, a Logical Tan will not usually join him. Not believing it is a safe activity, she sees no logical reason to participate. The Environmental Tan will usually experience these kinds of activities without his Logical Tan partner.

For the most part, these two are very much alike. Both are dependable, stable, and grounded. They both choose to analyze data and work with details. They share the same priorities. They may be interested in different projects and activities, but their different interests may help the relationship continue to progress. They can educate each other in different areas.

There may not be much passion or intimate communication in this relationship. Both tend to keep their feelings to themselves. Their relationship often resembles a business relationship. All the details and responsibilities are handled daily but rarely do they experience fireworks. Both can be content with these arrangements — neither feels compelled to be swept away by emotions.

Logical Tan and Sensitive Tan Relationship

See Sensitive Tan and Logical Tan Relationship.

Logical Tan and Abstract Tan Relationship

See Abstract Tan and Logical Tan Relationship.

Logical Tan and Green Relationship

See Green and Logical Tan Relationship.

Logical Tan and Blue Relationship

Blues desire a monogamous, committed relationship and are often drawn to the Logical Tan's stability and reliability.

Unfortunately, what typically develops in the marriage is a communication problem. Blues communicate from the heart — they want to bond emotionally with their mates. Logical Tans, on the other hand, process intellectually. These Tans prefer to analyze the situation and come up with a rational solution while keeping emotions and thoughts to themselves in the process. This can frustrate Blues, who feel isolated from the deepest part of their mates.

A Logical Tan does not intellectually understand the Blue's emotional unpredictability. She seems to be too intuitive and too illogical for the methodical and rational Tan. The Blue constantly wants to discuss the relationship and to talk about feelings. A Logical Tan can eventually become too emotionally unfulfilling for a Blue. The Blue feels she is often talking to a wall.

In this relationship, the Blue needs to become more emotionally mature so she does not wear out her Logical Tan mate by constantly requiring outside reinforcement to validate her self-worth. She must trust in the knowledge that she is loved. (That is the greatest lesson for a Blue — in or out of a relationship.) However, this Tan must also realize that the Blue must have emotional gratification, and he must learn the value of open discussions about feelings. If she is fulfilled emotionally, the Blue will go to the ends of the earth for her mate.

If both are looking for a traditional marriage, in which the Blue wife loves and nurtures the Logical Tan husband while he goes off to work and supports the family, then this relationship can work. With this Tan, the Blue has the comfort and satisfaction of knowing she has a stable, reliable, and committed mate. The Logical Tan knows that he has a loyal, loving, and devoted mate who will take care of him. The Logical Tan is the disciplinarian of the family; the Blue is the nurturer.

Although communication may be a problem, commitment and security are the rewards for this couple. Both fill different roles in the relationship. Logical Tans and Blues must realize that they each see the world differently, process feelings differently, and have different priorities. If a Blue can understand that this Tan needs to process information slowly and methodically (and if she can remain patient when he gets stuck), then she will have a secure marriage. If the Logical Tan can understand a Blue's emotional needs, and if he can learn to trust what she feels regardless of the lack of facts, then he will have a loyal, supportive, and loving mate. (One way in which this Tan can learn to trust a Blue is for him to observe and analyze her track record. Because a Blue's intuition is almost always right, the Logical Tan can learn to trust it.)

Logical Tan and Violet Relationship

Because the beliefs and behaviors of Logical Tans and Violets are at opposite ends of the spectrum, a relationship between them is challenging and only occasionally successful. Because the Logical Tan methodically and analytically processes every step between one and ten, she is appalled by the Violet's habit of trying to jump from one to fifty. A Logical Tan considers a Violet to be an unrealistic dreamer. These two commonly experience conflict with each other. When a Violet does accomplish his vision, however, the Logical Tan is impressed by the Violet's power and insight.

A Logical Tan is practical, analytical, and methodical; the visionary Violet is often scattered and far from practical in the normal definition of the word. In their relationship, problems can arise when the Violet wants to race forward, putting logic aside and risking everything on a dream. This usually upsets the Logical Tan, who values the security and the stable lifestyle she has worked so hard to establish. The Logical Tan can soon become frustrated and resentful of working so hard to financially support the Violet, who is off chasing dreams. Even the most patient Logical Tan will eventually want these dreams to materialize and produce real income. The Violet may want to travel, but the Logical Tan argues that taking time off from work would be irresponsible and impractical.

A Violet has profound emotional depth and can be completely moved to tears because of his compassionate nature. He wants to communicate with his mate with the same intensity. A Logical Tan tends to hold back her feelings. She does not usually care to explain them to anyone. A Violet is passionate, sexual, and creative; the reserved Logical Tan tends to withhold in these areas as well. These two have a difficult time communicating on the same level.

Although Logical Tans and Violets have completely different needs, they can benefit from each other if they stay centered and in power. The skeptical and cautious Logical Tan tends to ground the Violet and slow him down. The Logical Tan can also provide a stable and secure foundation to the relationship by adding common sense, reason, and practicality to the Violet's ideas. When she trusts the Violet, the Logical Tan can figure out the steps necessary to realistically actualize the Violet's dream. For example, the Violet can visualize an advanced form of media technology, and then the Logical Tan can develop the detailed technology to bring the vision into physical form. The Logical Tan can also provide a steady income so the Violet can fly with his ideas.

The Violet can keep the Logical Tan's life from becoming predictable. The Logical Tan frequently is enmeshed in repetition. The Violet can help the Logical Tan see life from other perspectives, thereby broadening her experience. The Violet can also help the Logical Tan explore and develop her emotions. While the Logical Tan can help the Violet keep his feet on the ground, the Violet can help to keep the Logical Tan from focusing only on the ground. They can provide a good balance for each other. However, it is more common for the Logical Tan's and Violet's differences to frustrate and annoy each other.

Logical Tan and Lavender Relationship

This is an interesting relationship, one that could either provide balance for the couple or cause them constant frustration. A

Logical Tan wants life to be rational, logical, and practical. The Lavender's life is anything but practical. She instead lives in a world of dreams, visions, and fantasies. A Tan judges this to be unrealistic and irresponsible. The Logical Tan must usually take care of bills, go to work, and handle the daily responsibilities in the relationship. This can eventually frustrate the Logical Tan unless he agrees to the arrangement.

The gentle Lavender can provide creative aspects to the relationship. She can inspire the traditional and oftentimes short-sighted Logical Tan to see things from a different perspective. She may also free him from some of his habitual behaviors. A Lavender can help to keep her Logical Tan mate from becoming too rigid. Her fantasies and unique perspectives sometimes fascinate the Logical Tan's otherwise analytical mind.

In power, the Logical Tan appreciates the sensitivity and gentleness the Lavender adds to his life. Out of power, the Logical Tan becomes quite frustrated with the Lavender's inability to function within a practical, logical, and economic system. The Lavender, who is much more sensitive and fragile than this Tan, can become quite hurt by the Logical Tan's inability to relate to her emotionally. Distressed by the situation, she withdraws into her own world. Communication between them then becomes difficult and sometimes impossible.

As long as the Logical Tan does not demand that the Lavender adhere to his set rules and disciplines, the Lavender can feel free to be her creative self. The Lavender often appreciates the practical and responsible abilities this Tan contributes to the relationship because his willingness to take care of business gives her the freedom to play. However, the Lavender can also find a Logical Tan too dogmatic and stifling for her taste.

Usually this couple will ultimately discover that they have no interests in common and that their styles of communication differ dramatically. A Logical Tan usually keeps his feelings to himself and discusses only rational information. When the Lavender shares her experiences, her descriptions are beyond this Tan's comprehension. He doesn't relate to her world. This relationship often takes the form of a responsible disciplining parent and a withdrawn yet sensitive child. These are not the ingredients that can create a mature, emotionally fulfilling, and intimate marriage.

The success of this relationship depends on both the Logical Tan's and Lavender's willingness to allow each to bring unique contribution to the relationship. One provides the secure and stable foundation; the other cultivates the emotional, creative, and spiritual aspects of the union.

Logical Tan and Crystal Relationship

See Crystal and Logical Tan Relationship.

Logical Tan and Indigo Relationship

See Indigo and Logical Tan Relationship.

ENVIRONMENTAL TAN
Environmental Tan and Red Relationship

An Environmental Tan and the Red would probably have more chances of success in a relationship than a Logical Tan and a Red. Both the Environmental Tan and the Red enjoy exploring and relating to the physical environment. Both tend to be the strong, silent type and so would have an appreciation for each other. However, both also tend to keep their thoughts and feelings to themselves, and so an intimate and emotional bond between these two would probably be lacking. Sexually, this pair is more compatible than a Logical Tan and a Red.

The Environmental Tan, just like his Logical Tan counterpart, would be able to make plans and organize information. The Red would use her physical energy to implement the plans. Because of their complementary skills, these two are a good working team. The Environmental Tan also has enough strength not to be intimidated by the Red's explosive power and energy.

A potential problem is that an Environmental Tan tends to live more in his head than a Red does, and the Red may not be able to relate to everything this Tan finds intellectually stimulating. On the other hand, the Environmental Tan's intellectual interests can add an extra dimension to the relationship. (See in chapter 6 the section on Red and Logical Tan relationships to learn more about the potential problems for Reds and Environmental Tans.)

Because neither is interested in sharing on an emotional or intimate level, these two would probably make better business associates than marriage partners. However, a successful relationship between them is not out of the realm of possibility.

Environmental Tan and Orange Relationship

See Orange and Environmental Tan Relationship.

Environmental Tan and Magenta Relationship

This combination is very similar to that of the Logical Tan and the Magenta. The Environmental Tan is much too stable, reliable, and logical for the Magenta's outrageous behavior and challenging ideas. This couple has very little in common. They find each other's attitude and behavior unappealing. (See in chapter 6 the section on relationships between Magentas and Logical Tans for more information regarding Magentas and Environmental Tans.)

Environmental Tan and Yellow Relationship

See Yellow and Environmental Tan Relationship.

Environmental Tan and Logical Tan Relationship

See Logical Tan and Environmental Tan Relationship.

Environmental Tan and Environmental Tan Relationship

This can be a great business relationship in which each respects the ideas and power of the other. However, there is not much emotional expression, tenderness, or intimacy between the Environmental Tans. They both tend to live their lives independently. Because they both keep their emotions to themselves, their communication is not very intimate or open. They respect each other for their mental abilities, stability, and common sense. However, there is not enough diversity between them to add depth to the relationship. This pair is too much alike. They make great friends or business partners, but they are traditionally not very emotionally intimate or sexually exciting as marriage partners.

Environmental Tan and Sensitive Tan Relationship

This couple has potential for compatibility. The Sensitive Tan desires a partner who has a sense of responsibility, reliability, and inner strength, and the Environmental Tan embodies those qualities. A Sensitive Tan needs a mate who is capable of commitment and will support a family. An Environmental Tan will choose to do this. Both prefer to communicate with others on a logical, mental level.

The Sensitive Tan provides the quiet, nurturing home environment for the Environmental Tan. She also provides the softness and emotional tenderness the Environmental Tan needs at times to balance him. She does not invade the Environmental Tan's need for privacy. Her style does not threaten him. Instead, he appreciates her quiet reliability, her sense of responsibility, and her subtle methods of nurturing. However, her gentleness is occasionally unchallenging for the Environmental Tan. He sometimes prefers a mate who is a bit more powerful and assertive.

A potential problem is that a Sensitive Tan, who has traces of Blue in her aura, occasionally needs someone she can relate to on an emotional and intimate basis as well. An Environmental Tan is not usually emotionally available. At times, the Environmental Tan is too gruff and regimented for the Sensitive Tan. The Sensitive Tan appreciates the Environmental Tan because she feels she can rely on him to handle daily matters; however, her emotional needs are not always met. If the Sensitive Tan can accept the fact that the Environmental Tan can give only on certain levels, and if she can relax and fulfill her own emotional needs, then this relationship has potential for success.

Neither Tan is outgoing or risk taking. Neither likes to socialize much, although the Sensitive Tan prefers to be with people more often than the Environmental Tan does. They both prefer to stay at home, creating a comfortable, secure, and private environment for themselves and their family. They relate to each other's need for security and consistency. Both are fairly stable; neither has emotional highs or lows that threaten or upset the other. Communication between them tends to be safe and predictable.

In many ways these colors have the potential for a harmonious relationship. They have the ability to complement each other and to provide the security and stability they both need.

Environmental Tan and Abstract Tan Relationship

This is not usually a very compatible couple. The Environmental Tan, who wants order and discipline in his life, is exasperated by the chaotic and haphazard behavior of the Abstract Tan. She is too careless and forgetful for his taste. The Environmental Tan prefers a partner who is more powerful and can stand on her own two feet. The gentle Abstract Tan is looking instead for someone to take care of her. The Environmental Tan has no respect for her inability to be responsible and reliable. Although the Abstract Tan has good intentions, she usually has too many things going on in her mind to follow through on many of them.

The Environmental Tan usually intimidates the Abstract Tan.

His power and strength can overwhelm her, and this increases her tendency to withdraw into her head. The Environmental Tan is a very private and solemn person who usually keeps his feelings to himself. Although the Abstract Tan will discuss the concepts of emotions, she tends to detach herself from her own feelings. Consequently, this couple can be emotionally unavailable to each other. Although the Abstract Tan's cheerful and optimistic attitude could benefit the somber Environmental Tan, he tends to reject her. The Abstract Tan's exuberant and scattered energy usually bothers the quiet Environmental Tan.

Even though the Environmental Tan appreciates the Abstract Tan's conceptual understanding of unconditional love for humanity, he prefers a mate who can help him take care of business. An Abstract Tan prefers a mate who will not require her to be so responsible or reliable and who will be more understanding toward her unique style.

Environmental Tan and Green Relationship

See Green and Environmental Tan Relationship.

Environmental Tan and Blue Relationship

See Blue and Environment Tan Relationship.

Environmental Tan and Violet Relationship

This is a very interesting combination. Although it has potential, this relationship does not usually remain a long-term, compatible one. Environmental Tans tend to be concerned about saving the planet's physical environment. Violets are usually concerned about saving the planet on a humanitarian level. Both are concerned about planetary problems, but from different perspectives. They can provide a good balance for each other. The Environmental Tan can bring practicality and reliability into the relationship, helping the Violet to focus and bring her visions into physical reality. The Violet can help the Environmental Tan see ideas and concepts beyond the limits of facts and proven information. Her visions can inspire and broaden his mind.

Problems often occur when the two attempt to communicate. They have different styles. The rational, unemotional Environmental Tan tends to keep his feelings and dreams locked inside; a Violet has great emotional depth and needs to relate with her mate on that level. To an Environmental Tan, a Violet appears to be an unrealistic dreamer with her head too often in the clouds. Her ideas seem unreliable and impractical. To a Violet, an Environmental Tan often appears to be shortsighted, unemotional, and overly cautious. A Violet requires passion and forward movement with her relationships. An Environmental Tan does not express passion or take leaps of faith easily, although he can learn to do so. His solemn behavior can eventually frustrate the Violet. Conflict and disagreements between the emotional visionary and the practical realist are common.

In a balanced, well-functioning relationship, the Environmental Tan is commonly the stable, consistent partner with the reliable job. The Violet focuses her attention on her dreams and visions, which can eventually elevate this couple into higher standards of living.

This couple will not compete with each other for attention because the Environmental Tan has no desire to call attention to himself. He is delighted to leave the role of entertainer to the charismatic Violet. However, with the Violet constantly wanting to be the focus of attention at social gatherings, this Tan may eventually judge her as being either insecure or pompous and egotistical.

Although this couple has the possibility of providing a good balance for each other, it is more common for them to become frustrated with each other's differences. An Environmental Tan feels more secure with his traditional, proven methods of living. Supporting a Violet's dreams may cause him financial hardship until the Violet is able to prove herself successful. A Violet needs to fulfill her dreams and live her potential. This Tan can analyze the Violet's visions so much that it slows her down or even causes her to give up. Being unable to live her dreams can cause the Violet unhappiness, depression, and confusion.

Although these two have potential as a couple, their differences usually become uncomfortable and limiting for them both.

Environmental Tan and Lavender Relationship

See Lavender and Environmental Tan Relationship.

Environmental Tan and Crystal Relationship

An Environmental Tan and a Crystal would probably not be able to create an intimate or emotionally bonded relationship together. Neither one typically seeks out relationships. The Crystal enjoys emotional communication, but is often too withdrawn to instigate conversation. The Environmental Tan is not interested in emotional discussions. Consequently, intimacy does not usually occur. Both individuals require time alone. Each tends to respect that need in the other, but these two can become too isolated.

Because an Environmental Tan does not display wild or outrageous behavior, the Crystal is not adversely affected by his energy. The Environmental Tan can provide grounded, stable energy for the fragile Crystal. However, the Crystal can also feel that the Environmental Tan is too emotionally unavailable, too practical, too stern, and too rigid for her gentle nature. He does not usually understand the Crystal's spiritual beliefs or her need to go within to meditate.

Both colors appreciate nature, which gives them something to share. However, the Crystal has a much more gentle, ethereal, and emotional approach to nature and to life in general. The Environmental Tan tends to appreciate life by analyzing it. A Crystal can contribute beauty and softness to the technical Tan; the Tan can add security and stability to a fragile and insecure Crystal.

If these two accept the balance that each adds to the other's life, they can build a fairly complementary relationship. However, because both tend to be introspective and quiet, the qualities often missing in this relationship are intimacy, emotional bonding, and open communication. The Crystal would probably have to adjust to the established, practical boundaries of an Environmental Tan's world, though she would be much happier living inside her own quiet world. Even though each personality can provide the qualities missing in the other, an Environmental Tan is usually too rigid, too logical, and too disciplined for the gentle, fragile, emotional Crystal.

Environmental Tan and Indigo Relationship

See Indigo and Environmental Tan Relationship.

SENSITIVE TAN

Sensitive Tan and Red Relationship

See Red and Sensitive Tan Relationship.

Sensitive Tan and Orange Relationship

This relationship can be challenging and uncomfortable for both partners. The Sensitive Tan tends to worry constantly about the Orange's safety and well-being. The Orange finds the Sensitive Tan's mothering behavior and nonrisk attitude boring and suffocating. A Sensitive Tan wants her companion to be at home doing practical, nurturing, and safe activities with her. The Orange has no desire to fulfill her needs. Living with the quiet stability of a Sensitive Tan is slow death for an Orange, who prefers to be much more adventurous and bold. The Sensitive Tan is usually consumed with dread every time the Orange walks out the door to challenge the physical environment or attempt a daring feat. After awhile, the stress is more than she can handle.

A Sensitive Tan needs to depend on her mate to be a provider.

Taking on traditional responsibilities is not an Orange's idea of really living life, however. If the Sensitive Tan married an Orange, she would spend most of her time alone. She needs more companionship from her spouse than the Orange is willing to give. Often an Orange is drawn to a Sensitive Tan specifically because she is willing to stay home and take care of business, freeing the Orange to be adventurous. Eventually, however, these mates are torn apart because the Sensitive Tan resents the abandonment and the Orange resents the suppression. These two do not usually meet each other's needs.

Sensitive Tan and Magenta Relationship

A Sensitive Tan prefers her life to be calm and quiet. Consequently, she is not comfortable with the Magenta's outrageous behavior. The Magenta is much too bizarre for her. Instead, the Tan needs stability, responsibility, and reliability from her partner. She needs someone who can provide security. The Magenta does not choose to fill this role.

The Magenta tends to find a Sensitive Tan too complacent. Although he knows she will take care of the details, run the home, and provide a loving, nurturing environment for him, eventually he becomes bored with her stability and predictability.

The Magenta needs a partner who is willing to be outrageous and fun loving with him and give him the freedom to be expressive. Although the Sensitive Tan does not stop the Magenta from expressing himself, his behavior often offends her. He easily embarrasses her. The quiet and respectful Sensitive Tan is much more interested in following the rules and complying with the standards set by society. A Magenta loves to challenge rules and live outside society's standards. He feels no need to be quiet or respectful.

Although the Magenta may have some daily needs met by the responsible Sensitive Tan, he usually finds her to be uninspiring. At the same time, the Magenta does not usually fulfill a Sensitive Tan's emotional or mental needs.

Sensitive Tan and Yellow Relationship

See Yellow and Sensitive Tan Relationship.

Sensitive Tan and Logical Tan Relationship

A Sensitive Tan and a Logical Tan can create a successful relationship. Both Life Colors have many of the same needs for security, stability, and reliability. Because of the subtle Blue characteristics in her aura, the Sensitive Tan will often bring more intuition, sensitivity, and warmth into this relationship.

A potential problem is that a Sensitive Tan wants affection, love, and emotional sensitivity as well as dependability and accountability from her mate. Although a Logical Tan can provide security and stability, he does not usually feel comfortable sharing on an emotional level. A Sensitive Tan will usually be patient, even though she misses the emotional bonding. Although she appreciates that her Logical Tan mate provides security by bringing home a regular paycheck, she can eventually be disappointed with the lack of emotional communication in the relationship. Although the Logical Tan may not understand his mate's emotional needs, he appreciates that she at least is calmer and more rational than most other people are. When a Sensitive Tan cries, there is usually a logical explanation behind it.

This is actually a good relationship. The Sensitive Tan provides emotional balance and warmth to the relationship; the Logical Tan provides security and stability. The differences in their emotional makeup do not usually outweigh their many compatible qualities.

Sensitive Tan and Environmental Tan Relationship

See Environmental Tan and Sensitive Tan Relationship.

Sensitive Tan and Sensitive Tan Relationship

A relationship between two Sensitive Tans is very comfortable and compatible. These individuals are content to have a warm, secure home together. They are also very loving and supportive partners. They both understand the need for quiet, calm, and privacy, and they can fulfill each other's need for commitment, security, and nurturing.

Although these two are emotionally and mentally compatible, a relationship between them can become complacent. Both hope and expect the other partner will take care of business and support them so that they can stay home and nurture the family. Although Sensitive Tans enjoy companions who are stable and realistic, they are usually happier with partners who have a little more ambition.

These two can communicate effectively with each other, but the element missing in this relationship is passion. There is usually a lack of drive, ambition, dynamic power, and sexual fireworks between them. Because Sensitive Tans do not like to take risks or initiate change, their potential for growth together is minimal.

Although this relationship is not very exciting, these two can be very secure and comfortable together. They often make better friends or roommates than marriage partners.

Sensitive Tan and Abstract Tan Relationship

A Sensitive Tan is one of the few personalities who understands and accepts the Abstract Tan's unique behavior. Both individuals process intellectually. They both prefer to work with details. The Sensitive Tan is fascinated by the Abstract Tan's ability to see all the details simultaneously, and she is patient enough to allow him the time he needs to put all the components together. The Sensitive Tan appreciates and shares the Abstract Tan's love of humanity. The Sensitive Tan will usually act on her love for people; the Abstract Tan frequently spends more time speculating and conceptualizing about humanity's potential. The Sensitive Tan can encourage the Abstract Tan to become more of an active participant in life and help him design the steps to accomplish his ideas.

The Sensitive Tan is very supportive and nurturing toward the frequently misunderstood Abstract Tan. She enjoys his innocence and optimism, although at times she can grow tired of the chaos he creates. She typically finds herself cleaning up after him, helping him locate his missing car keys, and reminding him of appointments. Although she is a nurturer, the Sensitive Tan can become exhausted being the Abstract Tan's mother and caretaker.

If the Sensitive Tan can maintain her patience and under-standing toward the Abstract Tan, and if the Abstract Tan can learn to focus his scattered energy and become more dependable, this couple can experience a compatible relationship.

Sensitive Tan and Green Relationship

Whether or not this relationship is compatible depends upon which roles the Sensitive Tan and Green partners are willing to play with each other. The patient and methodical Sensitive Tan can be a great secretary, bookkeeper, assistant, or helpmate for the Green. While the Green conceptualizes plans, organizes informa-tion, and manages the business, the Sensitive Tan takes care of all the details — very helpful to the Green. The Sensitive Tan respects the Green's ambition and intelligence. She also enjoys the financial results produced by his efforts. In this relationship, the Sensitive Tan feels secure knowing she will always be financially supported. In return, the Sensitive Tan provides a loving and comfortable home environment for the hardworking Green.

The powerful and dominating Green can often be too intense for the quiet Sensitive Tan, however. The ambitious and quick-thinking Green can make too many demands on her and take advantage of her willingness to help him. He can also be hard on her delicate emotional personality. Even though the Sensitive Tan is usually calm and logical and can rationalize much of the Green's behavior, she can also be easily hurt by his sharp criticism. The fast-paced Green can become impatient with the Sensitive Tan's slow, methodical processes. Usually the Green expresses his frustration; even if he withholds his judgments, however, the Sensitive Tan is intuitive enough to sense his disapproval. She can try repeatedly to keep up with his demands, only to become over-whelmed by his quick pace and high expectations.

The Sensitive Tan can also be disappointed by the Green's workaholic behavior. Although she enjoys his substantial income, she wants home and family to be bigger priorities to him. She is not interested in amassing a great fortune and owning expensive possessions. The Sensitive Tan wants to share a loving, comfort-able, secure, and modest home with her spouse. For her a home without a mate and family is just an empty shell. The goal-oriented Green, however, does not usually share the Tan's modest desires.

Although the Green appreciates the support he receives from the Sensitive Tan, he can also become bored with her. He desires a mate with whom he can have mentally challenging conversa-tions. A Green loves to debate. He loves to be inspired by new and progressive ideas. Making changes, taking risks, and learning new information are all exciting to the Green. The Sensitive Tan is more comfortable with the same, familiar environment. She is hesitant to take risks and is intimidated by arguments.

On the one hand, these two can provide balance for each other. The Green can support the Sensitive Tan and yet keep her from becoming staid and complacent. The Sensitive Tan can assist the Green by taking care of the mundane details that he abhors. She can also teach him to relax and be more patient.

On the other hand, neither may completely fulfill the other's needs. The Green can intimidate or emotionally wound the gentle Sensitive Tan; the Sensitive Tan can be too predictable and uninspiring for the energetic Green.

Sensitive Tan and Blue Relationship

See Blue and Sensitive Tan Relationship.

Sensitive Tan and Violet Relationship

See Violet and Sensitive Tan Relationship.

Sensitive Tan and Lavender Relationship

Although these are both gentle, loving personalities, they don't always fulfill each other's needs. Their relationship frequently evolves into a parent-child relationship.

A Sensitive Tan, who is one of the more patient and understanding individuals in the aura spectrum, desires a mate who is responsible and reliable. A Sensitive Tan needs a sense of security in her relationship. Being pragmatic, stable, and responsible are not on the list of Lavender personality traits. Unless the Sensitive Tan is willing to be the practical and dependable provider in the family, she will constantly worry about the Lavender's inability to be financially reliable. A Sensitive Tan feels safer with someone who understands the concepts of commitment and responsibility. The Lavender is too much of an irresponsible nonconformist.

A Sensitive Tan rarely understands the Lavender's preoccupation with other realities. She also becomes frustrated by the Lavender's frequent emotional withdrawals. She can feel abandoned and alone in this relationship. This couple does not communicate well with each other. The methodical Sensitive Tan wants a sense of order, logic, and practicality in her life. The imaginative Lavender prefers to live in his fantasies and dreams. The realistic Sensitive Tan is concerned with paying bills, buying food, and maintaining a stable job. The fanciful Lavender is more interested in having the freedom to be creative. The Sensitive Tan's expectations and concerns can eventually smother the simple Lavender. Being forced to focus energy on responsibilities in physical reality is uncomfortable and even painful for him. He ends up escaping the demands of the relationship by retreating into his own world.

If these two can stay balanced and in power, they can work out an equitable arrangement. The Sensitive Tan is able to provide a stable environment for the ungrounded Lavender. If the Sensitive Tan is willing to take care of the day-to-day details and responsibilities, her Lavender mate is allowed to be a creative dreamer. The appreciative Lavender then has the freedom to explore and bring back information from other realities to her. This information can sometimes help the Sensitive Tan see life from other perspectives and, therefore, broaden her horizons. The Lavender can lighten the Sensitive Tan's usually predictable life with spontaneity and creativity.

Usually, the quiet, unobtrusive Sensitive Tan will not force the Lavender to conform to her standards. She basically supports and nurtures her mate. However, the Lavender's irresponsible behavior will eventually disappoint the Sensitive Tan. Ordinarily these two do not fulfill enough of each other's needs to make this a very happy or successful relationship.

Sensitive Tan and Crystal Relationship

See Crystal and Sensitive Tan Relationship.

Sensitive Tan and Indigo Relationship

Even though this relationship can often be comparable to a mother caring for a child, it does have potential. A Sensitive Tan does not always understand the Indigo's surrealistic ideas or belief systems. The Indigo predominantly operates from his intuition and inner knowing. He has no facts to support his beliefs. The Sensitive Tan usually wants life to be more practical and realistic.

Although the Sensitive Tan has a difficult time understanding the Indigo, she continues to be very loving and nurturing, almost parental, toward her Indigo mate. The Indigo feels appreciative of the quiet love and acceptance he receives from the Sensitive Tan. In power, the Indigo is a very loyal and committed partner, which the

Sensitive Tan appreciates. These two typically have more of a mother-child relationship than a husband-wife relationship, and the Sensitive Tan usually ends up financially supporting them both.

For this relationship to be compatible, the Sensitive Tan needs to focus on the Blue aspect of her personality to enable her to bond with the emotional and spiritual Indigo. To communicate with the Indigo, she must be willing to put the rational Tan aspect of her personality on the back burner and trust the intuitive part of her soul. She must also be willing to provide the economic stability in the relationship while the Indigo explores his spirituality.

This relationship could be a challenge to maintain, because these personalities have very different approaches to life. Because they are both loving and sensitive individuals, however, they have the capability of working out their differences.

ABSTRACT TAN
Abstract Tan and Red Relationship

A relationship between an Abstract Tan and a Red is not typically compatible. Even though each personality has qualities that could provide balance to relationship, overcoming differences could be challenging.

The Red's energy is solid and reliable. He is a dependable, hard worker. The Abstract Tan's energy is scattered and often chaotic. She mentally travels in so many directions at once that she seems inconsistent and irresponsible. Even though the grounded Red could add a strong, stable foundation for the disorganized Abstract Tan, her random mental processes would eventually wear him out. This Tan's abstract theoretical discussions do not interest the practical Red. He instead prefers to work with tangible, physical reality. The Abstract Tan tends to live in her head, philosophizing and speculating over various concepts. Her tendency not to follow through on her ideas eventually frustrates the Red.

The Red's personality is action oriented. Although the Abstract Tan may benefit by having this practical worker in her environment, she could have trouble explaining her ideas to the Red. The powerful Red prefers to know what jobs need to be done so he can take action on them. The scattered Abstract Tan would typically have the Red doing a myriad of apparently unrelated tasks until he became frustrated by her disorganized plans. For instance, if the Abstract Tan wants all the living room furniture rearranged, she will tell the Red to move the couch by the stereo system and then ask him to repair the dishwasher. Later, as he is in the midst of his repair work, she will ask him to move the chair and the lamp to the place where the couch had been. The Red becomes frustrated as he jumps randomly from task to task. She should tell him where she wants all the pieces to be placed so he can then move them all. The Red is happier when he can see the tangible results of his completed project before moving on to the next assignment.

The Red's frustration and quick, volatile temper can intimidate the sensitive and childlike Abstract Tan. She typically withdraws from him. Because neither is adept at sharing feelings, there could be a shortage of emotional and intimate communication between them.

Even though the Red enjoys the Abstract Tan's optimism and appreciates her unconditional love and acceptance, he eventually becomes irritated by her scrambled behavior. Although the Abstract Tan enjoys being taken care of by the reliable and responsible Red, she realizes that her inconsistent behavior disappoints him. Consequently, she feels that she is incompetent and a failure.

This couple would be able to provide some missing elements for each other. However, both are usually happier with partners who can understand and be compatible with their lifestyles.

Abstract Tan and Orange Relationship

See Orange and Abstract Tan Relationship.

Abstract Tan and Magenta Relationship

See Magenta and Abstract Tan Relationship.

Abstract Tan and Yellow Relationship

These personalities are usually gentle and considerate toward each other, though they don't necessarily make practical or dependable marriage partners. They can feel safe with each other because neither would ever want to hurt the other. If the Yellow doesn't understand the scattered Tan's abstract theories, he usually just laughs them off rather than getting upset at her. However, in time the Tan's random mental speculations will begin to confuse and even bore the fun-loving Yellow. The Yellow prefers to spend time playing, exercising, playing sports, and experiencing physical reality. Although participating in physical activities helps an Abstract Tan loosen up and get out of her head a little, she is not apt to spend as much time being physical as the Yellow would like. The Abstract Tan enjoys theorizing and philosophizing.

Both personalities are energetic and optimistic, and they enjoy the company of other people. They are both curious and excited about learning new things. They are also both sensitive individuals who are very concerned about being liked by others. They have similar, childlike personalities. The Yellow prefers being physical and having fun, however; the Abstract Tan enjoys mental speculation and theoretical concepts.

Both the Yellow and the Abstract Tan tend to be like irresponsible children, so as a couple they can experience financial difficulties. Neither wants to handle the responsibilities of running a household.

This pair could be fun playmates. However, both tend to need responsible partners who can take care of business.

Abstract Tan and Logical Tan Relationship

Although both personalities prefer to work with the details of a project, the Abstract Tan's random style of choosing priorities can drive the Logical Tan crazy. The Logical Tan can become frustrated trying to understand the Abstract Tan's thought processes.

Rather than retrain the Abstract Tan, if the Logical Tan can just stand back and let her accomplish each step in her own scattered way, he will discover that she eventually does pull the whole project together. The Logical Tan cannot expect an orderly and sequential process from the Abstract Tan. He will be disappointed if he tries to reeducate her.

Neither personality likes to delve into emotional realms. Consequently, each is safe with the other, although a sense of emotional depth and intimacy will be continuously lacking in the relationship.

The Abstract Tan's tendency to misplace possessions can concern or annoy the conscientious Logical Tan. In addition, the Abstract Tan's scattered behavior, her incongruous stories, and her unreliable, forgetful nature can put the Logical Tan's life into a tailspin. He doesn't enjoy a disorganized lifestyle. He can also be worn out by the Abstract Tan's inability to efficiently handle her finances. In this relationship, the Logical Tan can quickly become a critical parental figure.

The Abstract Tan does add a sense of unconditional love and acceptance to the Logical Tan's otherwise straight-laced life. Even though the Logical Tan doesn't always understand or appreciate her ways, he does appreciate her optimism and her love for humanity. She brings these elements, which are frequently lacking, into his life.

The Abstract Tan appreciates the fact that the Logical Tan is able to create a stable, practical, and logical environment for the two of them. The Logical Tan is willing to be responsible, to work and provide for a family. The Logical Tan can provide a solid and reliable foundation for the flighty Abstract Tan, but he can also make her feel inadequate and incompetent because her style is so unusual.

These two can at least be compatible friends. If the Logical Tan is willing to be the more responsible partner and if he can learn to be patient while the Abstract Tan puts the pieces of the puzzle together in a less than methodical manner, this pair has potential together. If the Abstract Tan can learn to stay a little more focused and organized, then the methodical Logical Tan can feel more relaxed and secure around her.

Abstract Tan and Environmental Tan Relationship

See Environmental Tan and Abstract Tan Relationship.

Abstract Tan and Sensitive Tan Relationship

See Sensitive Tan and Abstract Tan Relationship.

Abstract Tan and Abstract Tan Relationship

Life with these two as partners would most likely be total chaos. They could have wonderful philosophical conversations about a wide variety of topics, but their home would be cluttered with clothes strewn everywhere, unpaid bills hidden under piles of unopened mail, and outdated memos reminding them of missed appointments.

Neither individual would be dependable enough to take care of business. In addition, because they both usually have hectic schedules and are running in many directions, they would rarely see each other. Even if they were to set up an appointment to get together, inevitably one of them would forget it. If they tried to do things together, they would just be adding more to their already heavily booked agendas.

Because Abstract Tans try to avoid dealing with their feelings, these two would not experience a great deal of emotional intimacy together. Even though they would be able to share their enthusiasm for knowledge and their optimism and love for humanity, they would be more compatible as friends. As friends, they could get together sporadically to discuss ideas. As friends, they would not have the same pressure to get together as they would have if they were married. Both would be better off marrying people who could provide them with a stronger degree of stability and commitment. They need partners who can take care of them and help stabilize and focus their lives. The Abstract Tans together are too scattered and unorganized to function efficiently as a team.

Abstract Tan and Green Relationship

Even though these personalities have abilities that could help each other, they are generally not compatible. The Abstract Tan's scattered and disorganized lifestyle irritates the orderly Green. The Green, who takes great pride that her environment is clean, organized, and elegant, is appalled by the Abstract Tan's disheveled surroundings and his obvious lack of respect for his possessions. The Green can panic every time the Abstract Tan goes near any of her priceless possessions.

The Green is fascinated by the Abstract Tan's ability to see an entire concept and each detail simultaneously. However, she often becomes frustrated by the scattered Tan's inability to explain the concept to her in an organized and rational manner. She also becomes impatient with the Abstract Tan's inability to follow through with many of his projects. Even if he does complete his many projects, they are frequently not done as quickly or as perfectly as the Green would like.

The Green is typically so intelligent, quick, and organized that the Abstract Tan tends to feel slow, inadequate, and inefficient around her. The friendly and sensitive Abstract Tan can also be so intimidated by the Green's power that he hides in his head, venturing out only briefly to talk about a new philosophical concept before retreating inside where he is safe. Although the Green may be fascinated by this Tan's ideas, she rarely sees any practical application for his unconditional love of humanity. She wants to know how the Abstract Tan's theoretical concepts apply to her daily encounters with work and life.

Even though the Green could provide structure and organization to the Abstract Tan's life, the Green eventually becomes frustrated and bored with the constant effort. Even though the Abstract Tan could bring an attitude of optimism, friendliness, and love to the Green's usually intense and serious world, the Abstract Tan usually feels intimidated, misunderstood, and unappreciated by the powerful Green.

The Green needs a mate who is powerful and ambitious and can take care of himself. The Abstract Tan usually needs someone to help her organize her life and who will be patiently understanding and supportive. Neither personality typically fulfills these needs for the other.

Abstract Tan and Blue Relationship

An Abstract Tan and a Blue are compatible in many ways. The Blue appreciates the Abstract Tan's understanding of unconditional love and acceptance for humanity. The Blue often wishes, however, that the Abstract Tan were more open and emotionally available on a personal level. As with all the Tans, the Abstract Tan tends to live too much in his head for the Blue's liking. He is not as willing or as able to experience the deep emotional bond that the Blue desires in a relationship.

The Blue does appreciate the Abstract Tan's sensitivity, his friendly personality, and his optimistic nature. Although few Life Colors understand or tolerate the Abstract Tan's scattered behavior, the Blue loves and accepts this misfit. She understands how it feels not to be understood by others. Like the Abstract Tan, a Blue doesn't have the facts to support what she intuitively feels. She also has difficulty explaining her feelings logically. The Abstract Tan has difficulty explaining his ideas logically because his mental pictures are scrambled and chaotic. The Blue is usually loving and patient enough to give the Abstract Tan time to bring all the details together. In return for the Blue's love and devotion, the Abstract Tan appreciates her and returns her love.

The Blue's natural mothering instinct causes her to take care of the childlike and sensitive Abstract Tan. She shops for him, cooks for him, listens attentively to his abstract concepts, and picks up after him. She can be a very faithful caretaker. However, even the long-suffering Blue can become overwhelmed and exhausted by the Abstract Tan's chaos. She occasionally tires of keeping him focused and organized so that he can stay on track. She also desires to be taken care of by her mate. She can often feel abandoned and disappointed by the Abstract Tan because his schedule is frequently so hectic that he rarely has time for her. The Abstract Tan loves and appreciates his Blue mate, but he forgets to make her a priority.

When this couple is finally able to spend time together, the Blue enjoys hearing about the Abstract Tan's many philosophical ideas about love and humanity. The Abstract Tan enjoys the warmth, acceptance, and attention he receives from the Blue. If the Blue becomes too emotionally needy, however, the fearful Abstract Tan may withdraw into the security of his mind, leaving the Blue alone and emotionally unfulfilled. To create a happy and successful relationship, the Abstract Tan must organize his life a little more and make his Blue mate a priority.

These personalities are sensitive and loving enough to create a harmonious relationship together. They must each learn to stay in power and in balance, however, to accomplish this goal.

Abstract Tan and Violet Relationship

See Violet and Abstract Tan Relationship.

Abstract Tan and Lavender Relationship

See Lavender and Abstract Tan Relationship.

Abstract Tan and Crystal Relationship

Typically, an Abstract Tan and a Crystal do not make a very compatible couple. The Abstract Tan's chaotic, unfocused behavior totally scrambles the Crystal's energy and causes her turmoil and frustration. The Crystal needs her environment to be quiet, clean, simple, and uncluttered. The Abstract Tan's environment is far from being clean and uncluttered. Although both individuals are sensitive and mean well, neither wants to be responsible for the other.

Emotionally, they are both withdrawn. The Crystal quietly stays in her inner spiritual world; the Abstract Tan safely hides in his head. They do not know how to experience intimacy with each other.

The Abstract Tan is very social and enjoys being around a lot of people. The Crystal shies away from people; being around too many people shatters her sensitive and fragile soul. Though both individuals love to learn, they have different methods of obtaining information. The Abstract Tan loves to research and gather information from other people and outside sources. The Crystal needs to calmly meditate for her answers.

The Abstract Tan, with his energetic and outgoing personality, doesn't know what to do with the delicate Crystal. If they were married, the Abstract Tan would tend to spend most of his time out of the house or constantly coming and going. The Abstract Tan's erratic behavior and chaotic lifestyle would irritate the Crystal. Frustrated, the Crystal would close herself off from the Abstract Tan, causing him to feel rejected and unloved. To keep from being hurt anymore, the Abstract Tan would then withdraw into his mental and philosophical world. With both partners isolated, there would be no hope for communication or intimacy.

These personalities would be happier with partners who are more similar and more understanding toward their unique behaviors and lifestyles.

Abstract Tan and Indigo Relationship

The Abstract Tan and the Indigo often create a harmonious relationship. They both have a similar quest for knowledge, for information that will help them understand humanity and universal principles. Others frequently misunderstand these two because their attitudes and behaviors are so unique. An Abstract Tan and the Indigo both experience unconditional love and understanding for humanity. Even though both are sensitive, caring, childlike, inquisitive souls, they are usually slow to develop deep relationships. Both need to trust the people they become involved with. These two can trust each other because they understand and appreciate each other.

The Abstract Tan, who is frequently a storehouse of information, can provide answers for the inquisitive Indigo. She can patiently teach him many facts and concepts about physical reality. In appreciation, the Indigo completely loves and accepts the Abstract Tan. The Indigo isn't tremendously bothered by the Abstract Tan's many ideas and tasks or by her disorganized behavior. The Indigo can gather information from a wide variety of the Abstract Tan's activities. These two can form a tight and devoted friendship. They can honor, trust, and teach each other.

The Indigo wants to bond on a deep soul-to-soul level with his partner. The Abstract Tan, however, is uncomfortable delving into such profound emotional commitments. The Indigo is usually patient and understanding concerning the Abstract Tan's fears. Given enough time and space to explore her feelings in her own way, the Abstract Tan may start to trust the Indigo enough to open up to him. If the Abstract Tan is never able to reach an emotional level at which she can bond soul to soul with the Indigo, the Indigo will still be accepting and loving, but also disappointed. The Indigo will always feel a void, being unable to connect with the Abstract Tan's soul.

Another potential problem is that neither is very adept at taking care of business. They both mean well, however, and if they learn to work out a plan together, they can create a happy life. They can keep each other focused and on track. These two can make a very loving and compatible couple.

GREEN

Green and Red Relationship

See Red and Green Relationship.

Green and Orange Relationship

A Green and Orange combination could be very fascinating. Greens are the business-oriented planners and organizers. Oranges could benefit greatly from relationships with these entrepreneurs. An Orange enjoys working for organizations that can sponsor him in such occupations as race car driver or stuntman. A quick-thinking Green can create business deals to enable the Orange to work for such a company. When the Orange desires to climb Mt. Everest, the Green can help the Orange create the financial support to take the trip. The Green is also smart enough to find ways the trip can benefit the sponsor. An Orange is impressed with the Green's mental skills. The Green is fascinated with the Orange's mental cunning, as well as his ability to plan and carry out daring feats. Although the feats interest the Green, she does not usually join the Orange on his dangerous adventures.

A Green and an Orange would have respect for each other's skills. Although they both love to calculate strategies, plan events, and test their skills, each has different goals. A Green loves mental challenges, accomplishing projects, and making money. An Orange loves the physical challenge of overcoming or outwitting his opponent. The Orange appreciates the money a Green can generate to enable him to pursue his desired challenges. This can be a great business partnership, with the Green's planning skills and money-oriented ideas combined with the Orange's cunning and physical abilities.

Both tend to be very self-sufficient and independent. Neither needs to be in a relationship. But each is fascinated and appreciative enough to know the value each brings to the relationship. However, because neither wants to be controlled, a conflict may arise with this relationship. Independence and desire to be in control could create power struggles.

With the intelligence, planning, and organizational skills they both have, this pair could easily become financially prosperous and free to do what they want. They would have respect for each other's mental capabilities, skills, and abilities to take on challenges. For the most part, this couple has great potential together.

Green and Magenta Relationship

A Green and Magenta relationship can be quite fascinating. The Magenta's creative and artistic imagination can fuel the Green's business ideas and entrepreneurial abilities. The Magenta's unique ideas and thoughts fascinate a Green's quick mind. The Green has the intelligence, persistence, and skills to pull off the Magenta's ideas. The Magenta, on the other hand, is fascinated by a Green's quick mind, her ability to see patterns, and her organizational skills.

The Green's ability to take care of business and provide financial security enables the Magenta to be creative, outrageous, and spontaneous. They both appreciate each other's ability to be independent. They do not want someone suffocating or depending on them.

This couple runs into problems when a Green needs to be admired and respected. The Magenta generally feels no need to respect or admire anyone or to behave at all in a respectable manner. His behavior often solicits quite the opposite reaction. The Green can become very embarrassed with the Magenta's disrespectful actions. A Green can also quickly lose respect for the Magenta because the Magenta does not choose to be as stable or take life as seriously as the Green does.

The Magenta, who does not like to be controlled, can end up resenting the powerful and domineering attitude of an out-of-power Green. While a Green likes to tell people what to do, the Magenta rebels and challenges her control. Both colors are fiercely independent and strong willed, which can cause power struggles and other problems in the relationship.

The Green wants expensive, quality items in her home — the nicest furniture, the finest clothing, and the most expensive jewelry. The Magenta prefers outrageous items, not necessarily expensive ones. The Green wants people to be impressed by her surroundings; the Magenta prefers to shock people. This difference in attitudes can become quite frustrating for the Green. Although they each recognize the ability of the other to fill needs in the partnership, this relationship could be very short lived if neither feels their strongest desires are being met. Although consistency and commitment are important to a Green, she is also one of the first to leave a relationship if it does not turn out the way she wants. These two may be better business associates than marriage partners.

Green and Yellow Relationship

Although nothing is impossible, and any couple can work things out with enough commitment and determination, this relationship can be an incredible challenge.

At first, a Green is drawn to the light energy of a Yellow. The Yellow's easygoing attitude and sense of humor help to balance out the Green's intense and serious attitudes. After awhile, however, the Green usually loses patience for the Yellow's lack of ambition. While pushing and demanding more from the Yellow, the Green quickly loses respect for him because he is not accomplishing something of value in his life. The sharp tongue of a judgmental, critical, out-of-power Green can inflict incredible scars on the sensitive Yellow. Being insecure about his abilities anyway, the Yellow finds it difficult to meet the high standards of the Green perfectionist. When a Green is frustrated, no matter what the Yellow does it is never enough. To further exacerbate the Yellow's sense of inadequacy, when the Green is angry she withholds affection and sex from her mate. Sex and physical touch are two of the greatest joys for a Yellow. If these individuals are out of power, the outcome of this marriage will probably be physical, mental, and emotional humiliation for the Yellow and disappointment for the Green.

While a Green loves to give orders, a Yellow hates to be told what to do. The Yellow, often feeling browbeaten, will resort to covert ways of rebelling against the authoritative Green. This serves only to irritate and provoke the Green even more. Hence, a vicious cycle of oppressive parent versus rebellious child begins.

For a Green and Yellow relationship to work, the Green has to realize that the Yellow does not have the same goals or priorities as she does. If the Green wants financial prosperity, she will have to create it herself. In balance, the Green can accomplish while the Yellow creates or brings joy to the planet. If a Yellow can make people feel better, he feels he has performed a valuable service. The Green needs to allow the Yellow to have his unique goals.

A Yellow, on the other hand, needs to understand that the Green wants to experience life to its fullest degree while accomplishing as much as she can. When she becomes frustrated and angry, the Yellow needs to realize that the Green is angry and frustrated with herself. The Yellow may be able to help the Green realize her potential and power and not be afraid of it. A Green just wants to be respected, admired, and acknowledged for what she has done. Acknowledgment is the greatest gift a Yellow can give to a Green.

Because the Yellow hates to be told what to do, the Green can inspire him into his creativity instead of pushing him. A Green empowers people by example and so could be an example to the Yellow.

In power, these personalities can benefit from each other. The Green can take a Yellow's creative ideas, formulate plans, and bring them into physical form. The artistic Yellow can benefit from the Green's organizational and managerial skills. As long as this pair can stay balanced and allow their unique talents, they can accomplish great creative projects together. However, it's more common for the Green to become frustrated and impatient and grow beyond the Yellow.

Green and Logical Tan Relationship

These two personalities have potential for a good relationship, because they both process intellectually and share many of the same interests. They both enjoy discussing ideas rationally and logically. They are usually intellectually compatible. However, the Logical Tan typically processes information more slowly than the Green, and this can cause the Green to become frustrated and impatient. While the Logical Tan processes information slowly and methodically, analyzing each step, the Green has already arrived at a final solution. A Green does not want to go into all the steps that the Tan insists are necessary. The Green usually mentally tunes out the Tan while he tells a story. She doesn't listen to all the details, but is off somewhere thinking about other plans. She reconnects to his story only when he has reached the punch line.

If the Green can realize the advantage of the Logical Tan's ability to be involved in details, she can learn to appreciate him. With a Logical Tan partner, the Green is free to plan ideas and concepts while the Logical Tan fills in the details. If the Green becomes impatient and tries to dominate or push him, he will move even slower. Their opposing behaviors can frustrate them both. A Green also tends to have an "I told you so" attitude, which irritates this Tan and prompts him to resist her even more. There is a simple solution, however. While the Tan methodically and precisely analyze every step, the Green should keep herself busy by mentally or physically working on other ideas.

These two frequently experience conflict over money. A Green wants to make a lot of money quickly. A Logical Tan believes he has to work a long time for money. He must save, invest wisely, and be patient. He wants to build a stable foundation. A Logical Tan, who does not like to take risks, will attempt to caution the Green. This only frustrates her. A Green is more of a gambler and risk-taker than a Logical Tan is. A Green likes to play the stock market. A Logical Tan prefers a savings account. A Green likes to spend money. She wants classy, expensive, quality possessions. A Logical Tan prefers items that are practical, functional, and less expensive. A Logical Tan is usually very frugal with his hard-earned money. These two often argue over the amount of money being spent in the home or in the business. A Green tends to overspend. She often lives beyond her means, which aggravates a Logical Tan.

Out of power, Greens and Logical Tans both tend to be judgmental and stubborn. A Green likes to be right. A Logical Tan will not move until the facts have been proven to him. Although they can usually discuss a problem rationally and intellectually, a Green can become sharp tongued during an argument. Whereas a Logical Tan tends to keep his emotions and thoughts to himself until he has analyzed the situation, a Green is quick to process and quick to lash out. Consequently, their dialogues can be one sided. The Green can be so quick and powerful that the Logical Tan does not have time to come back with a response. The Green is usually the more domineering and powerful in this relationship. When the Logical Tan feels overpowered, he withdraws in self-defense. This cuts off the communication between them, which further irritates the Green because she wants to be heard and respected.

To maintain harmony in this relationship, each must allow the other's method of processing. When the Green wants a lot of money, she must learn to create it herself. She cannot push a Logical Tan to make more money for her. If she has a goal or an idea, she must either accomplish it by herself or allow the Logical Tan to slowly process and achieve it.

The Logical Tan needs to compromise more often with the Green. He needs to trust the Green's track record and be willing to risk more often. He needs to respect the Green's quickness and intelligence, to be careful not to be so detailed and technical that he slows an entire project.

This couple has potential for success, provided the Green does not push the Logical Tan faster than he is willing to go, and provided the Logical Tan does not constantly slow the Green. If these two can perceive their differences as assets, then they can work well together. The Logical Tan can take care of each detail so the Green is free to create, organize, and plan strategies. Otherwise, their differences can create disharmony. The Green can appreciate the Logical Tan's stability, or she can become impatient with it. The Logical Tan can be frustrated by the Green's rash and impetuous behavior, or he can respect her willingness to act on her ideas.

Green and Environmental Tan Relationship

The Green is attracted to the mysterious demeanor of the Environmental Tan and considers his self-confident and aloof behavior to be a challenge. The Environmental Tan is fascinated with the Green's sharp intelligence and her ability to take quick, decisive action. These two are capable of accomplishing almost anything together. The Environmental Tan is a powerful personality and, therefore, one of the few who cannot be dominated by the strong-willed Green. Occasionally these two can butt heads, but the Green tends to respect the Environmental Tan's strength and tenacity.

Because they are fascinated by each other's style and presence and are excited by each other's power, they tend to be sexually attracted to each other. The electricity and magnetism between them creates energy that thrills them and can keep them tantalized for a long time.

They both respect each other's strong mental abilities. They both are intelligent and capable individuals who are self-motivated as well as independent. The Green and the Environmental Tan both want partners who are resourceful enough to take care of themselves. They admire each other's competence.

Problems arise when the Green becomes frustrated with the

Environmental Tan's slow, deliberate movements. She is impatient with his need to cautiously analyze information before making decisions. The Environmental Tan does not want to be rushed. When out of power, the Green can become critical, demanding, or intolerant. The Environmental Tan tends to withdraw inside himself, closing any possibility for communication between them. This behavior irritates the Green even more — she wants to be heard and respected. No matter how angry and frustrated the Green becomes, the Environmental Tan cannot be forced from his shell. The Green's only course of action is to back off and wait until the Environmental Tan decides to emerge again. If the Green lashes out too often, the Environmental Tan will eventually learn not to trust her and will remain permanently closed off from her.

The Green must learn to occupy her time with other projects while allowing the Environmental Tan the time he needs to process all the details. Fortunately, these two are independent enough to work alone. They don't need each other to feel successful or fulfilled. Because both tend to focus so intensely on their work, they can spend a great deal of time apart. Occasionally working on projects together can help to maintain communication and contact with each other. The Environmental Tan is more willing to calmly take care of the details of a project, which frees up the Green to develop ideas. The progressive Green can keep the Environmental Tan's life from becoming too rooted and mundane. She can add sparks and challenge to his otherwise routine life. The Environmental Tan can add a quiet stability to the frequently impatient Green.

Green and Sensitive Tan Relationship

See Sensitive Tan and Green Relationship.

Green and Abstract Tan Relationship

See Abstract Tan and Green Relationship.

Green and Green Relationship

This couple is potentially a powerful, ambitious, successful, and wealthy combination. They also have great potential to experience power struggles. Two Greens together may respect each other, but they may also butt heads. Greens like to be right. They hate losing arguments.

If both are in charge of their own areas in business, they can have a good partnership. If their jobs are clearly defined and if they can learn to respect each other's power, intelligence, and opinions, there can be admiration and compatibility between them. Problems surface when their goals differ or when one Green wants to dominate the other. A Green cannot tolerate being controlled but does, on the other hand, enjoy doing the controlling. Consequently, if one Green is married to another, they will each need to learn mutual respect and compromise to work out solutions.

When there is no respect between them, out-of-power Greens can be cruel to each other. They can also be very competitive, one always trying to make more money or be more successful than the other. Because Greens like to be right, they tend to have frequent and volatile arguments. Greens are usually very strong willed and tenacious.

If there is mutual respect and admiration, sex between these two can be quite powerful. However, if there is a disagreement, they will each withhold sex until the argument is satisfactorily resolved.

Greens love challenges. They can each encourage the other to learn, accomplish, and advance. Life will not be boring for these two. Their biggest problems are that they can both be competitive, strong willed, stubborn, and argumentative. They are usually intellectual equals, however, so their psychological battles can be exciting for them.

Both Greens love to win, so for there to be harmony and balance in this relationship, they have to create ways for both to win. Because they are both intelligent, finding a plan that allows both to win should be easy for them.

Greens need to admire and respect their partners. Fortunately, a Green is one Life Color that another Green cannot run over. Mutual respect is a possibility with this couple. Although a business partnership may have a better chance for success than a marriage, as long as these two see each other as equals, they have potential for harmony. Certainly these two will have money, an elaborate home, and quality possessions. They both have lavish tastes.

Green and Blue Relationship

See Blue and Green Relationship.

Green and Violet Relationship

A relationship between a Green and a Violet has excellent potential. A Violet is one of the few colors in the aura spectrum that a Green cannot run over. Even though a Green is powerful and bright and can quickly process steps one through ten, a Violet can jump from steps one to fifty. Consequently, the Violet can stay several steps ahead of a Green, which inspires and challenges the Green. However, for this relationship to succeed, the Violet must stay in power, remaining focused and centered.

A Violet has visions and dreams he wants to accomplish. An out-of-power Green can thwart a Violet by criticizing his visions, claiming they are not rational or practical. The Green often perceives the Violet to be an unrealistic dreamer. When the Violet wants to jump to step fifty, the Green will often challenge him and question his ability to accomplish that vision. If the Violet is not in power, he will doubt his ability to achieve his dream. The Green will then step on the Violet's idea and lose respect for him. If the Violet stays balanced and in power, when the Green challenges him he can stand firmly committed to his ideas. The Violet's power and commitment will then inspire the Green and motivate her to help him develop a plan to accomplish the dream.

Another conflict that may arise is the Green's desire to keep things orderly and efficient. An out-of-power Violet can become scattered and disorganized, causing the Green to lose tolerance and respect for him. Another potential problem involves their sexual attitudes. While a Violet is sexual and passionate, a Green can often be aloof and protective. When the Green is upset, she often puts up emotional and physical barriers. When both are happy and feeling respected, sex between these two can be passionate and fulfilling.

Greens and Violets are the wealthiest people on the planet, but conflicts can arise over their intentions and methods of obtaining money. A Green can do a job just because there is money in it. (An out-of-power Green can set up oil platforms even if it damages the environment.) However, when a Violet is in power, he has to believe in what he is doing, there has to be integrity and a higher purpose to it, and he has to enjoy the work. A Violet often judges a Green as being too materialistic, too cold, too calculating, and too concerned about money. A Violet wants money, but only because it gives him the freedom to accomplish things he really believes in. A Green wants money for material possessions and power. She wants classy clothes, elegant cars, and expensive homes. Ultimately, a Violet is not fulfilled by mere material possessions. If they can accept their differences or learn from each other, this couple has the potential of making enough money to make them both happy. The Green can have her quality possessions; Violet can afford to travel and be philanthropic.

One of the many positive aspects of a Green-Violet relationship is that a confident and centered Violet will allow the Green to be powerful. He is not intimidated by her need to control. The Violet will listen to the Green, then do things his own way anyway. In power, Violets lead and inspire others through their charm and intelligence. This allowing attitude creates less conflict between a Green and a Violet. However, when the Violet is out of power, this couple can experience intense power struggles because both want to be in charge. A Green must be in a relationship with someone she respects. As long as the Violet stays in power and focuses on bringing his dreams into reality, the Green will respect him.

Because both Violets and Greens want to be self-employed, they can make good partners. Even though the Violet has a vision, he is not always sure how to accomplish it. The Violet's vision can be planned, organized, and implemented by the efficient Green.

It is possible for this couple to achieve and maintain harmony in their relationship. When the Violet sees a vision, the Green needs to support it and to develop a plan to manifest it. In other words, the Green needs to trust the Violet's vision. This can be challenging when a vision does not look practical. However, the Green has the capacity to make dreams practical and financially rewarding. In turn, the Violet needs to focus his attention so that he does not frustrate the Green's need for order and discipline. A Violet does not want to be limited or restricted, but he does need to stay focused. While a Violet has a tendency to be idealistic or want to do ten projects at once, a Green can help him stay on target and focus on one project at a time.

A Green-Violet relationship has great potential for being dynamic, powerful, harmonious, and productive provided the Violet maintains focus and equal power and the Green stays set on accomplishing her goals and feeling good about herself. It is a good relationship as long as both partners stay in power.

The following are examples of Green-Violet relationships: Lucille Ball (Yellow/Green) and Desi Arnaz (Violet with Yellow), Arnold Schwarzenegger (Yellow/Green) and Maria Shriver (Violet), Nancy (Green/Violet) and Ronald Reagan (Violet), Elizabeth Taylor (Blue/Violet) and Richard Burton (Green/Yellow), Katherine Hepburn (Violet/Yellow and Green) and Spencer Tracy (Yellow/Green), Tom Cruise (Violet/Yellow) and Nicole Kidman (Green with Violet).

Green and Lavender Relationship

For the most part, the Lavender's fantasies and creative aspects will fascinate a Green, but he would eventually become frustrated with the Lavender's inability to take action. Their partnership could be a productive one if the Green could take the Lavender's creative ideas and put them into practical use. If the Green does not expect intellectual challenges from the Lavender, but instead accepts her creative ideas as stimulation, the two can work together. If the Green becomes angry or frustrated, his energy would be too intense and threatening for the sensitive Lavender. She would retreat into her fantasy world to escape his fury.

In power, this pair could add balance to each other's lives. The Green could add a practical and logical aspect to the Lavender's ungrounded and lofty fantasy world; the Lavender could add a fun and creative aspect to the Green's work-oriented and often stressful life. The Green would have to find intellectual conversation with other friends, not from his Lavender cohort. In this relationship, the Green would be the domineering, controlling mate.

Generally, these two are not the best marriage partners for each other. The Green is usually frustrated by the Lavender's lack of ambition and concentration as well as by her unreliable behavior. The Lavender is usually intimidated and overwhelmed by the Green's intense power and drive. The Lavender's emotional needs would probably not be met by a Green, who is not relaxed and open with his emotions. He prefers to stay in control, which could leave the Lavender feeling alone and unfulfilled. They would be more successful as business partners than as loving, intimate, sexual mates.

Green and Crystal Relationship

See Crystal and Green Relationship.

Green and Indigo Relationship

See Indigo and Green Relationship.

CHAPTER EIGHT

relationships with the emotional life colors

BLUE

Blue and Red Relationship

See Red and Blue Relationship.

Blue and Orange Relationship

This relationship would probably drive a Blue crazy and suffocate an Orange. The Orange's daring, life-risking behavior would put the mothering Blue into a constant state of worry about the Orange's physical safety. Orange tends to be independent and adventurous. A Blue wants her mate at home, being loving and emotional with her. The solitary Orange tends to keep his emotions to himself.

An example of a Blue-Orange relationship is a loving, nurturing woman married to an adventure-seeking policeman. The Blue is never sure if the Orange will come home at night or if he will be shot in the line of duty. After awhile, the stress and emotional drain are more than the Blue can handle.

An Orange prefers physical activity; a Blue prefers spiritual and emotional work. The sturdy Orange likes to live in his physical body and challenge his environment. The spiritual Blue does not usually focus on her physical body. The Blue likes to discuss spiritual and emotional concepts; the Orange is not interested in these topics at all. The independent Orange doesn't choose to talk about his emotions; emotions are the Blue's life source.

An Orange is a loner. A Blue needs to be around people. A Blue is a giver; an Orange seems to be more concerned with himself than with his mate or family. An Orange can often take advantage of a Blue's generous nature.

This couple has very little in common. If they were married, the Blue's role would be to pack food for the Orange as he prepared to climb a mountain or jump from a plane. Not being a daredevil or even a physical person, the Blue would choose not to accompany her mate. Instead she would stay home alone and suffer until the Orange returned. The Blue would spend too much time alone if she were married to an Orange.

This relationship is generally not compatible. Blues and Oranges do not have the same interests in life. They do not associate with the same kinds of people, nor do they share the same life purpose.

Blue and Magenta Relationship

This relationship can be quite challenging for a Blue. A Magenta is usually too bizarre for her. Because the Blue is very loyal and committed in her relationships, however, she will usually continue to love the Magenta regardless of his outrageous behavior. She tends to stand by him and to make excuses for his behavior, despite her embarrassment. The Blue remains loyal to her mate even when he is unfaithful or hurts her in another way.

A problem this couple may face is that whereas a Blue is very monogamous, the Magenta looks at most relationships, even marriage, as brief encounters — something to experience, enjoy, learn from, and then move away from. This attitude can emotionally devastate a Blue.

The Magenta, although appreciative of the unconditional love he receives from the Blue, can also tend to take advantage of that love. The Magenta does not relate to the Blue's deep, emotional spiritual needs or belief system. Although the Magenta may not try to change a Blue's belief system or spirituality, he also may not understand or agree with them.

Both colors enjoy being around people; they frequently attend social functions together. The Magenta's deviant behavior at these functions, however, often embarrasses the Blue, causing her to feel unaccepted by her peers. Although a Blue enjoys other people, she also likes to spend time alone with her mate. She enjoys cuddling, hugging, and being introspective. These activities do not interest the Magenta. He instead prefers to be around people and challenge the status quo by being outrageous. Because the Magenta prefers to be independent and uncommitted, the Blue can tend to feel abandoned in this relationship. The Blue is better off with someone who can be more loyal, supportive, and committed. The Magenta is happier exploring many relationships and maintaining his freedom.

Blue and Yellow Relationship

See Yellow and Blue Relationship.

Blue and Logical Tan Relationship

See Logical Tan and Blue Relationship.

Blue and Environmental Tan Relationship

Although a relationship between a Blue and an Environmental Tan is common, it is not always a very compatible one. Their daily, practical needs are met, but their deepest needs and desires can be unfulfilled.

The loving Blue is attracted to the Environmental Tan's stable and responsible qualities. She sees in his quiet and calm

personality the willingness to commit to a long-term, serious relationship. The hopeful Blue perceives that this Tan is both reliable
and responsible. She knows she will be able to depend on him to
be a solid provider and a faithful mate. The Environmental Tan
sees that the Blue will be a warm, loving, and loyal mate. He is
drawn to her willingness to be supportive and her dedication to
their relationship. He knows he can trust her. This relationship
often reflects the typical marriage of the 1950s, in which Dad was
the financial provider and disciplinarian while Mom nurtured the
children and took care of the home.

Eventually, communication can become a problem with this
couple. The Blue wants to discuss feelings and to bond emotionally with her mate. The Environmental Tan has difficulty
expressing his feelings. He prefers to keep his emotions to himself
and resents any attempts to invade his privacy. When an
Environmental Tan is upset, he withdraws into the solitude of his
mind to figure out a solution. The sensitive Blue, who wants to
share every thought and feeling with her mate, feels shut off from
him. She interprets his actions as a personal rejection. For the
Blue, communication and sharing should be a major part of a
successful relationship. While the Blue loves affection, the reticent Environmental Tan is not openly demonstrative. Feeling this
is an indication she is unattractive and undesirable, the Blue
retreats in sorrow to her room.

The spiritual Blue enjoys sharing thoughts about love, God,
religion, emotions, and relationships. The pragmatic Environmental Tan is more concerned with physical reality — economics,
government, data, logic, and tangible substances. These two do
not usually share the same basic beliefs about life.

The Environmental Tan believes that the Blue is too emotional and vulnerable. He cannot relate to her frequent torrent of
tears and her moods. He wants a partner who will quietly stand
beside him and not make emotional demands on him. He needs
his privacy. He also needs a mate who is practical and can deal

with the necessities of life. A Blue is not always practical; her intuition and her emotions rule her.

Although their basic needs for security, trust, loyalty, stability, and commitment will be met, some of their deeper needs may remain unfulfilled. The Blue's quest for emotional bonding and a deep, spiritual connection is often unrequited with this mate.

The Environmental Tan will experience frustration over the continuous emotional insecurities and neediness expressed by the out-of-power Blue. When he sees that the Blue is hurt and disappointed, he assumes he has failed one more time. He frequently feels guilty and inadequate. He feels that being an intelligent person, a committed partner, and a dependable provider should be enough to make his mate appreciate him.

While in power this couple has the capability of creating a balance for each other. The Blue provides the emotional nurturing while the Environmental Tan keeps the relationship grounded and practical. However, they usually do not relate well to each other's inner needs.

Blue and Sensitive Tan Relationship

This couple is quite compatible. Both colors require emotional bonding, stability, and commitment. The Sensitive Tan can add emotional stability to a Blue's life. Out of power, a Blue has a tendency to become moody and experience euphoric highs and severe depressions. A Sensitive Tan is much calmer with his emotional reactions. Both are very loving and nurturing people. While the Sensitive Tan is much more practical in the relationship, the Blue provides the emotional release. The Sensitive Tan gives the love and emotional bonding that the Blue so desperately desires. Although tending to keep his emotions to himself, the Sensitive Tan is not opposed to expressing how he feels to the loving Blue. The Sensitive Tan, however, does not want to discuss his emotions all the time. The Blue must be understanding and learn how to become more balanced with her emotional needs.

Both personalities love people. The Sensitive Tan, however, requires much more time alone. He needs peace, quiet, and order in his life.

The Sensitive Tan may have a difficult time understanding the Blue's emotional depth or the extent of her emotional depressions. The Blue's emotional reactions are not usually logical; consequently, the Sensitive Tan does not always understand the causes behind her irrational and erratic behavior. A Blue may experience hurt feelings because the Sensitive Tan is not always emotionally accessible to her. He is not quite as free expressing his feelings. However, the Sensitive Tan is usually gentle, calm, and realistic enough to help a Blue out of her depression.

Even though both colors are highly intuitive, the Sensitive Tan is usually able to produce facts and information to support his intuition. A Sensitive Tan can add practicality to the Blue's spiritual idealism. The Sensitive Tan can take care of running a home or supporting a family while the Blue is free to be the loving nurturer of the family. Both of these individuals believe in long-term commitments, and so this relationship has strong potential for fulfillment and success. If this couple marries, their relationship will probably last for life.

Blue and Abstract Tan Relationship

See Abstract Tan and Blue Relationship.

Blue and Green Relationship

A Blue and a Green are not usually compatible. They have strong conflicting priorities and methods of processing life. The workaholic Green tends to put his career before his relationship, which the Blue interprets as a personal rejection. The loving Blue feels that people, love, family, and relationships are much more important than money, possessions, and reaching the top of the corporate ladder. Although the Blue enters the relationship supporting the Green's ambitions and goals, she eventually becomes hurt and resentful when she learns that money and business are consistently his priorities. The Blue can even become a workaholic herself trying to win acceptance and approval from her Green mate. She soon learns, however, that no matter how much they accomplish or how hard they work, the Green still wants more.

The Blue's emotional needs are usually unfulfilled. The driven and ambitious Green has more important things to do. He does not usually relate to her emotional needs. Although the Green acknowledges that the Blue is more giving and patient than he is, he often loses respect for her because he considers her to be an emotional doormat. The trusting Blue is easily taken advantage of. She typically sacrifices her needs to help others. The Green is usually more self-centered and demanding. If these two go to a restaurant and the Green is dissatisfied with the quality of his meal, he will send the food back and demand better service. The apologetic Blue is embarrassed by the Green's behavior. The Green is too intolerant, outspoken, and unforgiving for her comfort.

The Blue's sensitivity and moodiness can irritate the powerful and self-controlled Green. He believes that such displays of emotions show weakness of character. The Blue, who craves warmth and affection, is frequently disappointed by a Green's aloof and emotionally disciplined behavior.

Both personalities value commitment and endurance. However, while the Blue will continue to hold on through emotional pain and suffering, hoping that some day her patience will pay off, the Green tends to be more logical. If he doesn't see the potential value in a relationship, he will leave it.

If the Green can learn to balance his life so that he spends time with his mate as well as with his business, then the appreciative Blue will lovingly support him in reaching his goals. When a Green is frustrated, he can either coldly and abruptly withdraw or become verbally abusive. Either behavior devastates the sensitive Blue. The Green must learn to communicate his feelings in a less hostile manner. The Blue, meanwhile, who can easily be hurt by his sharp tongue, needs to learn not to take the Green's outbursts so personally. His abrasive behavior usually signals frustration with himself rather than with his mate. The Blue can instead learn to leave him alone until the Green figures out a solution by himself or until he asks her for assistance.

The Green must learn to appreciate the Blue's ability to be loving and generous rather than criticize her for it. If the Green can become more emotionally available and less judgmental, he will have a very loving and devoted Blue mate. If the Blue can fill more of her own emotional needs, she can grow intellectually with the Green as well as be financially supported in style.

Although any relationship can work if there is enough love, commitment, and determination between the two partners, this relationship would require a lot of effort to be successful. Patience, compromise, education, and understanding are necessary components in this relationship. If these two are willing to work against the odds, they each have the capability to learn and grow in this relationship. If, however, they do not want to work quite so hard, other partners are more compatible and can better fulfill their emotional and intellectual needs.

An example of a Blue-Green relationship is Elizabeth Taylor (Blue/Violet) and Richard Burton (Green/Yellow).

Blue and Blue Relationship

A Blue can bond emotionally very well with another Blue. Two Blues often experience an instant connection. They tend to think and feel the same way. Blues can be best friends within their relationship. They can cry together over the same romantic movies. They understand each other's emotional needs, trust each other's intuitive thoughts, and share each other's spiritual beliefs.

Blues are very moral, monogamous, and loyal, so extramarital affairs would probably never happen in this relationship. In addition, neither wants to hurt the other by leaving. Although divorce is also rare for them, if it occurs, Blues would probably remain good friends throughout their lives, staying connected on some level by writing, calling, or visiting. Blues tend to put a lot of energy into their relationships; consequently, they tend to stay in relationship for a long time.

Out of power, Blues are very moody and tend to take things personally. A harmless comment can send a Blue into an emotional tailspin. Because they can each be so emotionally vulnerable and needy, they require constant emotional reinforcement. Fortunately, Blues are typically available to each other, so loving support and affection usually flow generously between them. Blues understand each other and are willing to lovingly fill each other's needs.

A potential problem can arise when one Blue plays the victim so often that the other Blue tires of having to take care of her. If they both play the victim at the same time, both will want to be rescued. The partner who rescues will then become the martyr and the other will feel guilty. A vicious cycle of victim, martyr, and guilt ensues. A Blue's natural weapon of guilt is very effective when used on another Blue.

Both Blues need to receive as well as they give. When one Blue attempts to give to the other, the other must learn to receive so the first feels fulfilled. Because Blues usually feel guilty asking for what they want, the other's intuitive abilities come in handy. Blues are able to know each other's needs without verbal communication. These two connect easily from the heart.

To stay balanced and in harmony, two Blues both need to realize that they are loved, that they do not need each other's constant reassurance to reinforce a sense of value or worthiness. They must both learn to love themselves as much as they love each other. Because Blues emotionally and intuitively understand each other and are both willing to give love, they tend to create very harmonious relationships together.

Blue and Violet Relationship

See Violet and Blue Relationship.

Blue and Lavender Relationship

Although both colors are very sensitive, loving, considerate, and compassionate, neither wants to be responsible for supporting a home. The responsibility would end up with the Blue because she is the ultimate doer and mother. The Lavender wants someone to take care of him so he can live effortlessly in a fantasy world. The Blue, who usually enjoys being needed, ends up feeling more like she is a mother than a wife. The Blue wants the Lavender to relate with her on a deep, emotional level. However, the Lavender is intimidated by such intense emotions, so he tends to withdraw from her.

The Blue tends to nurture, love, and support the Lavender. She is usually accepting and forgiving enough to let him do what makes him happy; however, her needs are not always met. The Blue wants emotional commitment and stability; the Lavender does not exhibit those traits. The Blue, when she is out of power, is filled with self-pity and plays the victim or martyr, which is too intense and serious for the Lavender. The Lavender usually escapes into a fantasy world, leaving the Blue with no one to listen to her or support her. The Lavender does not relate to the Blue's heavy, emotional behavior.

In a marriage, the Blue cannot usually depend on the Lavender for the emotional security and depth she needs. The Lavender can eventually feel trapped or smothered by the Blue. These two personalities are more emotionally compatible as best friends than they are as mates.

Blue and Crystal Relationship

See Crystal and Blue Relationship.

Blue and Indigo Relationship

This can be a very loving and nurturing relationship. A Blue is one color that can understand the Indigo's spirituality. A Blue also wants peace, love, and harmony on the planet, just as the Indigo does. A Blue is able to be very loving and accepting of the Indigo's need to live with higher ideals.

The Indigo needs people who can understand and support his ways, not reject, criticize, or try to stop him. The Indigo treasures the spiritual understanding and unconditional love he receives from the Blue. The Blue can often find herself taking care of the childlike Indigo, who is frequently misunderstood and sometimes frightened. She has compassion for the Indigo's plight.

Because Blues and Indigos are both intuitive, they appreciate each other's inner knowing, and neither asks for supporting scientific facts or details. The Blue also appreciates the depth to which the Indigo bonds emotionally, soul to soul, with his mate. Both personalities are very loving, warm, and committed in their relationships.

One of their few problems may be when the Indigo loses his center and withdraws. This is frustrating for a Blue, who wants to maintain emotional communication with her mate. The Blue's loving and patient gentleness can usually bring the Indigo out of himself and back to center.

It is challenging for the Indigo to relate to a Blue who is out of power because victims, martyrs, and self-pity are concepts he does not understand or tolerate. A Blue tends to use guilt to manipulate people. The Indigo does not respond to guilt or any other kind of manipulation. Communication can fall apart at this point. Both the Blue and the Indigo must stay in power as much as possible for this relationship to reach its fullest potential.

A Blue naturally wants to nurture and support the people she loves. The Indigo thrives on a Blue's emotional support and loving strength. An emotionally balanced Blue can also help facilitate the Indigo's way of living spiritually.

An example of a Blue and Indigo relationship is Michael Jackson (Indigo) with the mother of his children, Debbie Rowe (Blue/Yellow).

VIOLET
Violet and Red Relationship

This combination would be very interesting. With the Violet's strong leadership ability and her ability to see the future, she would give direction and vision to the Red's ability to bring ideas into physical form. With the Violet's head in the clouds and the Red's ability to keep his feet on the ground, this couple could create a good balance for each other. The Violet's charisma and dynamic energy would be fascinating and attractive to a Red, usually causing him to be sexually drawn to the Violet. A Violet is fascinated by the Red's ability to get things done.

Both personalities tend to be passionate, with a healthy sexual appetite. A Violet is sexual, but sex tends to be a universal, spiritual experience for her. For a Red, sex tends to be a very physical, lustful experience. Both would have their unique experiences while making love.

The downside of this relationship is that the Red may consider the Violet's visions to be unrealistic dreams and have a hard time respecting them. The Red likes to see and touch physical reality. Plans must make sense to him. A Violet tends to live in the future, seeing upcoming trends. A Red tends to live in the moment, the here-and-now. A Violet is often into ethereal ideas and concepts. The Red may mistrust what the Violet sees.

The Violet loves music and traveling. The Red is much more grounded and practical, preferring the comfort of home while working on realistic and applicable projects. Both individuals tend to be independent. The Violet enjoys the attention of others;

however, the Red is more of a loner. A Red tends to want to stay on the fringes at parties. Only when he knows people well will he take part in the conversation, provided the conversation is practical. A Violet's conversation tends to be about lofty ideals, spiritual possibilities, and saving the planet, which do not interest a Red. They seem impractical to him. Their conversation would be quite diverse, with neither person understanding or appreciating the other person's point of view.

A Violet out of power can become pompous or arrogant, and she may try to tell the Red what to do. This would not go over well with the Red, who would abruptly tell the Violet what he thought. Although the Violet may respect his honesty, she may also find his abrupt attitude abrasive. A Violet is usually very accepting of other people. A Red is much less flexible. His behavior may appear to be too rigid to a Violet.

The charisma, power, and sexual energy of a Violet and a Red can be well matched. However, their belief systems — one being spiritual and futuristic, the other being physically oriented in the here-and-now — can be quite different. There is also disparity in their emotional display. A Violet has great emotional depth and tends to be expressive. A Red has emotional power, but tends to keep it inside until he has an emotional outburst. If the Violet is able to lift herself above the Red's temper and see the bigger picture, when the Red has calmed down the two can be compatible again.

If these two can get along with each other, the Red has the power and physical energy to carry out the Violet's visions. The Red tends to take action; the Violet continues to dream up ideas. This couple can be well matched and compatible, provided they do not discuss spiritual beliefs or their concepts about reality.

Violet and Orange Relationship

See Orange and Violet Relationship.

Violet and Magenta Relationship

The Violet and the Magenta usually fascinate each other. The Violet's futuristic vision inspires the Magenta's quick and creative mind. Although the Violet can often see an extraordinary invention in the future, he does not always know how to create it. The Magenta can take the Violet's vision and create the invention using materials at hand.

Each color needs to respect the individuality and independence of the other. The Violet can be more accepting of the Magenta's outrageous behavior and attitudes than most Life Colors. The Violet can also find the Magenta's behavior quite bizarre. However, because people often find the Violet's ideas and visions unrealistic, he can relate to the Magenta.

It is possible for this couple to experience power struggles when each wants to go in a different direction, which could cause them to drift apart. This is fine if they are friends, but not if they are married. Neither wants to be dominated by the other or give up dreams. Because both colors enjoy being the center of attention, there can also be competition between them at social gatherings.

This couple can enjoy an exciting sexual relationship. The Violet and the Magenta both like options when it comes to sexual partners, so an open marriage could be quite possible in this relationship.

A Violet enjoys his world on a spiritual and emotional level; the Magenta experiences her world on a physical, tangible level. The Magenta does not share a Violet's desire to save the planet, but she does not usually question him or try to prevent him from accomplishing this task. A Violet is not interested in shocking people's moral standards or social behavior. He is more interested in inspiring and leading people to a better life. The Magenta is more excited about shaking up people and helping them realize their own unique styles and beliefs. A Violet envisions people living in harmony on the planet. Although both want people to be individuals and to live their individual desires and dreams, a

306

Violet also tends to see the bigger, universal picture and how everything works together. The Magenta tends to focus on what is in front of her and how she can make it unique and different. She tends to live more in the moment. A Violet tends to focus more on the future.

The Violet's visionary capabilities and his ability to keep moving forward fascinate a Magenta and keep her attention for much longer than most of the colors are capable of doing. A Violet tends to take his mission on the planet very seriously; however, the Magenta chooses not to take anything seriously. This relationship, oddly enough, has more potential of succeeding than many relationships in the aura family. As long as they do not compete for attention all the time, and as long as each allows the other the freedom to live life the way he or she chooses, this pair is compatible.

Violet and Yellow Relationship

See Yellow and Violet Relationship.

Violet and Logical Tan Relationship

See Logical Tan and Violet Relationship.

Violet and Environmental Tan Relationship

See Environmental Tan and Violet Relationship.

Violet and Sensitive Tan Relationship

This is a potentially strong relationship. The Violet provides the inspiration and vision to keep the relationship moving forward, while the Sensitive Tan supports and nurtures the Violet. Problems can arise when the Violet sees further than the Sensitive Tan is willing to go. Often the Violet has great ideas and business plans, but the Sensitive Tan fears taking a financial risk based on the Violet's unsubstantiated visions and dreams. However, when the Sensitive Tan feels that their combined income is stable and secure, she is more willing to allow the Violet freedom to experiment with his dreams.

The Violet's emotional depth and passion can sometimes overwhelm the shy and reticent Sensitive Tan. A Sensitive Tan has the ability, however, to adjust and even to expand her emotional boundaries to some degree. A Sensitive Tan does not always understand the Violet's desire to save the planet or to reach humanity. Although the risks involved in his vision may frighten her, the dedicated and loyal Sensitive Tan will tend to stand by her mate.

While the Violet wants to be the center of attention, the Sensitive Tan is content to stay in the background and emotionally support him. Consequently, these two do not compete with each other. Violets are natural leaders; most Sensitive Tans are natural followers.

If the Sensitive Tan criticizes or mistrusts the Violet, he may become unsure of his visions and thereby become scattered, insecure, and confused. The Sensitive Tan will then have to work even harder to encourage the shaken Violet to produce or to move forward with his career. The Violet, in turn, must learn to be patient and understanding with his Sensitive Tan mate. The Sensitive Tan does not see the bigger picture as easily as he does. She needs time to see the logic behind his dream and the steps that are necessary to fulfill it.

The Sensitive Tan can provide the stability for the relationship and also fill in the necessary details to accomplish the dream. When the Violet wants to jump from step one to fifty, it is more beneficial for the Sensitive Tan to help him plan the steps to get there rather than to oppose his ideas and dreams. This pair will accomplish more if they work together.

Violet and Abstract Tan Relationship

This relationship has potential for success, because the Violet is one of the few colors that is not concerned about the order in which the Abstract Tan finishes her tasks. Both individuals have a love for humanity and a love of knowledge. They enjoy searching for information that will unlock the doors of the universe. The Abstract Tan prefers to contemplate and discuss universal concepts; the Violet needs to take action and actualize the ideas. The Violet's dynamic energy often inspires the Abstract Tan to find ways to manifest her ideas. The Violet can see his visions, but dislikes taking care of all the details along the way. The Abstract Tan does not mind taking care of details as long as she can do them in random order. Taking care of details makes the Abstract Tan a good partner for the Violet.

At social gatherings, the outgoing and friendly Abstract Tan loves talking with a variety of people. She learns interesting and valuable bits of information this way. The Violet, on the other hand, prefers to be the center of attention. He can quickly become bored if the conversation is not meaningful or interesting to him. The Violet prefers to discuss world affairs, politics, spirituality, universal principles, the media, travel, music, the environment, or other topics that address the current transformation of consciousness on the planet.

The Violet wants passion and emotional depth from his mate; however, the Abstract Tan is often overwhelmed by such intensity. Therefore, the Violet can be somewhat disappointed by the emotional qualities of this relationship.

If these two are out of power, their relationship could be chaotic. Both individuals can see the entire picture at one time, yet they can't always figure out the steps involved in accomplishing the project. They can both become scattered and overwhelmed, and they must be careful not to feed off each other's confusion. An out-of-power Violet can quickly become intolerant of his confusion as well as the Abstract Tan's unfocused behavior. He can become frustrated, critical, and impatient. The Abstract Tan, feeling his disapproval, can withdraw from him. She will detach herself from her emotions so she will be safe from the

Violet's judgments. They then lose their connection with each other and the relationship will begin to suffer.

In power, both personalities are accepting of each other's shortcomings. Consequently, if they both stay in power, they can be a good team. The Violet can be the dynamic, visionary leader; the bright and perceptive Abstract Tan can take care of the details. She can also help the Violet maintain an optimistic faith in humanity. With their combined humanitarian idealism, this pair can help to change the planet.

Violet and Green Relationship

See Green and Violet Relationship.

Violet and Blue Relationship

A relationship between a Violet and a Blue has great potential. Blues have so much love to give that they can overwhelm most Life Colors with their affections. Violets, however, love being the center of attention and are capable of great emotional depth, so this relationship can be very compatible. While the Blue gives all her love and affection to the Violet, the Violet appreciates the attention and returns love to her. A Violet can be very demonstrative with his affections. A Violet is deep, compassionate, and understanding enough to allow a Blue to be overly emotional.

Both colors desire to help people. The loving Blue finds satisfaction in supporting the Violet's vision to save the world. When the Violet envisions a grand dream, the Blue, who trusts her inner knowing, can usually sense whether the Violet's dream is right. They can be a powerful team when the Blue supports and nurtures the Violet's dreams. Although some Life Colors, such as Green, tend to challenge the Violet's visions, the Blue usually encourages him. Both the Blue and the Violet personalities are intuitive. Spiritual growth and understanding are priorities for them.

A Blue loves the open, emotional communication that flows from a Violet. A Violet is willing to share his feelings with the devoted Blue. A Violet will openly reassure her that she is loved. A Violet is one of the only personalities who understands the Blue's emotional depth and insecurities and is willing to give her enough sincere love to bring her back to her center.

When a Violet becomes scattered and overwhelmed, a Blue usually comes to the rescue. When the Violet takes on too many projects, the Blue will jump in and help him. When the Violet loses his direction, the Blue intuitively helps the Violet find his center and refocus his energy.

One potential problem is that an out-of-power Violet can become self-centered, egocentric, and arrogant. A Blue, who tends to be so giving and loving that she can turn into a doormat, can be taken advantage of. A Violet's selfish and abusive behavior can hurt and confuse the loyal Blue. Her friends are often dismayed by how much emotional abuse she will take from the Violet because she loves him so much.

Another potential problem is in their sexual relationship. The Blue is very loyal, monogamous, and committed, and she desires the same commitment from her mate. A Violet, among all the Life Colors, has the most potential for being unfaithful in his relationships. A Violet is very sexually attractive; he radiates a sexual energy. If his appetite is not fulfilled at home, and often even when it is, he tends to stray. This, of course, can devastate a Blue.

For the most part, however, Blues and Violets are highly compatible. Both are spiritual, loving, emotional, and generous toward other people. A Blue desires a mate she can deeply and emotionally bond with. A Violet has the potential of creating this passionate bonding. These personalities are capable of fulfilling many of each other's needs. They are also able to help each other stay balanced and in power.

An example of a Blue-Violet relationship is Meg Ryan (Blue/Yellow) and Dennis Quaid (Yellow/Violet).

Violet and Violet Relationship

A partnership between two Violets can be extremely powerful and dynamic. When two Violets are in the same room sharing visions, the high energy in the room is compelling. Together they can inspire and empower each other's visions. With their strong energy, they could accomplish almost anything. Violets are also very sexually compatible. The sexual chemistry between them can be passionate and electrifying. They are drawn to each other like magnets. The chemistry can almost be overwhelming.

There are a few potentially negative aspects of this relationship. Because both enjoy being the center of attention, they can become quite competitive. They may each want to live a different powerful vision, which means they may go in separate directions. They can also become scattered as they try to accomplish too many projects at the same time, creating little opportunity for them to devote time to each other. (It is very common for two Violets in the entertainment world to be married yet live busy and separate lives.) Violets are also prone to extramarital affairs.

Another potential problem is that although they are both great at seeing future projects, neither is efficient at planning all the details. If at least one stays focused and in power, the projects will be completed.

For the most part, a Violet-Violet relationship is dynamic, charismatic, and powerful. They are both passionate about music, sex, traveling, and inspiring humanity. They usually have many interests in common. They must make sure they spend time together, however. By becoming too busy, they risk traveling in separate directions.

These teams are evidence of the dynamic power of Violet-Violet relationships: Cher and Sonny Bono; Steven Spielberg and George Lucas (the *Star Wars* movies); and John Lennon, Paul McCartney, George Harrison, and Ringo Starr (the Beatles). Coincidentally, each of these personalities is a Violet/Yellow. Comic Relief, the charity event for the homeless, was driven by the combined powerful energy of three Violet/Yellows — Robin Williams, Whoopi Goldberg, and Billy Crystal.

Violet and Lavender Relationship

See Lavender and Violet Relationship.

Violet and Crystal Relationship

See Crystal and Violet Relationship.

Violet and Indigo Relationship

With his visionary abilities, the Violet is able to relate to the Indigo's New Age beliefs. The Violet can see the future the Indigo intuitively feels is coming. (Indigos appear to be surrounding themselves with Violets who have the leadership ability, power, and strength to clear the way for the Indigo age.) The Violet clears the path, leading the way and keeping the Indigo safe from people who are not supportive or in harmony with her spiritual ways. The Violet also believes in the same higher principles the Indigo does. This relationship has tremendous potential, provided the Violet does not become so overpowering and dictatorial that the Indigo ends up rebelling or leaving him.

There are only a few areas in which conflict could arise. The two have different social needs. The Indigo prefers to connect with a few intimate friends, bonding on a soul-to-soul basis with each. At times a Violet loves performing and surrounding himself with crowds. Even though the Violet wants to be the center of attention, there is no competition because the Indigo prefers to stay quiet. A Violet, out of power and wanting to be the center of attention, will try to dominate the Indigo. The Indigo, however, will not be dominated, controlled, or manipulated in any way. This could cause power struggles and a strained relationship. If they both stay centered, they will accept and support each other.

For the most part these two create a highly spiritual and

visionary team. Both have a curiosity about other cultures. They enjoy traveling. They have great compassion for people everywhere. What they sense and see as higher truth can broaden the horizons of many people. The Violet and the Indigo both search for truth and higher consciousness. In power, they both have an inner sense of what is moral. This team works well together with common goals. They both want peace, compassion, and spiritual enlightenment on the planet.

An example of an Indigo-Violet relationship is Michael Jackson (Indigo) and Lisa Marie Presley (Yellow/Violet).

LAVENDER

Lavender and Red Relationship

Lavenders and Reds have absolutely nothing in common. Lavenders exist in fantasy worlds. They are not interested in physical reality. They live in their imagination more than in their bodies. Reds enjoy physical existence and expressing themselves through their bodies.

Lavenders are too fragile and childlike for the volatile and lustful Reds. Reds relate to power, vitality, strength, and courage. They love moving heavy mass in the physical world, working with the earth, and expressing their sensuality. Lavenders love fantasy, spirituality, sensitivity, and creativity. These colors would not know how to communicate with each other. They have no interests or beliefs in common, nor are they assertive conversationalists. Lavenders would not be able to relate to the Reds' powerful and lustful personality. The Reds would think that the Lavenders should be locked up in mental institutions.

Lavender and Orange Relationship

Lavenders and Oranges have absolutely nothing in common. Lavenders live in fantasy worlds and are not willing to spend much time in physical reality. Oranges live completely in the physical environment. Understanding why Oranges would risk their lives or face physically dangerous challenges is beyond the Lavenders' comprehension. The Lavenders prefer to escape into a fantasy world, and not take on physical challenges. They are much too sensitive, vulnerable, and mild for the Oranges' physical prowess and daring. Lavenders' are much too ethereal and unrealistic for the grounded, physical Oranges.

An Orange may be temporarily fascinated with the childlike Lavender, but this fascination would quickly pass. The Orange would end up ridiculing the impractical Lavender. Both personalities also have a great need to spend time alone, so neither would tend to instigate this relationship. The ungrounded Lavender often needs someone to take care of her. An Orange prefers to be free from relationship responsibilities.

These colors would rarely be in the same environment, so there is very little chance of their meeting. If they did, neither would understand the other.

Lavender and Magenta Relationship

See Magenta and Lavender Relationship.

Lavender and Yellow Relationship

See Yellow and Lavender Relationship.

Lavender and Logical Tan Relationship

See Logical Tan and Lavender Relationship.

Lavender and Environmental Tan Relationship

Occasionally, the Lavender and the Environmental Tan provide a good balance for each other. The Lavender helps to soften the Environmental Tan, and the Environmental Tan adds logic and stability to the Lavender's life. For the most part, however, these two frustrate each other. An Environmental Tan is too grounded, practical, and emotionally inflexible for the Lavender. An Environmental Tan judges the Lavender as being unrealistic and irresponsible. He doesn't relate to the fantasy world in which she lives. He prefers three-dimensional reality. The Lavender would fascinate the Environmental Tan for a short time, and then he would expect her to become more practical and realistic. The Environmental Tan usually tries to clip the wings of the Lavender.

The Lavender does not find any joy or excitement in an Environmental Tan's lifestyle. She is not able to explore life emotionally or spiritually when she is with him. She becomes bored with his inability or unwillingness to see life from other perspectives.

This couple has very little in common. Neither is able to relate to the other's perspective of the world.

Lavender and Sensitive Tan Relationship

See Sensitive Tan and Lavender Relationship.

Lavender and Abstract Tan Relationship

Although both are sensitive and kind individuals, this pair would not be able to take care of each other or maintain an intimate relationship. The Lavender spends most of her time daydreaming or fantasizing in her own world. She is not present in physical reality long enough to take care of household responsibilities. The Abstract Tan is just too busy and too disorganized to remember to pay the bills. He is usually too scattered and confused to be responsible for the ungrounded Lavender. Each hopes the other will take care of everything. Consequently, nothing is accomplished.

Neither personality is comfortable with emotions; as a result, this pair does not develop an emotionally intimate or bonded relationship. Although the Abstract Tan likes to share his thoughts and philosophies with others, these two rarely understand each other's language. The Abstract Tan is often fascinated by the Lavender's descriptions of other realities, but his already scattered mental processes can be blown out trying to understand her.

Both individuals are better off with partners who can add stability and focus to their lives. They need to be with people who are willing to take care of them.

Lavender and Green Relationship

See Green and Lavender Relationship.

Lavender and Blue Relationship

See Blue and Lavender Relationship.

Lavender and Violet Relationship

A relationship between the Lavender and the Violet is highly compatible. The Violet is the powerful, independent force who goes into the world to take care of business; the Lavender is free to stay at home and create a loving home environment. The Lavender sometimes adds her creative ideas to the Violet's visions. A Violet has great emotional depth and when in his power can be very accepting of others. He can allow the Lavender the freedom to spend time in her fantasy world. He is much more understanding of her behavior than many Life Colors are. There is no competition between these two. The Violet wants to be the leader and the center of attention; the Lavender shies away from attention and responsibility. The Lavender appreciates that the Violet takes charge.

A problem arises if the Lavender spends too much time in her fantasy world when the Violet needs communication and emotional depth from her. The Violet enjoys companionship, but the Lavender is not always available to him. Nor is she able to lend much guidance when the Violet becomes scattered. Another complaint the Violet may have is the Lavender's inability to make money. As long as the Violet accepts the role of moneymaker, however, they will not experience conflict.

A Violet seems to have much stronger sexual needs than the Lavender does. However, the Lavender can usually handle a

Violet's sexual power and chemistry. The Lavender merely moves into her fantasies when she is with him.

When they are in power, the Lavender and the Violet can complement each other's lives. The Lavender adds fantasy, lightness, and fun to the Violet's intensity and power. The Violet adds power, depth, and progressive movement to the sometimes ungrounded and scattered Lavender. The Lavender adds creativity and imagination to the Violet's visions; the Violet can actualize the Lavender's fantasies. Neither demands a great deal of time or attention from the other. These colors are emotionally and spiritually compatible as long as the Lavender spends enough time in her body to be a companion to the Violet. They both allow each other the space needed to explore their feelings, fantasies, and visions.

Lavender and Lavender Relationship

Two Lavenders together is a case of "nobody minding the store." Although sharing stories of wonderful adventures in other dimensions can be enjoyable for these two, their irresponsibility can get them into trouble. Neither wants to stay focused in this reality long enough to take care of everyday responsibilities. Each looks to the other to take care of business. Each can become disappointed and even resentful if the other doesn't fulfill the role of caretaker and provider.

Lavenders fare better in relationships with mates who are reliable, responsible, and action oriented — this relationship gives Lavenders the freedom to travel on inner journeys. Although Lavenders are sensitive and gentle toward each other and they allow each other time to be alone, they need mates who can provide them with some sense of stability, not add to their ungrounded and flighty world.

Lavender and Crystal Relationship

Both personalities tend to be too withdrawn and emotionally unavailable to have an intimate relationship with each other.

They spend too much time in their own worlds to effectively communicate with each other. Neither would have a grounded or practical influence upon the other.

Although both are gentle, sensitive, and intuitive beings who enjoy the fanciful things in life, neither is powerful or ambitious enough to deal with the real world. Neither wants a stable job to support the home or enjoys taking care of day-to-day responsibilities. Their home environment would be quiet because both would be meditating or exploring inner worlds. However, paying the rent on their peaceful home could be a problem.

A Lavender and a Crystal are safe with each other because neither makes strong demands on the other or is looking for an intense love affair. Neither intimidates the other. They appreciate each other's gentle nature. They can be quiet and considerate roommates; they don't have much to offer each other, however, in an intimate marriage relationship.

Lavender and Indigo Relationship

See Indigo and Lavender Relationship.

CRYSTAL

Crystal and Red Relationship

See Red and Crystal Relationship.

Crystal and Orange Relationship

See Orange and Crystal Relationship.

Crystal and Magenta Relationship

The Crystal and the Magenta are not very compatible. A Crystal requires calm and gentle behavior from her mate. The Magenta's behavior is much too offensive and bizarre for the sensitive, quiet Crystal. If the Magenta discovered that the Crystal does not like bugs, the Magenta would probably bring home giant bugs and decorate the house with them, just to shake up the Crystal. This attempt at humor would eventually shatter the Crystal.

A Crystal's priority is to get in touch with her spirituality and her intuitive understanding. The Magenta has no time or desire to deal with the spiritual level. He would become easily bored with a Crystal, although at first he would be tempted to figure out what makes her tick.

Excitement, crowds, and parties are what thrill the Magenta. A Crystal, on the other hand, prefers a peaceful, calm home environment, a healing atmosphere, and a few close friends. The Crystal would be overwhelmed by the Magenta's outgoing and outlandish behavior. The Magenta would eventually become indifferent and uninterested in a Crystal's point of view. These two would rarely be in the same places, let alone marry or have friends in common. Neither personality would understand the other.

Crystal and Yellow Relationship

A Crystal and a Yellow are both very sensitive, loving personalities. What these two have in common is their natural healing abilities. They both enjoy healing, working in gardens, and connecting with nature. They are both physically and psychically sensitive through touch. Both the Crystal and the Yellow understand the need to have quiet time alone.

Problems arise, however, because a Yellow is often too energetic, much like a rambunctious young child, and can upset the Crystal's delicate nature. While the Yellow wants to be outside playing and having fun, a Crystal wants to be quietly meditating and reflecting on life. A Crystal is soft, gentle, and introspective; a Yellow is more fun loving and outgoing. After awhile, the Yellow may become disinterested in the Crystal's need to have peace and quiet. A Yellow needs physical activity and play. Although a

Crystal enjoys the Yellow's natural enthusiasm and carefree attitude, eventually his energy would exhaust her and she would need to withdraw from him.

Neither of these childlike personalities wants to work or be responsible for paying the bills. Although they would be kind and sensitive to each other, they wouldn't be grounded enough to support each other financially. Each would also tend to shy away from the responsibility and commitment of marriage. They would prefer to stay innocent and childlike throughout their lives. Both would be better off finding partners who would support them financially and be more emotionally stable.

Crystal and Logical Tan Relationship

Because both the Crystal and the Logical Tan prefer to keep their thoughts and feelings to themselves, they tend to be separate from each other. There is usually very little communication between these two.

A Crystal is usually too fragile for a Logical Tan, whose rigid rules, standards, and beliefs are too limiting for her. A Logical Tan has difficulty understanding the Crystal's spiritual personality as well as her need to be introspective and commune with God. A Crystal seems like a piece of fine china to a Logical Tan.

A Crystal needs to trust and bond emotionally with her mate. A Logical Tan does not tend to bond emotionally with anyone. He prefers instead to have an intellectual companion, someone he can discuss factual, logical ideas with. Sharing emotional intimacies is threatening for a Logical Tan. A Crystal has no desire to discuss the problems of the world or the current economic conditions, whereas these are areas that interest a Logical Tan. A Crystal prefers instead to spend her time and energy contemplating spiritual ideas and the purpose of life. A Logical Tan is much too analytical and logical to relate to the spiritual Crystal.

If these two were to marry, they would spend most of their time in separate rooms at opposite ends of the house. Although this could make them very compatible roommates, it does not do much to create an intimate and loving marriage.

If this couple can stay in power, however, it is possible for them to provide an interesting balance for each other. The Logical Tan can provide a stable environment and financial security for the Crystal. The Crystal can bring gentleness and beauty into the Logical Tan's often logical and mechanical world. The Crystal can inspire this Tan to consider inner and spiritual ideas rather than focusing only on logic and data. The Logical Tan can help the Crystal to stay more grounded and to feel safer in the physical world.

If they slipped out of power, they would probably withdraw from each other, making it difficult to maintain or continue a relationship.

Crystal and Environmental Tan Relationship

See Environmental Tan and Crystal Relationship.

Crystal and Sensitive Tan Relationship

A Crystal and a Sensitive Tan are very sensitive, nurturing, compassionate, and quiet people. They both prefer to keep their feelings and thoughts to themselves. Because they are calm, loving, and caring, they tend to be gentle with each other. A Sensitive Tan often wishes that the Crystal were a bit more practical and logical, but she is loving and accepting enough to let the Crystal be who he is.

One challenge for this couple is that a Sensitive Tan, with her Blue aspect, needs an emotional commitment from her mate. A Crystal, however, does not always want someone depending on him or turning to him for emotional support. If a Crystal withdraws too often from meeting his mate's emotional needs, the Sensitive Tan can feel abandoned. Nevertheless, if the Sensitive Tan can stay balanced and secure, understanding that the Crystal is giving as much as he can, this couple can be compatible. The

Sensitive Tan must learn not to demand too much from the fragile Crystal, and the Crystal needs to be more giving toward his mate.

Another problem that may arise is that a Crystal does not like to be practical or pay attention to details. The responsibility of maintaining the home, business, or family tends to fall on the Sensitive Tan, who may find these responsibilities burdensome after awhile. A Sensitive Tan prefers a mate who is a reliable partner, who shares the duties and responsibilities of supporting a family. A Crystal is not typically a proficient provider — he can barely support himself. An agreement must be made between these two regarding the division of obligations.

For the most part, however, these two make a compatible couple. They respect each other's sensitivity and need for quiet, reflective time. They are loving and considerate toward each other. A Crystal and a Sensitive Tan both want a calm, secure home and a pleasant, understanding relationship.

Crystal and Abstract Tan Relationship

See Abstract Tan and Crystal Relationship.

Crystal and Green Relationship

A relationship between a Crystal and a Green can be too harsh for the Crystal and too frustrating for the Green. A Crystal is introspective, quiet, calm, peaceful, and not motivated to accomplish. She has no concept of earning money. A Green is ambitious, outgoing, and driven to accomplish. A Green's energy can be too powerful and intimidating for the Crystal. A Green thrives on action and challenges that would overwhelm a Crystal. She needs solitude, meditation, and harmony to feel centered. The Green does not understand the Crystal's spiritual needs, nor does he relate to her spiritual personality. The quiet Crystal would be overrun by the Green's strong, businesslike attitude. She would tend to shy away from his intensity. A Green needs a partner who can match his power, someone he can have challenging, intellectual discussions with. A frustrated and angry Green, who can be abrupt and brutally honest when he communicates, could very well devastate the sensitive and fragile Crystal.

If this couple were to work out at all, it would be only if the Crystal were to add some of the Green's energy to her aura and become more powerful, stepping into the world with more dynamic force. (A Crystal's tendency is to hide out.) The Green's influence could help the Crystal become more secure and self-confident. If the Crystal were not overwhelmed by the Green's energy, it could add power, direction, and stability to her life. The Green would also have to be in power and not be too abrasive or demanding on the Crystal.

Both colors have a need to be independent and to have time alone, so they would understand and respect this need in each other. A Green is one of the few personalities who could handle the Crystal's withdrawing without feeling rejected. Although both personalities enjoy having their environment clean, tidy, and organized, these two prefer different items in their environment. While a Green likes elegant furniture and expensive art objects, a Crystal likes simple possessions. On the positive side, however, the Green would take care of business, allowing the Crystal time to stay quietly home alone. The Green enjoys having a career and making money.

A Green may be fascinated by the Crystal's spiritual ideas, though he would challenge many of them. Emotionally and sexually, both colors tend to be aloof. A Green prefers a partner who can be powerful and passionate. Sexual intensity with a Green could overwhelm a Crystal if she were not careful. Only if the Crystal could take on the Green's energy and match his standards would they be compatible. More often, the Green tends to dominate the Crystal, becoming easily frustrated by her lack of drive and ambition. A Crystal does not challenge or inspire a Green, and the Green tends to intimidate and overwhelm the Crystal.

Crystal and Blue Relationship

This relationship has the potential to be very harmonious. Both the Crystal and the Blue have an appreciation for the esthetic and spiritual things in life, so they can create a harmonious and beautiful environment together. A Blue is loving and sensitive enough to support and protect the Crystal's emotionally fragile nature. However, the Blue must also be very patient and understanding because Crystals are often withdrawn and tend to keep their deep emotions to themselves. The Blue, who wants to connect and communicate with her mate on an emotional level, can often become frustrated by the Crystal's need for solitude.

Occasionally, problems can arise with this couple. When the Blue loses her center and sense of self-worth, she becomes needy and moody. The Crystal then typically withdraws into his private world, which leaves the Blue feeling abandoned and unloved. A Crystal is not a rescuer. When a Blue loves someone, she wants to be around him all the time. A Crystal needs to spend a great deal of time in solitude to meditate, to cleanse and balance his aura. A Blue needs to be careful not to smother the Crystal with her emotional needs. The Crystal needs to emerge from hibernation more frequently to be with the Blue. A Blue loves having people around her and usually has an abundance of friends. A Crystal tends to shy away from people and social activities. The Blue may need to go to social gatherings herself and allow the Crystal time to stay home alone.

The Blue, being a natural nurturer, can help the Crystal become clear and centered by loving and protecting him. His energy is fragile and easily shattered. The Blue can help create a safe home environment for the Crystal. If she tries to over-mother the Crystal, however, he can feel invaded. He often just wants to be left alone.

For this couple to be compatible, the Crystal must learn to express appreciation to the Blue. The Blue must learn when to gently give love and when to be still. She needs to learn not to feel rejected when the Crystal needs time alone. A Crystal does appreciate unconditional acceptance and love, which the Blue is very capable of giving when she is in power. For the emotional Blue to feel fulfilled and appreciated, the Crystal needs to share his feelings with her more often. Together they can be a very gentle and loving couple.

Crystal and Violet Relationship

This relationship has both positive and negative aspects. These two can provide a good balance for each other, though they can also feel they do not meet each other's needs. The Crystal tends to withdraw from the world. The Violet needs to be out saving the world. A Violet has a desire to be the center of attention. A Crystal withdraws from having any attention focused on her at all. Though both are very spiritual, they live in two separate worlds. The Crystal lives in an inner world. The Violet lives very much in the outer world and wants to help improve it.

A Violet loves music and traveling. A Crystal prefers quiet solitude and staying at home in her own little haven. The Violet can offer a balance to the introspective Crystal by bringing home information concerning the outside world. This can enable the Crystal to become better educated and informed. If the Crystal can absorb some of the Violet's energy, she can become more powerful and less fragile. She must, however, be careful not to also take on the scattered attributes of an out-of-power Violet.

In this relationship, the Violet is definitely the powerful leader. The Crystal appreciates the fact that the Violet is out in the world, taking care of business and being productive so that she is allowed to stay home and be financially supported. When the Violet comes home after a day of saving the world, the Crystal has created a serene, nurturing environment for him. This couple can be very compatible when they fulfill these needs for each other. If the Violet can refrain from being so powerful that he intimidates the fragile Crystal, she can show her appreciation by creating a loving home for him. Often, though, her typical emotional and physical withdrawal leaves the Violet no partner to interact with. To have those needs met, the Violet should depend upon communicating with others in the outside world.

Crystal and Lavender Relationship

See Lavender and Crystal Relationship.

Crystal and Crystal Relationship

Although two Crystals can be compatible, with similar needs and beliefs, they have very little to learn from each other. They both understand the need for meditation and quiet solitude. Their home can be very peaceful, simple, and quiet. Because they both tend to be withdrawn and introspective, however, neither would be the first to instigate a relationship. They understand each other's need to work with nature for inner balance. They both want peace and harmony in the home; however, neither wants the responsibility of traveling outside the home to work for a living. Crystals are often shy and lack self-confidence. They are not very social. They tend to stay isolated in their own worlds, hiding in their own rooms.

This relationship has very little potential for growth; neither has anything to bring back to the other from the outside world. They are both better off finding mates who are more self-confident and can take charge.

Crystal and Indigo Relationship

See Indigo and Crystal Relationship.

INDIGO
Indigo and Red Relationship

Indigos and Reds would have very little in common. Indigos sense that life and matter are energy. The Reds feel that the

Indigos dropped from outer space. Reds could not relate to the Indigos' different approach to physical reality or their inability to see life as tangible.

Indigos are much too sensitive and spiritual to deal with the Reds' explosive physical energy, power, and strength. Indigos tend to challenge humanity's limited concepts of physical reality. Reds prefer to see reality as entirely physical.

Indigos have a difficult time dealing with their physical bodies. Reds relate mainly to their physical bodies. Sexuality to Indigos is a soul-to-soul experience, where two souls can soar together on a higher spiritual level. For Reds sex is a lustful, physical, and tangible experience. Reds would not be able to understand the Indigos' language, ideals, or spiritual beliefs.

The Indigos' apparent aloofness would not bother Reds because Reds tend to be loners anyway. But if they strike up a conversation, they would not have much to say to each other. Indigos are much too ethereal for the Red's physical, grounded personality. They are too much New Age children for the practical, sensible, realistic Reds.

Indigo and Orange Relationship

See Orange and Indigo Relationship.

Indigo and Magenta Relationship

See Magenta and Indigo Relationship.

Indigo and Yellow Relationship

The sensitive Indigo and the friendly Yellow can be great friends. The Indigo's view of life is a novelty for the Yellow. The Yellow's playful attitude interests the curious Indigo. A Yellow is so easygoing and playful that she enjoys the Indigo's different approach to life and his unusual beliefs about reality. With her creativity and curiosity, the Yellow can have a great time exploring some of the Indigo's ideas. Both Life Colors are sensitive and want people to like them, but they are also stubborn — neither likes being told what to do. Because of this, they understand and respect the other's need for space and freedom. Neither has a desire to control the other.

Although both are sensitive and considerate of the other's feelings, the Indigo wants to relate to his mate on a deep, soul-to-soul level. A Yellow tends to take relationships and sex rather lightly, having meaningless, playful sexual encounters with one person after another. The Indigo cannot even consider such behavior. A Yellow believes that life is to be lived in the moment, with the freedom to make spontaneous choices. Although an Indigo also believes that life is to be lived in the moment (for that is all there is), he also believes it is to be lived from deeper levels of compassion and commitment.

The Yellow tends to live in her body and relates mostly to physical reality; the Indigo has a challenging time relating to his body at all. The Yellow wants to be more physically active; the Indigo wants to focus more on understanding spiritual truths, moral issues, and ethical concepts. The Indigo prefers to be more contemplative and subdued. During those times, the Indigo needs to retreat to his spiritual studies and allow the Yellow to go outside and play. The Indigo has to understand that it is not the Yellow's need or purpose to focus so intensely on higher concepts. The Yellow can help the Indigo understand his body better while adding a dimension of fun and enjoyment to the Indigo's experience. The Indigo can teach the energetic Yellow about the spiritual aspects of life. These personalities can provide a good balance for each other.

The Indigo and the Yellow enjoy the nonjudgmental, accepting nature of each other's personalities. But when the Indigo needs to know he can trust and depend on those closest to him, the Yellow is not always there when he needs her. A Yellow does not enjoy the heavy responsibility of people depending on her. This can create ill feelings and disappointment for the

Indigo. He can lack trust in her. The Yellow needs to be more dependable and responsible within relationships. Because neither wants to hurt the other and neither enjoys conflict, the Indigo and Yellow couple will probably be intent on maintaining a harmonious relationship.

Relationships between an Indigo and a Yellow include Michael Jackson (Indigo with Violet) and Lisa Marie Presley (Yellow/Violet); Michael Jackson and the mother of his children, Debbie Rowe (Blue/Yellow.)

Indigo and Logical Tan Relationship

These personalities have great difficulty understanding each other. The Indigo challenges most laws and limiting concepts on the planet. The Logical Tan believes laws and standards are not only common sense, but they are necessary for our very survival. This pair can be in constant conflict. The Indigo needs someone she can relate to on an emotional basis. Emotional bonding is not a priority for a Logical Tan; he tends to keep his feelings to himself. The Indigo's ideas seem unrealistic, impractical, and often bizarre to the Logical Tan, who needs everything to be logical and analytical with supporting proof. Everything for a Logical Tan must be a factual, realistic experience. Life for the Indigo involves energy, emotions, and spirituality. A Logical Tan is the typical disciplinarian; the Indigo is the antithesis of discipline. The Indigo challenges old ideas and standards. This upsets a Logical Tan's structured way of life. Far from the Logical Tan's ideals is the Indigo's New Age concepts, spiritual ideals, and unique ways of looking at life.

If these two were in power, with the Logical Tan open minded enough to at least discuss different ideas, they could possibly be friends. The Indigo could help the Logical Tan explore other possibilities. The Logical Tan could help the curious Indigo understand three-dimensional reality by giving her facts and information. (However, the Indigo would probably believe the Logical Tan's facts were not conclusive.) The Indigo believes there's more to reality than physical appearances. The Logical Tan wants the Indigo to be more realistic and practical, not question reality in the face of obvious facts. The Indigo's inability to conform or to be practical and logical eventually upsets a Logical Tan, whose purpose is to figure out and analyze three-dimensional reality. The Indigo wants to show people that their limited concepts of three-dimensional reality are probably not reflective of reality's true nature. Most likely, these two would be constantly questioning and refuting each other's beliefs.

Indigo and Environmental Tan Relationship

This is not one of the most compatible relationships. The Indigo seems to understand life beyond physical reality. The Environmental Tan grasps his sense of reality from his physical environment. The Environmental Tan wants life to be logical, analytical, and grounded. The Indigo is the first to challenge traditional, rational belief systems. The Environmental Tan, however, prefers to follow rules and live by set standards. He becomes agitated by chaos.

Both personalities, however, have a high regard for nature. They are both inspired by the beauty and magnificence of trees, animals, and the earth, which could be the common ground for their discussions. An Indigo is too different, too New Age, and too spiritual for an Environmental Tan. The Environmental Tan wants structure and discipline; the Indigo wants people to free themselves from their limitations. These two would be better off if they found mates who shared their beliefs.

Indigo and Sensitive Tan Relationship

See Sensitive Tan and Indigo Relationship.

Indigo and Abstract Tan Relationship

See Abstract Tan and Indigo Relationship.

Indigo and Green Relationship

These personalities are absolutely fascinated by each other — up to a point. At first, the Indigo is a curiosity for the Green. The Green, who loves to be quicker and smarter than everyone, is fascinated by the Indigo's quick mind, advanced ideas, and unusual concepts. However, she also constantly challenges and questions the Indigo. She becomes frustrated if the Indigo is not able to produce rational explanations to support his beliefs.

Considering that a Green has a strong need to control her life and the lives of those around her and that the Indigo refuses to be controlled, there could be conflict between them. Although the Green can be frustrated by the Indigo, she also respects his refusal to be dominated.

The inquisitive Indigo can learn a lot from the intelligent and well-informed Green. But the Green must be careful not to be too harsh or too pushy with the sensitive Indigo. The Indigo's emotions run deep, and he needs to trust the people around him. A Green can be very impatient, always in a hurry. The Indigo needs to move at his own pace. He will not be rushed or forced into anything. Another problem arises when the Indigo's desire to emotionally bond with his mate runs into a Green's protective walls. The Green has to be in control, causing her to protect herself emotionally.

The Green is definitely the moneymaker in this partnership. The Indigo does not prefer to deal with money. He can explore creative ideas instead while the Green takes the ideas and transforms them into physical and practical form.

Conflicts can arise because of their different views and attitudes regarding people, money, and business. An out-of-power Green can often operate outside the Indigo's moral belief system, not thinking twice about stepping on others as she climbs the corporate ladder. Indigos believe such actions are contrary to the spiritual nature of evolved beings on the planet.

This team can be very effective at facilitating each other's growth. They can also butt heads and become frustrated. A Green usually does not have the same spiritual goals or understandings as the Indigo, and this frequently causes them to go in different directions. Although the information each brings to the relationship can enhance and inspire the other, a Green has a tendency to be too powerful, bold, and brash for the Indigo. While an Indigo in power is one of the few Life Colors who can stand up to a Green's power, an Indigo who is out of power can become easily crushed and intimidated. The Indigo then retreats within himself and finds it difficult to regain trust for the domineering Green.

Indigo and Blue Relationship

See Blue and Indigo Relationship.

Indigo and Violet Relationship

See Violet and Indigo Relationship.

Indigo and Lavender Relationship

Spiritually and emotionally, these two have similar characteristics. Both can be very sensitive and gentle. They both believe there is more to life than physical reality, and they allow each other the room to explore that belief. These childlike souls both live from their intuition rather than from logic or intellect. Because they both are highly creative, developing artistic projects together could be fulfilling and profitable for them.

Neither the Indigo nor the Lavender wishes to control or dominate anyone else. They are each very accepting and undemanding toward others. They allow each other the space they need to live their lives. They understand the need to be individualistic. Typically, other people can misunderstand them, so their mutual understanding is appreciated.

Although they are both sensitive individuals and are compatible in many ways if they stay balanced and in power, they don't always have much to offer each other. The Indigo needs to be with someone who can discuss and validate what he senses about physical reality. The Lavender is not usually capable of providing answers to the inquisitive Indigo because she doesn't spend much time in physical reality. The Lavender could give the Indigo a warped sense of the world by describing the fantasy world she experiences.

The Lavender is not usually capable of reaching the emotional depths the Indigo requires from a mate. The Indigo wants to bond with someone on a soul-to-soul basis. The Lavender prefers life to be less serious. The Lavender spends so much time withdrawn in her own world that the Indigo tends to feel alone and abandoned.

Although the Indigo may be intrigued by the Lavender's other worlds, he is more interested in exploring this one. The Lavender cannot relate to the intensity of the Indigo's need for truth, so she usually floats into other dimensions, leaving the Indigo to live the truth on his own. The Indigo gains little understanding from the Lavender about life on this planet.

Indigo and Crystal Relationship

The Indigo and the Crystal have very similar needs and beliefs. Their energies are compatible. Although these two can be gentle and sensitive beings who are easily affected by other people, they can be very soothing for each other.

Their priority in life is to connect with their spiritual sources and knowledge. The Indigo has a great desire to understand and live his life by higher principles and higher consciousness. The Crystal's life revolves around her spirituality. They can have wonderful, enlightening discussions about spirituality and inner reality. Both share the need to spend quiet, reflective time in meditation. They understand the importance of going within to find answers. They also both understand the need to feel emotionally secure, and they prefer spending time with sensitive and trustworthy people. In power, the Indigo and the Crystal feel they can trust each other. Although they are both sensitive personalities who have highly charged physical and emotional systems, their energies are compatible with each other. The independent Indigo seems more capable of dealing with the intensity of the outside world, however, so it is usually he who brings worldly information home to the vulnerable Crystal.

The Crystal's natural ability to be a clear channel for universal energy has a healing and energizing effect on the Indigo. It helps him stay centered and connected with his sensitive physical body. They both understand they are unusual individuals, and they allow and accept each other's uniqueness.

Both the Indigo and the Crystal have great emotional depth. While the Indigo has a need to bond strongly on a soul-to-soul level, however, the Crystal has a fear of connecting so intensely, of being hurt or shattered. The delicate Crystal often withdraws so far within herself that communication becomes difficult or even impossible. Even though the Indigo is gentle and understanding, he can feel lost if the Crystal withdraws too often. Usually, these two are sensitive and patient with each other's needs. They can help each other stay secure and balanced, and consequently the Crystal can stay more open to the Indigo. Because both operate so much from their intuition, each one typically knows what the other needs to feel safe.

Out of power, they can both tend to become lost, frightened, and confused. If either withdraws too often, they could lose trust in each other. If, however, they maintain their spiritual understanding and their gentle communication with each other, these two are emotionally, spiritually, and physically compatible.

Indigo and Indigo Relationship

Two Indigos together are definitely able to understand each other. They are emotionally and spiritually compatible. Both experience similar challenges as they make their way in the world.

In power, they would both expect and provide honesty and high integrity in their relationship. Both are highly psychic and intuitive, so their communication and mutual understanding would be strong.

Indigos make very compatible friends, mates, confidants, and lovers. Neither tries to run the other's life because each respects the other's experience of life. They are able to bond with each other on a soul-to-soul level. Their emotional and spiritual understanding is very compatible. Their inability to take care of everyday responsibilities, however, can cause difficulties. Neither usually wants to stay home to handle the details.

Each would need to stay balanced and in touch with inner knowing or the confusion that would ensue could upset them both. When Indigos lose touch with their inner sense of truth and higher principles, they can become self-destructive or hyperactive. Indigos are too physically sensitive to have this kind of disruptive energy in their environment. One partner remaining aware and centered would most likely be able to help the other become centered again.

Emotionally, Indigos are more compatible with each other than they are with any of the mental or physical colors. They can provide great comfort, appreciation, and understanding for each other.

CHAPTER NINE

conclusion

FREQUENTLY ASKED QUESTIONS

Can I change or add colors to my aura?

The outer bands in the aura change frequently. The Life Colors typically do not change. However, because we have free will, we are free to do anything we desire. We have no limits. Refer to the Introduction for more information about why people change their Life Colors.

You constantly add and change your outer bands of colors, though you are usually unaware you are doing so. The colors reflect your state of consciousness at the time. If, for example, you decide you must become more responsible and hardworking and that you must earn more money and accomplish a financial goal, green will begin to develop in the outer bands. Your Life Colors usually remain intact, but your behavior temporarily shifts into more Green aspects. You may find yourself uncharacteristically more driven, more concerned with money, and occasionally more frustrated with other people's lack of ambition.

A few methods can help you add colors to your aura. Your

thoughts and imagination are your most powerful tools for creating what you want. Imagining and declaring that you have a certain color in your aura instigate the process, and that color will begin to develop. You can imagine or visualize yourself surrounded by that color. Add that color to your environment. Wearing a certain color does affect your aura and may add that color to your aura. Inhaling and imagining you are breathing the color into your body will also help you become the personality of that color.

When you decide to add certain qualities and behaviors into your life, the corresponding colors begin to evolve in your aura. If you decide, for example, that you are going to relax and have more fun in your life or maybe design some creative project, yellow will begin to emerge in your aura. If you decide you want to begin helping the planet by becoming involved in a humanitarian, environmental, or political cause, violet will appear in your aura. The more determined and dedicated you are with the new concepts and the more action you take in those directions, the brighter and more intense the color becomes.

Even if you unintentionally develop a behavior, the corresponding aura color will develop as well. For example, if you suddenly become outraged and angered, red will begin flashing in your aura. If you become pregnant and notice mothering instincts developing, blue will most likely also become apparent in your aura.

To consciously add colors into your aura, you must either visualize the specific color around you or develop the behaviors and qualities associated with that color. If you desire to be more loving and nurturing toward your family, either visualize blue around you or start behaving in a more loving way. Either method will add blue to your aura.

Be aware that if you add a color to your aura, you may easily experience that color's out-of-power characteristics as well as its in-power traits. If you add violet, you may become scattered and overwhelmed by the number of new projects you have recently undertaken. If you add blue, you may discover that you are suddenly a great deal more emotional. By adding yellow, you may find that you are unmotivated to accomplish anything or that you have an unusual craving for sweets.

When you introduce new colors into your aura, you must learn to stay in power with the new personality traits, just as those who have had the Life Colors since birth must do. When you develop a balance all of the individual colors, they form the perfect white light.

People often ask if adding green to their auras will stimulate healing. Many healers use green in their work. They paint their offices green or ask their clients to visualize green. This is not related to the Life Color Green. Healers use green because it lies in the middle of the color spectrum and therefore promotes the balance that is necessary for self-healing.

Can I learn to see the aura?

We all came into this lifetime with the ability to see the aura. As we grew older, we learned not to see it. Infants and animals still see the aura because they have not been taught otherwise. That is why a dog will differentiate between strangers, growling and barking at one person yet befriending another, and a baby will smile and reach out to one person, but cry and pull back from another. We may each see the colors differently, just as we probably taste foods differently. Not all people experience the same taste when eating liver or asparagus, for example, as evidenced by the fact that some people actually enjoy the taste of these foods.

People often learn to see the aura through different methods. Trusting what you see or feel is the biggest step. Those with Physical Life Colors often sense the aura first through their physical bodies. Some are able to feel the heat from a person's aura through their hands. You may experiment with this tactile sensing method by holding the palms of your hands approximately three feet from a person's body and slowly moving in toward the body until you feel the sensation of heat or energy. In the beginning you may experience the sensation in your hands only when you are a few inches away from the body. However, with trust, patience, and practice your sensitivity will increase and you will learn to feel a person's aura from a greater distance.

People with Mental Life Colors frequently learn to identify a person's Life Color by comparing language and behavior with what that they have learned about each Life Color. For example, they will conclude that someone who is an exercise fanatic, who has a childlike, playful personality, and who doesn't like to work probably has a Yellow Life Color. Those with Mental Life Colors can be some of the least trusting of their intuitive abilities. They feel more comfortable analyzing the facts regarding a person's lifestyle, behavior, and occupation and often learn to "see" the aura intellectually.

Many with Emotional Life Colors intuitively sense a person's Life Color before they physically see it. They can feel whether the person is an insecure and sensitive Yellow, an emotionally depressed Blue, or a powerful Green by tuning in. Blues, for example, are able to become quiet inside, ask their higher selves about another person's Life Color, and usually receive the correct answer. Because Violets are such visual personalities, they tend to actually see the aura before most people do. Their third eye seems to be more developed. It appears that Indigos, the new psychic children, also have retained their ability to see or sense the aura.

A simple exercise to help you see the aura is to have someone stand in front of a white background while you focus just above and beyond the person's head. After awhile you will be able to see a soft white glow around the body. Many people assume that what they are seeing is an optical illusion, an afterimage of the physical body. (For example, if you stare at something red for awhile and then look away, the opposing color green will appear before your eyes. This is an optical illusion.) To prove to yourself that you are seeing the aura, ask the person to concentrate energy and imagine an intense beam of light shooting from the top of the person's head. You should be able to see that white glow expand, intensify, or fluctuate.

The key is to ask your higher source to help you see it and then to trust what you see. Make sure you are not afraid to see the aura, because fear can hold you back. Are you concerned that your friends and family will think that you are crazy? Are you afraid they will stop loving you? Are you afraid of your own power or your psychic abilities?

There are five basic steps in learning to see auras or in developing any intuitive or psychic abilities:

1. willingness (many people are afraid to develop these abilities)
2. learning to quiet the mind
3. trusting what you see (or hear or sense)
4. practice
5. acknowledgment and gratitude (acknowledge when you do see the aura and do not discount or dismiss your experience).

We are moving into an era in which we will become aware that we are unlimited beings. We have many more abilities than we believe we have at this time. The ability to see the aura is a natural one we have forgotten how to use. It can be easy to reawaken that ability.

Learning to see the aura will help us understand that we have more talents and abilities than we realize. It will also help us better understand others and ourselves. If we are ever to experience peace and harmony on the planet, understanding one another and accepting our differences as well as our similarities are major steps toward reaching that goal.

Are there other colors in the aura besides the basic Life Colors?

People frequently report seeing white, gold, or pink in the aura. The Life Color Gold can be seen around highly evolved spiritual masters and usually signifies a very high vibration. Pink is often seen in the outer bands, not as a Life Color. Pink signifies that the person has a strong desire for love and romance.

Seeing white in the aura signifies something entirely different. For every inch of white seen next to the body, a major life question has been answered for that person. If the question is being asked, but has not yet been answered, white is outside the Life Color bands. The most common major life questions asked are, Is there a God? Does God know who I am? Now that I know the answers to those questions, what do I do with the information?

Typically, when people are first learning to see the aura, they observe a white glow around someone's head or body. This is different from having white in the aura.

People also report seeing gold around someone's hands. What many experience as gold I experience as yellow. Yellows are very powerful healers and frequently have strong energy emanating from their hands. Whatever colors you see, trust what you see and ask yourself what those colors mean to you. Even if people see different colors, the information about the person should match.

Some wonder if people can have black or "evil" auras. Black is the absence of color. I have never witnessed black in someone's aura. Whenever I see people who are angry (which I believe stems from hurt or fear) or violent, they usually have Red Overlays.

Faded auras usually reveal a serious illness, a lack of life energy circulating through the body, or a desire to no longer be on the planet.

Do animals have auras?

Yes. However, with the exception of dolphins, animals have colors different from people's auras. Animals have either silver blue auras, which means they believe they are animals, or they have golden yellow auras, which means they believe they are humans. Most pet owners will probably know their pet's aura colors by their behavior. Probably not a surprise to dolphin lovers, dolphins have the same aura colors as humans do.

Do different cities and countries have different aura colors?

Yes. Even though people with different aura colors are in every city, state, and country, different areas tend to attract certain aura colors. For example, Yellows are typically drawn to warmer climates and natural environments. Yellows do not function well where there are a lot of buildings, traffic, and concrete. Breathtaking scenery or dramatic weather appeals to Violets. They also need access to interesting cultural, political, or spiritual events and people. Violets can become bored in small, sleepy communities unless they travel frequently. Greens need to live in or near larger cities where there is action and the potential for making a lot of money. Lavenders and Crystals are attracted to quiet, simple, and pretty environments. Oranges prefer to live where there is nature but where they also have easy access to their favorite daring sport. They may live close to high mountains, along racing rivers, or near Hollywood so they can work as stunt doubles. Magentas tend to live in larger cities where their bizarre behavior is usually more tolerated.

The following locations resonate predominantly with these aura colors. If you live in any areas, it doesn't necessarily mean that you have these colors. However, if you feel drawn to one of these areas, it may mean you have at least one of the colors in your aura.

Many Violets aren't sure where home is right now. Because Violets are global, they need to understand that the world is home and that they may be traveling extensively in this lifetime.

Sample countries:
Africa — Yellow and Violet
Australia — Yellow
Brazil — Red and Yellow (with some Blue)
England — Logical Tan
France — Green/Violet

Germany — Green
Italy — Yellow/Violet
Japan — Green with Violet
Mexico — Yellow
Russia — Violet with Logical Tan
Spain — Violet/Yellow
US — Yellow/Violet (A Yellow/Violet country that thinks it's supposed to be Green, Logical Tan, and Blue. This creates conflict. Violets desire freedom and global peace; Yellows are rebellious youth who want to play. Tans think they are supposed to focus on security and jobs. Greens are workaholics who want to be wealthy. Blues constantly try to rescue everyone.)

Sample sections in the US:
East Coast — Green and Violet
West Coast — Yellow and Violet
Northeast — Green
Southeast — Yellow, Tan, and Blue
Midwest — Tan and Blue
Northwest — Violet
Southwest — Yellow and Tan (with some Violet)

Sample states:
Alaska — Red and Yellow
Arizona — Yellow and Tan
California (southern) — Yellow (with some Violet)
California (northern) — Violet and Green
Colorado — Yellow and Tan
Florida — Yellow and Green
Hawaii — Yellow, Blue, and Violet
New Jersey — Green and Blue
New Mexico — Yellow and Tan (with some Violet)
New York — Green

Sample cities:

Detroit — Green and Tan

London — Tan and Violet

Los Angeles — Violet, Yellow, and Tan (Beverly Hills — Green)

New York — Green

Paris — Violet and Green

Rio de Janeiro — Red and Yellow

San Francisco — Violet and Green

Seattle — Violet

Tokyo — Green

Washington, D.C. — Violet

about the author

Pamala Oslie is a popular professional psychic, speaker, lecturer, and consultant. Her work with auras has proven highly effective for her clients and those who attend her workshops. The information she provides regarding the personalities of each of the aura colors has helped thousands understand their lives with greater clarity and has empowered them to live happier and more fulfilling lives. Her advice has helped them improve relationships, parenting skills, career and work, and family life. She has presented her work on auras to The International Association on New Science, a group of scientists, physicists, psychologists, astronauts, and authors.

Pamala is also the author of *Make Your Dreams Come True: Simple Steps for Changing the Beliefs That Limit You,* available from Amber-Allen Publishing (800-624-8855). She lives and works in Santa Barbara, California.

VISIT PAMALA'S WEB SITE FOR MORE INFORMATION ABOUT LIFE COLORS AND PSYCHIC ABILITIES

TO ORDER OR FOR INFORMATION ABOUT AUDIO AND VIDEO PRODUCTS, FUTURE WORKSHOPS, OR LECTURES, CONTACT PAMALA AT:

Post Office Box 30035
Santa Barbara, California 93130-0035
Telephone and fax: (805) 687-6604
Web sites: www.auracolors.com
www.pamoslie.com
E-mail: auracolors@auracolors.com